Short Chic

Short Chic

*The Everything-You-Need-to-Know
Fashion Guide for Every Woman Under 5'4"*

Allison Kyle Leopold and Anne Marie Cloutier
Illustrations by Durell Godfrey

RAWSON, WADE PUBLISHERS, INC.
New York

Library of Congress Cataloging in Publication Data

Leopold, Allison Kyle.
Short chic.

Includes index.
1. Fashion. I. Cloutier, Anne Marie.
II. Title.
TT560.L46   646'.36   80-5999
ISBN 0-89256-173-4   AACR2

Published simultaneously in Canada by McClelland and Stewart, Ltd.
Composition by American–Stratford Graphic Services, Inc.
Printed and bound by R. R. Donnelley & Sons Co.,
Harrisonburg, Virginia
Designed by Jacques Chazaud
Fourth Printing May 1982
Revised Edition

ACKNOWLEDGMENTS

In addition to those people whose names and comments appear throughout this book, and the hundreds of women who answered our questionnaire and whom we interviewed in the course of our research, we would like to thank the following for their invaluable help: Thomas Cohen, Eleanor Rawson, Miriam Arond, Marilyn Cooperman, Deborah Geltman, Gayle Benderoff, and Durell Godfrey.

We would also like to express our appreciation for the help and support of Nancy and Dick Abrams, Kathleen Beckett, Audrey Brooks, Pamela Choy, Robert Cloutier, Donna Cowen, Mary Anne Diorio, Sheila Eby, Diane Forden, Bert Greene, Nancy Handelman, Michelle Hillman, Jody M. Leopold, Camille Martinetti, Robert Masello, Nonnie Moore, Beth Terrell Prest, Edward Primativo, Catherine Sabino, Francine San Giovanni, Phillip Schulz, Jody Shields, Jane F. Templeton, Christina Thorp, Barbara Wagh; to the many, many editors who contributed thoughts and ideas; and to the representatives in stores all over the country who contributed their time and effort to this project.

And, finally, a heartfelt thanks to both our families, who saw us through the best of times and the worst of times during the writing of this book.

Contents

Short
Chic

1. Short Chic

hort Chic. It used to be that the two words were mutually exclusive. But no more. Because if you're one of the fifteen million American women under 5′4″, then this book has been written specifically with you and your fashion needs in mind.

Just who is the *Short Chic* woman?

- *She is the woman under 5′4″ with an average figure* who's tired of wearing small-sized fashions that really have been scaled down from fashions for the taller woman.
- *She is the adult woman* who's never been quite comfortable shopping in the teen sections of department stores.
- *She is the discriminating woman* who refuses to wear cheaply made "little girl" fashions featured in all but a few of the specialty petite shops.
- *She is the working woman* who wants more feminine options than dark suits, plain pumps, and a pile-on of status symbols.
- *She is the executive woman* who wants to be taken seriously—who's had it with the figurative—or actual!—pats on the head that her small stature seems to inspire.

- *Most of all, she's the woman who cares about fashion.* She wants to look chic, elegant, and sophisticated in her clothes without being overwhelmed by them. And she wants professional advice on how to achieve that goal.

We came to write *Short Chic* after many years of writing for fashion magazines. During that time we've often seen fashion stories directed to the shorter woman—mostly the result of overwhelming requests by readers.

The stories have been unsatisfactory from several standpoints: (1) Most stick to the simplest fashion ground rules—reiterating the same tired basics that the shorter woman has known since the first day she ventured out from under her mother's wing to buy her own clothes; (2) finding an adult 5′3″ model as an example is a difficult task indeed; but mostly (3) the fact that, since most designers admit to cutting their size 4's and 6's to enhance the proportions of a *tall* slim woman, the clothes usually don't look well on shorter women, and it takes a whole lot of effort to make them look well.

We also noticed that even in the best fashion books, the short woman receives, at most, just a few pages worth of random information, most of it running along the following lines: "Stick to simple, basic styles"; "Stay away from big patterns"; and "Keep everything to scale" (so what else is new?). In sum, divorce yourself from much of the fun and freedom that fashion has to offer.

But we weren't interested in writing about *that* kind of fashion. The reason: We never believed it was true.

- The petite and fashion-conscious women we worked with and met day to day didn't "stick to basics"—and they looked sensational.
- Our under-5′4″ friends didn't always "stay away from big patterns"—and they looked terrific.
- Both of us, at 5′2″ and 5′3″, felt little compunction about toting an oversized "out-of-scale" bag every now and again—and we thought we were coming along okay, too.

In fact, all of us dressed pretty much the way our taller counterparts did. As far as height is concerned, it would seem, anybody can wear anything.

At first glance that is.

Because, on closer inspection, a pattern emerged: Though the clothes worn by a 5′2″ woman may *look* as freely put together as those worn by someone 5′7″, actually they have to be subtly tinkered with to suit a shorter body. For example . . .

"There's nothing wrong with a short woman wearing horizontal stripes," one 5′2″ fashion editor told us breezily. "I wear them all the time."

But, when pressed, she admitted, well, of course not *big*, *bold*, *wide* stripes in contrasting colors like red and white. What the editor *really* meant were tiny pencil-thin horizontals in muted, close-to-each-other colors. And no, she added, they weren't all-over stripes either—only across the neck and shoulders. Aha!

Another short woman said she had no qualms at all about wearing low-heeled shoes and still looking leggy. Really? we asked. But was there anything special about the way she wore them? Well, now that we mentioned it, she did *religiously* match her shoe color to her sock color whenever she wore low heels . . . and another Short Chic principle came to light.

Most short women, however, turned out to be exceedingly timid in their approach to fashion. Asked if she'd ever consider wearing a cape, a 5′1″ marketing manager looked at us in horror.

"That's because most short women dress scared," explained a 4′10″ designer. "They've tried so many things that didn't work that they've been discouraged from experimenting with clothes altogether."

In order to zero in on the questions and feelings shorter women have about fashion, we designed a seven-page questionnaire and sent it out to nearly one thousand 5′3″-and-under women all over the country. Told to expect an average 15 percent return on an unsolicited questionnaire of such length, we were delighted when the first returns started to trickle in, and we were overwhelmed as everyday, six days a week, our mailboxes overflowed with returning questionnaires. The tally: more than twice the projected response! At this writing, the figure is still climbing. Note: According to Washington D.C.'s National Bureau of Standards, 39.6 percent of American women between the ages of seventeen and seventy measure in at 5′3″ or under. Furthermore, the average woman's height is only 5′3½″, not 5′5″ or 5′6″ as commonly supposed—which is why we had decided on 5′3″—under-average height—as our cut-off point. But many questionnaires came back filled out by women who were 5′3½″ and 5′4″. "We feel we have the same problems as women who are 5′3″ and are just as interested in looking taller" was the gist of what they said. So because the rules in this book actually apply to *any* woman who wants to look taller, we upped our cut-off to include women up to 5'4" (which, incidentally, coincided with the fashion industry's own standards, for the petite woman, of 5'4" and under).

What the Questionnaires Told Us

What the *Short Chic* questionnaires revealed, first of all, was that there's a hefty lot of frustration out there—with clothes, with designers, with the fashion industry in general. Women reveled in the novelty of a bona fide sounding board—at last!—and more than half of them made considerable use of the blank half-page we provided for additional comments on which to vent their personal feelings. . . .

"Inside we're tall and respond to the same fashion influences as everyone else. We have the same taste levels—just shorter bodies."
38-year-old, 4'10" Copy Chief, Washington, D.C.

"It seems sometimes that the fashion industry supports the tailors of the world at the expense of shorter people. It hurts the old pocketbook when I have to spend an additional $15 or $20 on alterations for every piece of clothing. *That's* discriminating. What I wouldn't give to be able to buy a garment in the morning and wear it in the afternoon!"
40-year-old, 5'1" Project Coordinator, Detroit, Michigan

"We may be short, but we're not built like broomsticks. We have as shapely figures as tall women do, just in smaller proportions."
24-year-old, 5'1" Sales Assistant, Boston, Massachusetts

"It's high time someone realized that being short is not synonymous with being young, cute, or frivolous or, the other extreme, dull, dreary, and ultra conservative. And too many designers assume that the average consumer for size 5's and 6's are the tall slim women, not the short ones."
36-year-old, 5'3" Business Executive, Philadelphia, Pennsylvania

But Would They Choose to be Taller?

Surprisingly, there was a dichotomy of opinion on that subject. "I don't waste time wishing for the impossible, but if I had a choice,

I'd be a few inches taller so I wouldn't have to put up hems," wrote a practical soul from Virginia. In contrast, a 4'8" lawyer from Ewing, New Jersey, found her height "perfectly satisfactory"; a 5' California physician called being short "rather novel." A 5'2½" housewife from Dayton, Ohio, however, felt that she would have had "a better view of the world" were she 5'6". All in all, the comments were as varied as the women themselves.

All well and good, we thought, but how about height when it comes to fashion? *Would the women dress differently if they were taller?* we queried. That's when the fantasies came pouring in. Yes, yes, yes, we heard over and over again. Capes. Furs. Wide pants. Skinny ones. It seemed as though we had opened the lid on a Pandora's box of small-sized fashion cravings, unleashing a horde of closet fashion fans.

"Suits are smarter-looking on taller women. I'd wear bulky knits and more dramatic clothing, trendy pants and blousey tops, all kinds of exotic fabrics and styles if I were tall."

> Elaine M., 5'3", Oceanside, New York

"I feel I'd have a more graceful appearance and wear more stylish clothes if I were tall. I'd leave my stilts behind (high heels) and wear pretty flat-heeled shoes in the summer, tapered pants, and slinky things that require height to hang gracefully."

> Beverly H., 5'2", Kansas City, Kansas

"I'd dress more flamboyantly for sure. I'd wear flared skirts, jump suits, jodhpurs, big bold prints, lots of pleats, bulky sweaters, and high turtlenecks."

> Joy W., 5'1", Bennington, Vermont

But aren't there any fashion advantages to being short? we then asked.

A 4'10" Connecticut accountant, who "likes being petite," put it this way: "Because of the difficulties we have, I think we're more aware of dressing in appropriate styles. Being short also forces you to develop a strong personal style." A short Atlanta homemaker felt she could "save money by buying things in the pre-teen and teen departments." But most of the responses ran along the lines of "You must be kidding"; "No way"; or just plain "No." A 5'1" teacher from Long Beach, Long Island, wrote in, saying: "I'm sure there are some advantages because tall people say so, but I really can't think of any." Others requested that we write them back: "I would really love to know what they are, if any," penned a doubting Florida respondent.

Some answers, however, were especially insightful. . . .

"Because of the so-called difficulties that are related to fashion and the shorter woman, she can open the door to a more creative side of her fashion moods. She shouldn't let size hinder the possibilities of the joy that is connected with looking good."

5'1" Boutique Owner, Carmel, California

Others went into specifics, many bringing up the fact that it is much easier for the shorter woman to look feminine.

"Being short is a plus when it comes to evening clothes. A short woman can more easily appear feminine, delicate, and fragile. And she can wear revealing or dramatic fashion without looking overpowering."

5'2" Regional Sales Manager, Chicago, Illinois

"Because I'm small, I can wear things like down vests, jackets, and Frye boots, and not look huge and horsey."

5'1½" Teacher, Lake Forest, Illinois

"We can enjoy fashion fads that are appropriate to our size. Little lace collars are okay on 'little women,' absurd on big Berthas."

5'2" Editorial Assistant, Boston, Massachusetts

"Although cute and innocent looks are carried off more easily by short women, we don't always want to look like ingenues—we have to fight all our lives against looking cute and childlike. We also like to look elegant and sometimes sophisticated and fashionable without looking ridiculous. I think this is possible, but it is hard for shorter women to adapt a fashion and silhouette that glorifies height, into terms that make *us* confident in our clothes and comfortable in our bodies."

5'1" Newspaper Correspondent, Saint Louis, Missouri

The responses to the questionnaires led us to thoughts about how shorter women came to be second-class citizens in the world of fashion.

One factor, we believed, could be the insulation of the fashion makers—the designers themselves. We looked into this possibility.

Mollie Parnis, a very friendly and down-to-earth lady who says she is 5′5″, told us she makes her clothes on a 5′8″ model, then grades them down to smaller sizes. But she doesn't think of her size 4 as being for a short woman but rather for someone 5′5″ or 5′6″. "Do you ever really see any short women around?" she asked us with genuine but incredulous interest. "Because I don't. Not among my friends or the people I do business with," she said firmly.

Perry Ellis is a designer whose clothes we unstintingly admire but who is generally considered to be "hard-to-wear." No wonder, we learned: "Being short is all in the mind," he told us. "It has nothing to do with height." (Sorry, it has everything to do with height. It simply—is—height). He feels that the only mistakes short women make are *mental* mistakes and that short women should dress just the way tall ones do. "My size four is made for a tall, thin woman, but all a short woman has to do is take up the hem to proportion it to her size," he stated. Really? But when he designs does he consider his typical customer and think of how the clothes will look and fit on her body? His response: "When I design, I design in the abstract, looking at the design in terms of shape and fabric, rather than how it would look on the typical customer I am supposed to cater to."

Well, now we understand. . . .

One question we asked provoked an interesting batch of responses. In a culture that seems to glorify "tall" as "beautiful," *had any one of the women felt put-down socially because of her height?*

Some, to our delight, reported an opposite reaction.

"I love being short. Believe me, people don't know what they're missing. In high school, when the boys were shy, perhaps I didn't date as much as I would have liked because of my height. But now, of course, it's having the opposite effect!"

4′9″ Law Student, New York, New York

"I'm very pleased with my height and size. The only reason I would ever envy a taller woman is that she can carry extra weight better than I can. Otherwise, I enjoy being 'small.' I have less of a problem getting in and out of cabs, I fit into crowds on the bus during rush hour, and I adore being shorter than the majority of men."

5′3″ Sportswear Designer, Fort Lee, New Jersey

* * *

But many—too many, we were dismayed to learn—said that they felt a subtle and sometimes not-so-subtle negative reaction where men were concerned. "When the ideal woman is considered to be five foot seven, it's like being looked over and found wanting," wrote one petite respondent. Another commented: "It's just a sense I have that men are being turned off to short women. My ex-husband is six foot two; his new wife is five foot nine. He met me, you see, in an earlier era, when being short was 'in.' "

Some women felt the pressure outright.

"I've actually been told by a man that I'm not attractive to men because of my height and that men prefer tall women regardless of their own heights."

4'11½" Nutritionist, Baltimore, Maryland

"The male-oriented world has fitted me with a sense that no matter how well dressed or beautiful I look, I could never compete with a woman who is tall."

5'2" Saleswoman, Riverdale, New York

So how did "tall" come to be synonymous in the public eye with "beautiful"? Darned if we can figure it. For almost all of the last century, petite women were admired (after the example of diminutive Queen Victoria). Heelless slippers were even worn, for a time, in imitation of the small but royal stature.

As for our own century, whatever happened to songs being sung to sweethearts who measured "five foot two, eyes of blue" or to "Honey Bun" (who was "only sixty inches high")? And—how could it be forgotten—a good many of our most admired beauties and famous sex symbols all happened to be short.

Tiny Mary Pickford is an early example. The screen idol of her time, she was said to have worn Paris fashions to perfection—off-screen, that is, when she wasn't turning out the highly successful little-girl portrayals that earned her millions in those pre-income-tax days. (One of the special advantages of being short is that you manage to look a lot younger than you are for a longer period of time. Mary was one woman who recognized her doll-like height as the *asset* it really was. More than that, she played on it: We read of her traveling the country, exhorting citizens to buy War Bonds. "I'm only five feet tall," she cried, "but every inch of me is fighting American!")

Gloria Swanson was another extraordinary beauty of the same vintage, who epitomized for many the apex of screen glamour. Her height, 5′1½″, never seemed to interfere with her larger-than-life screen image or with her penchant for daring, dramatically styled fashions. (After all, wasn't this the woman who became known for the line "I'm still big; it's the pictures that have gotten small," in *Sunset Boulevard*?).

Swanson, you see, was an early proponent of "tall" body language, it seems. "I was only a half inch taller than Mary [Pickford]," she is reported to have said, "but I'd wear enormous heels and I'd tower over her. Then I'd say, 'Get out of my way, you little shrimp.' "

Looking over the roster of celebrity names, it's hard to believe that short women aren't considered to wear clothes well. During *her* decade, 5′4″ Joan Crawford set the fashions, too: the elaborately ruffled organdy gown she wore in *Letty Lynton* totally belies the fact that short women are supposed to be overpowered by ruffles and flourishes. Macy's claimed to have sold more than fifty thousand inexpensive versions of the Lynton confection. We think, too, that Crawford's Adrian-inspired broad-shouldered silhouette was one of the factors that contributed to her being remembered as looking taller than her actual height.

Need we say, too, that short women are amply represented in the sex appeal department? Lest anyone forget, the fabulous Mae West was only a little over 5′ tall. Aside from incredibly clever dressing (high heels and feathered hats, gowns with sinuous, elongating details), Mae "acted" big. Seductive Veronica Lake was also a five footer. And Jean Harlow, at 5′2″, was acclaimed to have a "photographically-perfect body," despite, or as we prefer to think, *because* of her scaled-down height. Other examples? How about petite Claudette Colbert as Cleopatra in *The Serpent of the Nile*, her small figure draped and wrapped in shimmering lamé, an irresistible queen. Another unforgettable—though short—Cleopatra: 5′2″ Elizabeth Taylor.

The vogue for petite beauties isn't just a fancy of days gone by, either. The young actress chosen to represent the perfect "10," Bo Derek, is just 5′3″ (she was filmed tall and towering next to 5′2″ Dudley Moore), as is rock star Debbie Harry of Blondie. Bardot-like Pia Zadora is 5′2″; Linda Ronstadt also measures in at a captivating 5′2″; sexy, raunchy Bette Midler at 5′1″; Dolly Parton at just 5′.

Of course, many of the stars you see on television are also short —sometimes you know it and sometimes you don't. Country singer

Barbara Mandrell shows off her petite proportions by casting super-tall chorus boys behind her. But others contrive to keep their heights under wraps. A call to a major TV station inquiring about under 5′4″ actresses brought this response from the network exec: "We really can't give out anyone's height," he told us, "because most press agents have gone to a lot of trouble either to fabricate a new height on their client's official bios or to simply keep it quiet. They just don't want it getting around that they [the actresses] are short."

"I'm sure I've lost jobs because of directors who preferred taller women," a 5′2″ actress/dancer told us. Cheryl Ladd, at 5′4″, admitted that her height almost kept her from winning the part of Kris Monroe in TV's *Charlie's Angels*.

With many TV personalities, height is disguised: It's hard to tell how tall they are or aren't, depending on how skillfully they're dressed or how they've mastered their own body language.

"There is a general tendency for shorter people to compensate for their heights by being more expansive and verbal and by using more body movements, as if to signal, 'I'm here,' 'I'm visible,' 'be aware of me,'" said Dr. Barry Lubetkin, clinical director of New York's Institute for Behavior Therapy. "Of course there is also an opposite reaction, that of being reclusive and 'invisible.'

"Frequently, shorter women look younger than they really are," Dr. Lubetkin continued, "and if their young little-girl image met with approval as they were growing up, they may play it up with such 'cute' mannerisms as childlike giggles, coquettish turns of the head, wide-eyed eye contact, and, when they walk, a mincing step rather than a more mature stride. On the other hand, if they've been made to feel humiliated because of their size, they may try to appear older instead."

Dr. Lubetkin emphasized that this doesn't apply to all short women, of course, and that it all depends on the particular individual's social history.

Petite Patti Lupone, who originated the role of Evita on Broadway, is a perfect example of the results of positive body language. When she showed up at a fashion sitting for a magazine one day, the editors (who didn't know in advance how tall she was), were sure that the lavish ball gowns they had chosen would overwhelm her completely. But once she put on her makeup, reported one editor, and turned on her star quality, her presence dominated the sitting.

Actress Linda Kelsey, who plays reporter Billie Newman on TV's *Lou Grant* is also just 5′3″, but so devoid of such aforementioned "cute" mannerisms that the only time you become even remotely aware of her height is when she stands next to tall Art Donovan, the dapper assistant city editor. Billie is also skillfully dressed, almost never appearing in clothes that are too big for her delicate frame, whether she's in jeans and a top or, as in more recent episodes, in casual but carefully pulled together "working woman" combos: skirts, jackets, and small-collared soft blouses.

Suzanne Pleshette, as Emily on the old *Bob Newhart Show* is another example of a short woman with tall body movements, plus a knack for carrying off fashion. As a result of that combination, the audience was left with nary a clue that she's only 5'4". Her character was superbly dressed, always chic. (She wore the clothes; they didn't wear her.)

On the other hand, 5'3" Bonnie Franklin's Anne Romano on *One Day at a Time* consistently dresses wrong for her height: Her overtailored working suits, overly long jackets, and mannish fedoras only accentuate her petiteness.

Try seeing if you can be clued into height with other personalities by either gesture or wardrobe. Kittenish Charlene Tilton of *Dallas* is 4'11". Linda Lavin, who plays Alice on the TV series of the same name, is 5'3". So is Isabel Sanford of *The Jeffersons*.

Interestingly, just as there's a body language of height, so there seems to be a verbal or written one. When we read that one state senator was described as having "perky good looks," we would have bet our boots that the lady was short. Similarly, in his book on height, *The Height of Your Life*, author Ralph Keyes related this anecdote about a 5'1" actress who heard that a new show was looking to cast a "very elegant woman." What constituted "elegant," the woman asked. Well, for starters, tall. That ended the conversation. When you're short, you can be "cute" or "perky," even "lovely," but never "elegant," she explained.

Work and the Shorter Woman

"Being short and being a woman is professional hell." That was how one disgruntled questionnaire respondent summed it up. Others talked about "lack of respect," the desire to be "taken seriously," and having "suggestions trivialized because of my height."

What it all adds up to is this: Despite the growing influx of women into the working world, women in business are *still* given second-class treatment because of their sex. Old prejudices die hard.

The woman who is short, however, has two strikes against her. Not only is she female, but she's also up against another obstacle: In the business world, there's an acknowledged stigma against those of less-than-average height (something shorter men have been combating for years). Studies show that employers unconsciously seem to equate taller with better, rewarding higher salaries, bigger raises, and quicker promotions to the tall.

All of which is all the more reason that the shorter woman, smaller even than the shorter man, has to dress to heighten her image —authoritatively, positively, femininely—making the most of every inch she's got. "I may have short legs," fumed one 5'3" Ph.D. candidate, "but my brain is full-sized!"

In nearly all fields, short women run up against a credibility gap owing to the stereotype of their size: Their petite looks seem to suggest "young" and "little girlish," decidedly hampering their acceptance both as effective co-workers and as managers.

When 5'2" Jacqueline McMickens became the first female chief of operations of the New York City Department of Corrections, she was described as "looking more like a college sophomore than a police chief," although, at the time, Mrs. McMickens was wearing a stylish and businesslike tan Calvin Klein suit. She admitted that because of her *youthful looks*, her *height* and her *sex*, many of her male subordinates were at first reluctant to accept her.

Congresswoman Shirley Chisholm, a petite ninety-pounder couldn't find work after college, even as teacher's aide, until she finally told an interviewer in frustration: "Don't judge me by my size." Then, given a tryout, she was a success.

Several women wrote us about the different forms of job discrimination they felt they had been subject to because of their size. One 5'1" woman recalls being turned away from a major banking institution's trainee program because she didn't have "the right image." Others mentioned jobs they would have liked to have tried for but couldn't because of official height requirements. "I would love to have been a stewardess but couldn't because I'm only five feet tall," wrote a woman from Seattle. (Ironically, the original stewardesses back in 1930 had to be graduate nurses—to give the passengers a feeling of safety—and, because the planes were small, they were required to be under 5'4" and less than 115 pounds.)

Other jobs that have height requirements are various areas of law enforcement and the armed forces. But most job discrimination is more subtle than official.

* * *

"When dealing with taller people, it is sometimes difficult to project professional stature if one lacks it physically."

31-year-old, 5'2½" Lawyer

"A taller woman just looks more authoritative. She can wear more stylish clothes and flat shoes without looking young and unprofessional and look men right in the eye."

42-year-old, 5'3" Sales Representative

Of course, there are exceptions—dynamic women under 5'4", who, with talent and persistence, have succeeded in all fields of endeavor: lyric soprano Teresa Stratas, barely 5' tall; Helen Galland, president of the nationwide eleven-store Bonwit Teller chain, 5'4" (a previous Bonwit store president, retail whiz Mildred Custin, was 5'); Matina Horner, president of Radcliffe College, about 5'3"; Jean Rosenberg, vice-president and merchandising director of Bendel's, 5'4" (one of her first finds: Sonia Rykiel, "because her clothes are great on small people like me," she said); Muriel Siebert, 5', the first woman to obtain a seat on the New York Stock Exchange; Chicago's Mayor Jane Byrne, 5'3"; gymnast Cathy Rigby, 4'11½"; writers Joan Didion, Erica Jong, and Lillian Hellman, 5'2", 5'3", and 5'4" respectively. Film critic Pauline Kael is 5'. Dancers Patricia McBride and Natalia Makarova, 5'2" and 5'3"; Oscar-winning costume designer Edith Head, 5'1" . . . and others.

"I wear appropriate clothing, practice good posture, and don't feel I'm perceived as a mini-sized person," said Barbara D., 5'2", a thirty-seven-year-old financial consultant. Lawyer Liz T., 5'3", put it like this: "Walking tall has always been my approach to life, and being short gives me an edge in the world of business—the element of surprise. Business is still a man's world, and working within it daily I see the impact the element of surprise a small attractive woman can have when she presents a nice package—neat and well dressed—*and then whams them with her knowledge.*"

Keep in mind, however, that style isn't the same as substance. Looking the part isn't going to make a whit of difference if you can't back it up with performance. But all other things being equal, an attractive personal appearance can serve to give you an edge—and tip the scales in your favor. On the job, making the most of every inch can change the way others see you and the way you see yourself.

What You'll Find in *Short Chic*

Effective dressing, however—*effective* meaning that it works for you and that you look good and feel comfortable in what you're wearing —applies not only to shorter women with paying jobs but to any woman, however she spends her time—in the office or at home, during leisure hours, in all areas of her life.

But up until now, except for a few token nods from the fashion-powers-that-be, the shorter woman has been practically ignored by the fashion industry. Key words: *until now.* As one woman put it, "We are a mini-army, eager to be recognized as fashion-aware, not as stepsisters in hand-me-downs."

Realistically, we want to emphasize that *Short Chic* is not a guide on how to look tall. If you're 5'2", there's no way in the world you're going to look 5'8". What you can look is not shorter than you really are, that is: Although what you wear won't necessarily add more than an inch or two to your appearance, the right clothes can prevent you from losing any of the precious inches you already have and can enable you to look good *as you are*, petite, sure but stylish, fashionable, comfortable also.

What you're going to find in these pages is information you're not going to find anywhere else: *professional fashion advice tailored specifically to you*, garnered from hundreds of experts in all areas of fashion—fashion designers (especially those who are under 5'4" themselves), clothing manufacturers, retailers, fashion and beauty editors, stylists, and professional fashion consultants.

What you're going to find are *solutions* to putting clothes together so that they work for you, not against you.

- You'll find the rules, plus the know-how to get around them so that you'll come out looking better than ever.
- You'll learn how to train your fashion eye to see clothes in terms of *yourself* and *your* needs.
- You'll discover how to adapt the styles that suit your size to the changing eye of fashion (like the reasons, for example, some short women can wear longer skirts and look good and some can't—and which category *you* belong to).
- The special needs of the two most prevalent short figure types.
- The all-important rules of scale and proportion, this time explained as they pertain to women under 5'4".
- How to determine your most flattering hemline range and most workable pants shapes.

- When to listen to the dictates of designers and when to ignore them.
- How to choose a fur coat that doesn't dwarf you.
- How to stretch your height with the right accessories . . . and more.

Plus, we think you'll find *Short Chic* is a guide that lasts. Fashions change, but the basic principles here will remain the same, i.e., red will always be an eye-catching color, and the long, narrow lines of a coat like the reefer will always make the wearer look longer and slimmer. The same principles that can be used to interpret fashion now will hold five years from now as well.

A note about Short Chic *shopping tips:* Throughout *Short Chic*, we've made an attempt to offer tips on just *some* of the American (mostly) designers and manufacturers that we and others have generally found to work well for shorter women. Bear in mind that this is by no means intended to be an all-inclusive listing; doubtless you will want to add your own personal favorites to the roster. Moreover, depending on your own proportions, some will work for you and others won't. In addition, recognize that styles, cuts, and prices change; some manufacturers mentioned may no longer be available; new ones—good ones, we hope—will crop up to take their place. These recommendations should not be construed as implying failure on the part of those not mentioned to provide clothes suitable to the shorter woman.

2. The Height of Chic: Starting from Square One

"One side will make you grow taller, and the other side will make you grow shorter."

"One side of *what?* The other side of *what?*" thought Alice to herself.

"Of the mushroom," said the Caterpillar. . . .

Alice remained looking thoughtfully at the mushroom for a minute. . . . at last she stretched her arms round it as far as they would go, and broke off a bit of the edge with each hand.

"And now which is which?" she said to herself. . . .

—Lewis Carroll,
Alice's Adventures in Wonderland

Poor Alice. Only three inches high and nowhere to go for a straight answer on how to get any taller. It's a plight, no doubt, that would be recognizable to any under-5'4" woman who's ever tried to get some usable fashion advice on the same subject. Nothing will make you physically taller, of course (magic mushrooms exist only in Wonderland); but you'll find that clothes can go a long way toward making you *look* taller.

How Can You Dress Tall?

Most short women with an interest in fashion already know the basic rules: "Don't wear horizontal stripes"; "Match your stocking to your shoes"; and so on and so on. True, the rules work; they will help you to look taller. We'll be discussing them all later on. But there's a lot more to a tall fashion image than *just* looking taller. The shorter woman also wants to look chic. Sophisticated. Glamorous. Sexy. *Interesting.* In other words, she wants—and has every right to expect—the same fashion options that taller women have always had.

Coming to Terms with Proportion and Scale

As the first step toward recognizing your options, read the following paragraph and commit it to memory:

> *All other things being equal, there is no reason a short woman can't look just as terrific in clothes as a tall woman. It's not a question of your actual height (which is a fixed factor)—it's a question of proportion and scale (which are both controllable factors).*

Got that? Now, we know that those two words *proportion* and *scale* are always being thrown at you by fashion experts. And by now, when you see them coming, you may experience an overwhelming urge to run in the opposite direction. But wait! Come back! Because those are two of the most important things that are going to help you achieve a taller, more fashionable image. And the one you have to consider first is proportion. *Yours* . . .

Proportion: According to the classical Greek definition, the ideal stature for a woman measures seven and a half times the length of her head. If you'd like to test the theory, measure the length of your head (top of forehead to chin) and multiply that figure by seven and a half. Ideally, the result should equal your height in inches. Example: If your head length measures eight inches, your height (ideally) would be 5', or 60 inches (which is seven and a half times eight). You don't measure up? Don't worry—few women do exactly. But the point is this: an ideally proportioned body has nothing to do with height. A woman can have ideal proportions whether she's 4'11" or 5'10"!

The second part of the proportion question deals with the placement of the waist and the length of the legs. You're either:

1. equally proportioned (average waist length and leg length for your size),
2. short-waisted and long-legged,

or 3. long-waisted and short-legged.

If you can't decide which you are, ask yourself: If you could add one inch of length to either your waist or your legs, which would it be? If you said "waist," you're probably short-waisted. If "legs," long-waisted. And if you had difficulty making up your mind, you're most likely equally proportioned. But whatever your body type, you should always keep it in mind when choosing clothes.

Other proportions count, too: The width of the shoulders, hips, and waist; the size of the bust; the length of the neck; and the upper and lower proportions of the leg—all have to be considered when you're thinking tall, and many of the aforementioned will probably fall into the category of assets. You don't believe it? Read on.

- *A small head* makes the body below it look taller. (Most models, if you'll notice, have small heads.)
- *A long neck* instantly creates the illusion of height.
- *Straight, slightly broad shoulders* are a fashion asset because clothes will drape gracefully down from the shoulder.
- *Long legs* always make a body appear taller (and always look terrific in pants).
- *A short woman with a long waist* will have much less trouble than her short-waisted sister when it comes to finding tops and dresses that fit and look well on her.
- *A narrow waist and ribcage is another plus.* When you're little in the middle, it's easier to make the rest of you look slimmer, and looking slimmer automatically means looking taller.
- *Narrow hips* mean that you can indulge in clothes with full pleats and gathers and still look taller and slimmer. You're also a natural in pants.
- *Legs that are longer from the knee down* than from the knee up are also an asset: Skirt lengths will be less of a problem for you. And whether the fashions call for long skirts or short, you can wear either and still look taller than you are.
- *And last, but certainly not least: A slim or average figure* is the best possible asset you could have when it comes to looking taller. To quote one of our questionnaire respondents; a 5', ninety-two pound art gallery worker: "As long as a woman is thin and well proportioned, she has only to be reasonable in her choice of clothes. A short heavy woman looks one hundred percent worse than an average heavy woman." It's true that extra pounds add up more quickly on a short woman than the same number of extra pounds do on someone taller. If you really care about heightening your fashion image, you've got to keep yourself in good shape. Not thin, necessarily (though it's a plus if you are), but not more than

ten pounds over the mark.

Scale (the second controllable factor) is the size of a thing in its relation to something else. In fashion terms, that usually means the size of the details on a garment (a print, a lapel, a pocket, and so on) in its relation to the garment itself *and to the wearer.* Note the emphasis on the last four words. For the shorter woman, that consideration is essential because, although a piece of clothing—a jacket, say—may be scaled down to her size, the details on that jacket may not necessarily be. And if they're not, she should have the details altered to scale or avoid the jacket altogether.

As an example of what we mean, look at the figure at right (also shown on the cover). You can't tell just by looking at it whether the woman is supposed to be short or tall—and one reason you can't is because every clothing detail is scaled to the size of the figure.

- The model is dressed in just one color—in this case, shades of gray ranging from pale pearl gray to deep charcoal. The fashion interest created by the mix of texture—the slick leather sheen of the coat, the tweed of the scarf, the downy cashmere of the sweater, keeps such a color pallette from being monotonous.
- Proportion helps. The three-quarter-length coat could look choppy, but it doesn't because it's worn with a color-matched gray skirt, which is also slim and narrow.
- The unbroken line of color from the sweater to the skirt continues right down to the steel-gray of the boots, a more elongating choice than a pump.
- The sweater is striped in thin, low-contrast tones of gray-on-gray (bold, broad stripes *wouldn't* have worked); the turtleneck is scaled smaller, neater.
- The knitted muffler creates a long, vertical line.
- The two patterned bangles carry the eye out to the wrist, adding interest without cutting height the way a belt would.
- The model's hair is perfectly proportioned at chin-length, neither too long nor too short.
- The brim on the hat is jaunty enough for style but far from wide and overpowering.

If you don't trust yourself to judge scale correctly, you can start intensive training in that area just by scrutinizing the models in fashion magazines or the fashionable women you see on the street. When you do, be thinking along the lines of such scale questions as:

- How wide is the lapel of the jacket in relation to the width of the shoulder?
- How far above the waist does the breast pocket fall?
- How long is the skirt in relation to the length of the jacket?

In no time, you'll find yourself evaluating the scale of any detail, like a pro. With that talent in your possession, you'll be able to judge how any fashion should look when it's scaled down to your size.

The Checks and Balances Dressing System

Throughout this book we'll be giving you rules, tips, dos, don'ts and how-tos for dressing tall and perfecting your fashion image—and, quite frankly, if you tried to follow every one of them, you'd never find a thing to wear! The rules are there to be used, of course. But rather than have you attempt to obey every one to the letter, we suggest you think of them as data to be fed into an eight-point clothes-evaluating system of Checks and Balances. The importance of the system can't be overemphasized because it will tell you not only whether a particular garment works on you but also why it does or doesn't.

How the System Works   Try on the garment, look at yourself in a full-length mirror, then evaluate the garment in terms of the following eight points, letting each point count as a plus (+) or a minus (−), depending on whether it contributes to a tall image or detracts from it. Points to consider include:

1. your height
2. your weight
3. the color of the garment
4. the texture of the fabric
5. the pattern of the fabric
6. the line of the garment (verticals or horizontals contributed by the neckline, the seams, or a striped pattern)
7. the cut of the garment
8. the drape of the fabric.

To get you acquainted with the general idea, here's an example of the Checks and Balances System in action.

Anne Marie once found a dress that, at first glance anyway, should have been a no-no for any short woman. The checks against it:

1. The dress had a horizontal neckline. (*Remember: horizontals shorten you, verticals lengthen.*)
2. It was patterned with medium-sized horizontal stripes.
3. The colors were bright and bold.

Now, all of the above, as you'll learn in upcoming chapters, are supposed to make you look heavier and/or shorter. Usually, they will. *But* those three minuses happened to be balanced (and ultimately vetoed) by five elongating pluses:

1. Anne Marie herself is on the tall side of short (5'2").
2. She is slim.
3. The dress was made of a fluid silk knit.
4. The texture of the knit was flat.
5. The cut of the dress was straight and close to the body.

Result of the Checks and Balances evaluation: The five pluses override the three minuses—which explains why the dress looked sensational on her. Now, if you translate all that information into chart form, it would look something like the chart below.

Short Chic Checks and Balances Chart

Points to Consider	Elongating (+)	Shortening (−)	Rating (+)	(−)
1. Height	Over 5' tall	5' or under	√	
2. Weight	Slim or average	Overweight	√	
3. Color	Dark or grayed	Bright or light		√
4. Texture	Flat	Deep	√	
5. Pattern	Solid or miniprint	Medium/large print		√
6. Lines	Verticals	Horizontals		√
7. Cut	Close to body	Full, stands away from body	√	
8. Drape	Soft/fluid	Stiff/bulky	√	
		Totals	+5	−3

The pluses have it!

After you've read our book and become more familiar with all the rules we'll be talking about, you should refer back to this chapter and devise a Checks and Balances chart for yourself. Once you get used to it, you'll be able to do it in your head anytime, anywhere, for any piece of clothing you want to evaluate. As you get more proficient, you'll realize that some points may carry more weight than others (which you'll want to consider in case you wind up with a tie score of pluses and minuses). You may even want to list additional factors in the Points to Consider column: special figure problems or assets when they are applicable. (If you're evaluating a skirt and you're slim but have heavy thighs, you'll want to take that into consideration. Or if you have a long graceful neck, and you're evaluating a blouse, you'll want to count that graceful neck as a plus.) The point of the whole system is that it reduces some of the mysteries of fashion to a logical, surefire formula you can use every day.

Developing Your Style Sense

A woman can spend a fortune on designer clothes, but if she hasn't got style sense, the result can be very bargain basement.

Style is what gives fashion individual character. It's a special way of putting things together. It can be sophisticated or romantic, elegant or amusing—but real style is always in good taste and always expresses something unique about the wearer. How do you go about developing this sixth sense?

An eye for fashion is an inherent part of style. When a woman has a good fashion eye, she has the ability to look at an outfit in terms of its own appeal *and* in terms of the times. Fashions change, after all, and your way of looking at them should change, too. A skirt that looked too long to your eye one season may look just right the next. Reason: Sometimes the eye is meant to assess "length lines" from waist to hem (as when long skirts are in), sometimes from neck to hem (when short skirts are the thing). Focus will change, too. One year the bust may be the center of attention; another year the buttocks. Whatever the given focus at any given time, your eye should be judging fashion from that viewpoint. When it does, not only will you appreciate what's being said in fashion terms, but you will also understand why certain accessories shown with that fashion-look work and why others don't.

As a good for-instance, let's go back to the twenties. During the flapper era, busts were flattened, dress lines were straight, accent was on the hip (via dropped waists and hip sashes), and heels were of low-to-medium height to accommodate the shorter skirts. Now imagine the same look worn with a pair of stiletto heels and a waist-cropped jacket from the fifties. *Disaster!* The dress and the accessories would be speaking two different fashion languages. Which certainly isn't to say you can never mix pieces from two different eras: You can and should, if that's the way your style sense takes you. But just make sure that the pieces aren't working at cross-purposes and that they don't contradict one another in the process.

The virtues of patience and discipline can't be ignored when you're talking about style. Most fashion mavens know that when a woman looks wonderfully turned out, it often means that she had the patience and discipline to *wait* until she found exactly the right dress, bag, or scarf, and the willpower to not settle for "almost right." At 5'3", Marilyn Cooperman, the former fashion director of *Seventeen Magazine* (now editor-in-chief of Simplicity Patterns), is a woman with terrific personal style who agrees with the wait-until-you- find idea completely.

"Over the years I've learned to be very careful and selective about fashion. I think you should always wait until you absolutely love a thing and not make do. That's discipline. . . . For example, I once made a blouse from some exquisite Liberty fabric my husband bought for me in Italy, and when I was choosing the buttons for it, I wouldn't settle. I own hundreds of beautiful buttons, and I selected some from those. But, as it turned out, the buttons were *too* wonderful; they had too much personality for the blouse. So, in the end, I bought buttons especially for it. . . . A friend of mine is another good example of the kind of self-discipline we're talking about. She has impeccable taste and style sense, especially about jewelry. It isn't always the most expensive, but it is always the most interesting and refined because she'd never settle for something less."

Quality, another inseparable part of good style sense, refers to the excellence of a thing. And when it comes to fashion, the quality of the clothes you wear is always a direct reflection on you. But, you may protest, is it fair to judge a person's quality by the way she dresses? Of course it isn't. But let's face it, most of us do just that— even if only on an unconscious level. Yes, it happens, and more often than any of us would like to admit. So rather than chance it, best play safe and opt for the best quality you can afford. How **can you** recognize good quality when you see it? Well, some positive indications would include:

- The superiority of the materials from which a thing is made (the real and natural as opposed to the synthetic).
- The amount of craftsmanship that went into its making (faultless stitching lines, reinforced seams, etc.).
- The attention paid to small details (evenly matched pleats, beautifully made buttonholes, the matching of a lining's pattern along a hidden seam).
- And, finally, quality can refer to the uniqueness of the design (so when you wear the item, you won't meet yourself coming and going on the street).

The best quality isn't always the most expensive, and the most expensive isn't always the best quality. You've got to use your head; when you do, we think you'll discover that there are still plenty of great things out there that can be had for a reasonable price. Because, in the final analysis, quality clothes may speak for themselves, but they also say some very complimentary things about *you!*

Our last word on style: Study the classics. Now when we say "classic," some women automatically think "boring." But you have to remember that classic clothing can be tailored, romantic, sophisticated, or offbeat and still hold onto its title. What makes it a classic is its sense of timelessness—the ability of the design to "hold" and still look good from year to year. The characteristic that keeps such a classic from becoming dull and repetitive is that it always expresses the individuality of the wearer. This has to do with the way the classics are combined when they're worn. For example, instead of adapting a single classic look (like preppy) from head to toe, add a dash of the unexpected. Instead of topping a tartan skirt with a blazer, make it a black wool melton jacket from the thirties. Or pair a lacy Edwardian blouse with gray flannel men's trousers from the forties. That element of pleasant surprise is where real style sense expresses itself.

If you hang around fashion magazines, you'll begin to notice that fashion editors themselves dress in classic pieces most of the time. Not that they ignore the trends; it's just a matter of not getting too carried away by them. When they do want to update their look, they may buy a few separate pieces of the current fashion or add a few new accessories and *voilà!*—the classics are turned into trendy.

When the Rules Count

You're not always going to care about looking taller or more fashionable. When you're running in the Boston Marathon, shoveling out the driveway, or mopping up the baby's lunch from the floor—who cares about tall? But when you do care—on the job and angling for a promotion, out for a special evening, or making a speech in front of three hundred people—then it's nice to know that the rules are there to help you look your tallest, your chicest, your best ever!

Making Friends with Your Mirror Image

First of all, we're assuming you own a mirror to have an image in. What you need is a reliable, *full-length* mirror that will enable you to see yourself from head to toe. Even if you're just checking to see how you look in a hat, you need the long view to see how that hat works with your height and your entire outfit.

Once you have acquired the mirror in question, stand in front of it *sans* a stitch. (Yes, we know it can be painful, but think of it this way: If you like what you see, your ego will get a boost. And if you don't, it may prompt you to swear off brownies and sign up for that exercise class you've been thinking about. So either way, you win.) As you look at yourself, be as objective as possible (pretend you're looking at another woman's body), and take note of everything: the length of your neck, the width of your shoulders, waist and hips, the size of your bust, the length and shape of your legs. All these things will be taken into account later on. The important thing is not to cheat and not to assume you already know what you're going to find. Women are notoriously astigmatic when it comes to their own bodies (usually veering toward the negative). For example, don't think your hips are too big just because they're larger than your bust. It may be that your hips are fine and your bust is small. And that kind of distinction is important when you're choosing clothes to correct figure flaws and build up height.

---

3. Fabric as Image-Maker

Fabric is one of the most important secrets of Short Chic, and this is the chapter that will introduce you to its hidden mysteries. Once you've learned them, you'll be able to use fabric in ways that work for your height instead of against it . . . to create illusions about your proportions . . . to change your fashion image from subtle and safe to downright dynamic. With the right fabric know-how, you'll also be able to experiment with different looks the same way tall women do—by layering, mixing patterns, playing with color, breaking the rules even—but in special ways that flatter your height. In other words, when you know the potential of fabric, you'll discover that it's the next best thing to having a magic wand!

Feminine/Dressy vs. Tailored/Casual

The first thing to remember is that each fabric, because of its texture, pattern, color, weight, or finish, projects a certain image that can be classified as feminine/formal or tailored/casual—regardless of the piece of clothing it's been made into. For example: a blazer in velvet is usually considered to be dressy, romantic, "for special occasions," whereas the same blazer in tweed comes across as sporty, hard-edged, or practical. The key is to use a mixture of those qualities in a way that achieves the image you want to project.

We know whereof we speak when we say that many 5'4"-and-under businesswomen make a fabric mistake toward one extreme or the other. One young executive woman we know measures 5' tall in bare feet, looks younger than her twenty-eight years, and is a genius in public relations—a combination of factors that could be lethal where acceptance on the job is concerned. So what did she do? Under the impression that looking authoritative meant dressing to kill, she filled her closet with silk blouses, wool crepe de Chine suits, and lots of showy jewelry (on her salary she could afford to) . . . until she got tired of people asking her if she had a special date that night. Finally she got the message and switched to tweedy blazers, un-matched wool suits, and the like. As a result, she found that people seemed to be a lot more comfortable around her. She also started getting more professional responses from the male clients she worked with.

From this we can only conclude that although dressing to the nines has its place, the office is not usually it. When a small woman bedecks herself with romantic, feminine fabrics in a work situation, she can give the impression of being a fluffy-headed female—an image that short women can all too easily fall into if they're not careful.

And then there's the short woman who shoots for the other end of the pole: pin-striped menswear suits, white Oxford shirts, ties, and pants. The theory here, we assume, is that if you look like a man, men will treat you as an equal in spite of your sex and height. Another mistaken idea, which usually just plays up what you're trying to play down.

Naturally your choice of image will depend largely on the position you hold and the traditional dress requirements of that position. A banker isn't going to dress like an art director or a kindergarten teacher. But generally, what you're aiming for here is a happy compromise between the two extremes. By learning to work with the two categories of image-making fabrics, you can hit just the right note.

Some examples: a soft silk blouse or an angora turtleneck (both feminine fabrics) can soften the hard-edged look of a classically tailored wool tweed suit. Conversely, wool trousers or a simple tweed skirt can be dressed up with a velvet blazer.

* * *

If you're unsure about the image you've been projecting, **run** your eye down the following list to see if you've been playing it to extremes, that is, choosing too heavily from one column or the other. If you have, try mixing a few from column A with a few from column B. You may be pleasantly surprised at the result.

A. *Feminine Fabrics*	B. *Tailored/Casual Fabrics*
silk crepe	twill
velvet	solid, medium- to heavy-
challis	weight wools
soft knits	corduroy
velour	denim
satin	poplin
jersey	canvas
suede	khaki
lace	leather
voile	flannel
taffeta	tweed

Here are a few more examples of how to mix both types successfully:

1. *A skirt combo for office wear*
    1. a silk crepe de Chine blouse (A)
    2. a paisley wool jersey skirt (A)
    3. a brown leather vest (B)
    4. a tweed hacking jacket (B)

2. *A casual pants combo*
    1. khaki cotton canvas army-style trousers (B)
    2. a twill shirt-jacket (B)
    3. a Victorian cotton and lace blouse (A)
    4. a multicolored flannel challis neck scarf (A)

Note: Some fabrics, of course, can go either way, and the image they project will pretty much depend on the style of the garment, whether tailored and hard-edged or more fluid and feminine.

Texture: Using It to Create Optical Illusions

You've probably noticed that in combining feminine fabrics from column A with tailored/casual fabrics from column B, we're combining textures. And texture is what gives character to a fabric: softness or crispness, stiffness or fluidity, smoothness or roughness, dullness or shine. As far as the shorter woman is concerned, it's a top priority when choosing clothes. Forget the fact that you've finally found a skirt whose plaid perfectly matches the tweedy sweater your cousin Audrey gave you for Christmas. If the skirt's not the right texture, it won't feel right or look right—and it probably won't do a heck of a lot for the sweater either. The reason for being choosy: *Texture has the ability to emphasize or deemphasize the wearer.* If you use your smarts, you can make both eye-deceiving abilities work to your advantage.

DO opt for soft, fluid fabrics instead of stiff ones when possible. Generally speaking, shorter women need fluid fabrics that gracefully skim the body and create a narrow profile. As a matter of fact, the softer and more fluid the better. When a woman measures 5′7″ and upward, she's got the length required to carry off the heavier, stiffer versions of cotton, linen, wool, and such. On a short woman, these textures can add bulk and in some cases look downright silly. The best example of what we mean: Remember when you used to make clothes for your doll? After a few false attempts you probably discovered that a skirt made from a scrap of Harris tweed didn't work half as well as one sewn from pliable cotton jersey. And, on a larger scale, the same general principle holds true: The smaller and shorter you are, the softer the fabric should be.

DON'T make the mistake of thinking that heavy, stiff fabric is just what your small frame needs to appear larger; it doesn't work that way. If a woman is small-boned, bulky fabrics can overwhelm her and make her appear even smaller by contrast (imagine slim, small-boned legs stemming out from under a stiff, heavy skirt. *Uh-unh!*) And on a heavier woman, bulky fabrics only accentuate what's already there. This is especially true if the stiff fabric happens to be in a skirt. (It helps if the skirt is full-length because the material will be covering a greater area, but even here, a softer fabric is preferable.)

DO keep your eyes open for clothes made from soft cottons (broadcloth, Oxford cloth, muslin, and damask, for example, as opposed to stiffer polished cottons and poplins), fine-weave linen, sheer (sheer as in "lightweight," not as in "see-through") wools, silks, challis, and just about anything knitted—as long as it's not too bulky.

* * *

DO be careful about the heavy fabrics you do wear. If you happen to be terribly fond of richly woven brocade, crisp linen, and sturdy wool melton, there's no reason to avoid them altogether if you're short. But try to confine the stiff or bulky fabric to the upper part of your body in a jacket or vest or to a coat. Another qualifier: Make sure the piece is cut close to the body, and that it's made with a minimum of fabric needed for the style.

Flat vs. Shiny, Thin vs. Thick

Another point about texture concerns the effect of light on the fabric. Fact: Shiny textures (satin, silk, polished cotton, and such), as well as deep-pile fabrics (terrycloth, velour, velvet, chenille, wide-wale corduroy, and so on) reflect light in such a way as to make the garment—and you—appear larger. Not taller. Just larger.

On the other side of the coin, flatter weaves and matte-finish fabrics (cotton pique, lightweight wool jerseys, raw silk, and so on) absorb light—which means they don't add unwanted bulk. Does that mean you're confined to a life of flat, thin textures if you want to dress tall? Not at all. If you want to wear velours, wide-wales, or any heavily textured fabric, just follow the stiff-fabrics rule: Use them in a jacket, vest, or coat, and save the smoother weaves for a dress, skirt, or pants. Another tip: To add interest to those smooth weaves, look for detailing in the design and cut (top-stitching, pleats, and so on).

Pattern: Scaling Its Size to Yours

"Short women should stay away from large patterns." How many times have you heard that one from your friendly neighborhood saleslady? Well, in this case, she's right . . . mostly. Super-sized plaids, overblown flowers, polka dots the size of dinner plates . . . naturally you can't wear them if you're short. You probably couldn't wear them if you were anything under 5'10"! The whole trick is in making sure the patterns you wear are scaled down to your size. Here's how it works:

- For the most part, it will behoove you to go for the smaller checks, the more diminutive prints, the scaled-to-size plaids and stripes—not only because pattern works best when it's kept in proportion, but also because any pattern adds *some* bulk. And, naturally, the more noticeable the pattern, the heavier it will make you look.

- When bold patterns are in vogue, look for a slightly reduced version of what they're showing on the fashion runways. The pattern will still be bold, but it will be proportioned to you.
- Large patterns (if you like to wear them) should be confined to the upper portion of the body in a jacket or vest that falls close to the body.
- When the pattern itself is large, its colors should be muted. (By following this last rule, you can even get away with using a big print in a body-skimming gathered skirt.)

It always pays to experiment, however, because sometimes you never know about pattern: While modeling for a petites story in *Harper's Bazaar*, actress Morgan Fairchild (who is only 5'4" as well as small-boned and petite) hesitated when confronted with a voluminous silk Michaele Vollbracht dress in a brightly colored, circus-poster print. Being very savvy about fashion and about what did and didn't work on her small frame, she said, "I'm too small-boned for a dress like that." But she was game enough to try it, and when she did—surprise! The material was so soft and fluid that the amount of fabric made no difference. And once the dress was belted, the pattern turned into an abstract print that came across as a fabulous play of color. So you never know!

Pattern Mixing: How to Mix Patterns the Way Models Do and Make It Work for Your Height

Even though dressing in patterns will add some degree of bulk, it also adds a high degree of chic to your look. If, like many short women, you've admired the mixed pattern look but shied away from mixing patterns because of your height and size (or simply because you never knew how to do it), consider giving it a try. We think the fashion image you'll project will be worth the risk of looking a wee bit bulkier.

If you're thinking (as you glance at your lunch of cottage cheese and grapefruit) that this is a rather cavalier statement, rest assured, it's not. Case in point: Suzanne B., a thirtyish, 5'2" gallery owner who showed up for her *Short Chic* interview wearing black-and-white mini-herringbone-checked pants, a red/green/black/white plaid taffeta blouse with a ruffled neck, tied together with a longish black wool wrap sweater. While she readily admitted she wouldn't raise a protest at losing five or six pounds, she explained, "I'm sure I'd look thinner in a solid color wool pants and sweater, but frankly I don't think I'd look half as attractive or interesting. And I'm more concerned with that—and with experimenting with different pattern and color combinations—than in looking stick-thin." So, with that sentiment in mind, here's how to wear pattern on pattern and make it work for your height:

Rule 1: It can't be denied that the thinner you are, the more easily you can carry off this look. (While five pounds or so over the mark can be a slight disadvantage, fifteen pounds or more can be a major problem in pattern mixing, if you're short.)

Rule 2: Keep in mind what we said about scaled-down pattern; when you're mixing several together, it's a must.

Rule 3: Stick with the classics: multicolor tweeds, mini-herringbone tweeds and houndstooth checks, polka dots, paisleys, and skinny stripes. As a rule, florals usually sit this one out because they're harder to work with. But even they can join the classics group if they're used in a diminutive geometric-type print—the "shower of flowers" that you often see in the better wool challis skirts, shawls, and scarves.

Rule 4: Never use more than three, possibly four, coordinating colors at a time, or you might end up looking as if you dressed on your way out of a burning building.

Putting the Rules into Practice   The simplest form of pattern mixing would involve a very limited colored scale—say, black and white. Here's how to combine different patterns of those colors in a sophisticated evening look.

1. Tapered evening pants in white pin-dotted black crepe.
2. A white crepe blouse scored with thin black pinstripes.

You might take this combination to the second level by adding . . .

3. A black-and-white bird's-eye check jacket.
4. A black/white/gray/red paisley scarf.

As you get more advanced at pattern mixing, you might try something along the lines of the daytime combinations that follow. The colors are all toned down and muted (which means they won't overpower a small frame), and all the patterns used are simple menswear classics.

1. A blue/brown/cream tweed blazer
2. A blue/brown/cream Argyle vest

3. A brown/cream pin-striped shirt
4. A blue/brown herringbone skirt

You could even stick a paisley hankie in your breast pocket (say in a fourth coordinating color, like cranberry with some blue and brown in it), and the whole thing would work beautifully.

If you're still convinced that pattern mixing will make you look short and dumpy, here's a modified version that confines the pattern interest to the upper part of the body while drawing focus away from your hips.

1. Solid grayish green trousers
2. A maize/cream checked flannel shirt
3. A gold/green/red wool paisley vest
4. A green/gold tattersall wool scarf

Pattern mixing can be a little tricky at first if you're new to it, but study these combinations and the fashion magazines for direction, and you'll find yourself catching on in no time.

Layering with Fabrics

We were surprised at the number of women whom we surveyed who said they loved the layered look but avoided it because of their height. The truth is that you can dress in layers—*if* the fabrics are thin (so you won't have to worry about excess bulk on your smaller, shorter frame) and *if* the colors you use are in the same tonality (so you won't chop away at your height with distractions of color). An example of the technique:

Carla D., 5'2½", works at a real estate developers office by day and studies at night for her own agent's license. Since her schedule is tight (she's also the mother of two sons, Bryan, age eight, and Jay, thirteen), she's got a minimum of time to shop for clothes. But she manages to pull together a casual but professional office look that a taller woman would envy. Her strategy: She works with a small wardrobe based on thin, easily piled-on layers designed to work with her height. "I mostly buy neutral-colored classics, all in the same general color scheme, then switch them around to suit my needs and my schedule. By sticking with just one basic tone, my shopping is simplified and I know that everything works either over or under everything else as well as all together."

Her typical look might include a camel-colored light wool jump suit, layered over a thin yellow cotton-knit turtleneck. Over the jump suit, an unlined chamois shirt-jacket ("a basic piece—I wear it belted so I feel more dressed-up"), plus an elongating accessory—a cream-colored cashmere scarf ("bought years ago at the men's department at Brooks Brothers"), worn untied.

More Tips on Layering

When your base is a skirt, be sure it's a style that fits smoothly around the waist and hips. Layering over a dirndl with a lot of gathering at the waist won't work if the fabric is something heavy (like a tweed), whereas one in narrow-falling wool jersey will.

When your base is pants, be sure they're classically tailored pants with a smooth, flat front.

Color: Bending the Rules

We've often referred to color in this chapter, and we'll be bringing it up again frequently throughout this book. The reason is simple: Color is such an integral part of the fashion picture that it refuses to stay put under one neat heading. With color you can express your moods and your personality. It's that aspect of fashion that holds everything together, the element that makes clothes fun, sexy, glamorous, exciting. And once you learn to use color to your advantage, it can be an indispensable tool for creating the illusion of height. But first, a look at the long-standing color rules.

Almost every short woman has heard the one about dressing in one long line of color to establish a taller image. And then there's the "Stick with dark colors" rule, usually recommended for the shorter woman who wants to look taller and more authoritative. And let us not forget the short-woman's commandment that says: "Thou shalt not wear contrasting-color belts." Pretty limiting, don't you think? We do too. Now let's talk about the loopholes.

Old Rule 1: Dress in One Long Line of Color

According to this one, you're supposed to wear a sweater, belt, skirt, stockings, and shoes all in the same shade. You could, of course, and it's true that this ploy will make you look taller. And allowing for a variety of texture to add interest, the result could look fabulous. But it's not the kind of dressing you want to attempt every day of the week. So here's an alternative that's equally valid: Instead of all one shade, work with a spectrum of related shades that are basically the same tonality and capable of blending into one another. Example: A pale russet blouse that goes into a darker russet belt that goes into an equally dark or darker russet tweed skirt into equally dark or darker russet tweed stockings and shoes.

Of course, you don't have to be restricted to just one color family. If you want to pair, say, an apricot string-knit sweater with brown tweed trousers, or a mustard-color blouse with a green plaid skirt—fine. Just make sure the color value or weight of each color is about equal or at least not too contrasting. That is, wear a pale with a medium shade or a medium with a deep, but not very pale with very deep or you're back in short city. Because although it's perfectly all right to bend Rule 1, you don't want to break it outright—wearing a white blouse with a black skirt, for instance. Not only will you put yourself in danger of being mistaken for an usherette, you'll also be misusing color to divide your body into two distinct sections—and a body divided cannot stand tall. Exception: a white top with black *pants* (the length of black cancels out the contrast-color negative).

The reasoning behind that peremptory statement goes something like this: Whatever's dark is less noticeable because, whereas light, bright colors clamor for attention, dark ones behave as meekly as a ten-year-old girl at a dancing school tea. Therefore, if you dress in dark colors, you'll diminish yourself by looking thinner, and by looking thinner, you'll look taller.

Old Rule 2: Always Wear Dark Colors

As far as it goes, it's true. You will. In addition, dark colors (that is, your navys, blacks, grays, and browns) will make you appear more somber and, because of that, more businesslike and authoritative. That's no lie. But while dark colors can do wonderful things, this doesn't mean you have to own a whole closetful of them. What this rule does suggest: grayed-down shades will make you look thinner (and therefore taller) than pure, unadulterated colors. By "grayed-down," we don't mean dull and washed out. We just mean colors that are slightly muted: a grayed pink instead of a screaming bubble-gum pink. A softened red instead of the stoplight variety.

Now, about the "authority" of dark colors.

If yours is the kind of job that requires somber hues and a sub-dued manner, and you're getting sick and tired of gray pin-striped suits, consider this: If the clothes themselves are clean-cut and classic (and you've got the self-confidence to carry it off), a pale color could be just as authority-commanding as a dark one. An image that comes to mind is of a lawyer we once saw at a large after-hours cocktail party. She was about 5'3" and still dressed in her business clothes—a perfectly tailored wool gabardine suit in a delicious pale rose that was slightly reminiscent of Häagen-Dazs raspberry sherbet. And she looked smashing! So impressive, in fact, that we assumed any woman who knew how to look that chic just had to be smart. One just took her capability for granted.

Old Rule 3: Don't Wear Contrasting Color Belts

If you're decked out in a cobalt blue jersey dress cinched with a shocking crimson belt, you've just broken Old Rule 3. But there *is* some logic behind the rule: An eye-catching belt rivets the gaze to that spot immediately. And although this tactic may be a great way to play up a Scarlett-O'Hara-sized waist, it does nothing to increase your height. The loophole for this one is based on the same principle as for Rule 1: If you want to wear a contrasting belt, keep it in the same tonality as the dress, skirt, or pants. In the case above, a cranberry belt would have worked better than a bright red. Cranberry is still a shade of red (if red is the contrast color you're going for), but it's the blue side of red, making it a first cousin to the cobalt and therefore related to that family, too. Result: The eye notes a slight contrast but not enough to arrest it at that one area and cut the figure in half.

Coming on Hot and Cold

There's another aspect of color you'll want to consider, and it's this: The warm hues on the spectrum (red, orange, and yellow) are advancing colors and hence carry the illusion of weight. Cool hues (blue, green, and violet) are receding colors and tend to minimize the size of the wearer.

Shopping for Color

Because colors do play such an important role in Short Chic dressing, you'll want to be especially careful when choosing them. When you're looking for a particular shade to match something you already own, don't try to memorize the color and hope for the best. On the other hand, you don't have to schlepp the piece of clothing around with you to match it either. The easy way: Go to a stationery or art supply store and buy a small color sample booklet (the kind artists use for choosing colored papers). To use it, just snip off the postage-stamp-sized swatch of the color you want to match (there are plenty of shades to choose from) and Scotch-tape it onto a little white square of cardboard that you can slip into your wallet for handy reference when needed.

Again, a reminder about how to read this information: A color that maximizes isn't going to make you look taller; it's going to make you look heavier. So unless you're thin to begin with, you'll want to lean toward the deemphasizing shades. You say you're fond of warm colors and you're ten pounds overweight, and what have we got to say about that? Just this: Wear them, by all means, but try to avoid the *pure* reds, yellows, and oranges. In their muted versions, warm colors will lose some of the weight-adding illusion—and probably look a lot richer besides.

Take a Spin on the Color Wheel

The color wheel is a simple and graphic way of studying color relationships and learning basic color-harmony principles. By using one of the three methods described below, you'll be able to coordinate all your fashion colors, whether you're mixing solids or patterns, whether you're working with two, three, or four colors at a time.

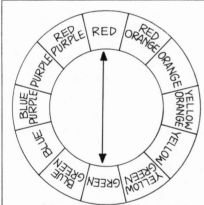

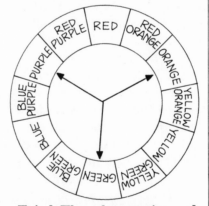

True complement: Two colors of the wheel that lie directly across from each other form a true complement. In the example above, the two colors are red and green, but by "spinning" the arrow you can determine all the other complements as well: blue and orange; blue/purple and yellow/orange, and so on around the wheel.

Triad: Three harmonious colors that lie at equidistant points on the wheel (in our twelve-color wheel that works out to every fourth color) form a triad. This example shows a triad of green, purple, and orange. Other examples of triads: blue, yellow, and red; red/purple, blue/green, and yellow/orange, etc.

The first thing you have to realize is that all colors are not created equal. Our color-wheel illustrations, for example, are meant to represent full-strength, pure colors. But other versions to consider are *tints, shades, and tones:*

- *A tint* is a pure color to which white has been added. (E.g., pure red plus white equals pink—a tint of red.)
- *A shade* is a pure color to which black has been added. (E.g., pure blue plus black equals navy—a shade of blue. And pure orange plus black equals brown—a shade of orange.)
- *A tone* is a pure color to which black and white (or gray) have been added. (E.g., pure purple plus black and white equals a grayed purple which is a tone of purple.)

It's good to keep that information in mind when you spin the imaginary arrows on the color wheel. If you were working with true complements like red and green, for instance, you wouldn't necessarily want to use them in their pure state. A bright red blouse and a bright green skirt would make you look like a glaring traffic light. *But* a pure full-strength red shirt paired with a skirt in olive drab (a *shade* of green) would look sensational. Or you could try it the other way: a shirt in pale pink (a *tint*) worn with a bright full-strength green skirt. That would work, too.

That's not to say you should never mix pure hues. Let's say you're working with a triad color harmony, as many fabric designers and clothing designers do. A dress that's patterned in pure full-strength red, blue, and yellow could be terrific. Ditto a dress in a solid full-strength blue/green, topped, say, with a scarf that's striped with the same blue/green, plus red/purple, and yellow/orange.

What you sometimes have to be careful about . . .

- *Mixing pure hues (whether they're full-strength, tinted, or shaded) with toned or grayed hues.* A pure pastel, for example, doesn't usually work with a toned pastel—they represent two conflicting "moods" of color.
- *The rule above especially applies when you're juggling with patterns.* Say you're pattern mixing with a three-color scheme of black, white, and red. In that case, the mix will coordinate much more successfully if the red in each pattern is *either* a pure, bright red *or* a toned, grayed red.
- *Another thing to check when color mixing with solids or patterns is the color itself.* Again, using red as an example, an orange/red is not the same as a blue/red—even if they're both

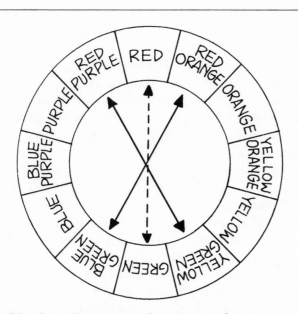

The Double Complement involves four-color harmony (indicated by the solid-line arrows in the illustration above. To determine a double complement, simply find the true complement (shown above as the broken-line arrow) then split both ends of the arrow to both sides of the colors it points to. In the wheel above, for example, the true complement is red and green. If you split the "red" end of the arrow into two parts so it points to the colors on both sides of red, and then split the "green" end of the arrow so it points to the colors on both sides of green, you get a double complement—in this case, red/purple, red/orange, yellow/green, and blue/green.

There are other methods for determining color harmonies, but the three above are the most common and easiest to use. Also to note: Any of the colors on the wheel will harmonize with black or white, as well as a go-with-everything neutral like beige.

pure or both toned. If the color or pattern mix you're trying doesn't work, mistaken color-identity could be the reason why.

Fabrics: The Naturals vs. Synthetics Debate

Good fashion starts with the fabric. If it's cheap, even the most creative designer would have a job making something from it—and the best designers wouldn't try. What we're talking about here is quality. (Remember what we said about that in the first chapter: If a short woman wants to establish credibility for herself in her job, good-quality clothes are essential.) And what it means is natural fabrics or convincing look-alikes as opposed to inferior man-mades.

If you don't already know it for yourself, the difference between natural and synthetic is enormous. Natural fibers, that is, those derived from plant or animal sources, will fit better, fall better, look better and feel better than any inferior synthetic. What's more, naturals are more comfortable, both in hot weather and cold, than test-tube fabrics. The reason: Since cottons, wools, linens, and silks are all derived from living things, they're all porous and allow the skin to breathe. This means that they also allow perspiration to evaporate on your skin so that you don't feel damp and clammy in hot weather. Synthetics, on the other hand, are not nearly as absorbent and don't breathe as well as natural fibers (if at all). Which means that synthetics are warmer in the summer, cooler in the winter, and, on the whole (given the chemicals that go into their making), not terrific if you happen to have sensitive skin.

On the negative side, natural fabrics are usually more expensive than synthetics—for the present at least. (But times are changing. Since all synthetics use petroleum or a petroleum derivative in their making, there's a good chance that they will eventually cost as much as or more than naturals.) And although it's true that naturals are more durable than synthetics, they're also more trouble to care for. Most wools, silks, and linens have to be dry-cleaned, and cottons have to be ironed and, unless preshrunk, carefully washed. And we'd be foolish to deny that some people have allergic reactions to some natural fibers—wool, in particular.

So where does all this leave us? Preferably with the best of both worlds. Because although we still shout the glories of natural fibers and will continue to do so until dissuaded by men in white coats, we do believe in compromise. What we're saying is that no, Virginia, there's no need to rush into your bedroom and burn every synthetic fiber in your closet. There are many man-mades you couldn't easily learn to do without. Your underwear is probably made of nylon, for example. And then there's your Lycra/spandex swimsuit. And your brushed nylon bathrobe. And if you check the labels on some of your blouses, you'll probably find that some percentage of the fabric is synthetic—which is fine. Synthetics can add durability and care convenience to natural fibers. They can give them more stretchability and keep them from wrinkling too heavily. *But*—and this is an important *but*, so pay attention—the percentage of the synthetic fiber should, preferably, be a comparatively small one. Just enough to do its thing but not so much that it corrupts the inherent qualities of the natural fiber.

Our last word on synthetics and naturals: As of this writing, there are murmurings among fashion people about new improvements in synthetics as science comes closer and closer to imitating the attributes of natural fibers in the laboratories. Perhaps in a few years we'll be seeing cotton, silk, wool, and linen look-alikes that are every bit as appealing (practically and aesthetically) as the real thing. In the meanwhile, however, we advise going by the following standard rules where fabric is concerned.

Always look for: Natural fibers, good natural/synthetic blends or *convincing* synthetics (which is to say they should look, feel, and drape as well as the natural fibers they imitate).

Stay away from: 100 percent polyester double knits, gabardines, and twills, most 100 percent acrylic knits, fake suede, and anything Qiana. To our way of thinking (and most top fashion editors agree), fabrics like these will make anything fashioned from them look cheap and second-rate.

Cotton   This includes broadcloth, Oxford cloth, terry, damask, muslin, corduroy, canvas, denim, voile, and velvet, to name a few. The most comfortable of the natural fibers, cotton is either woven or knitted and can be comfortably worn all year round. It's washable, and if it's Sanforized as well, shrinkage will be minimal.

Linen   Made from the flax plant, linen is twice as strong as cotton, and like cotton, extremely comfortable to wear. It does crease easily (you can't have everything), and treatments for crease resistance can weaken the fabric somewhat. But chances are you won't be wearing your white linen suit on a daily basis, so better go for wrinkle-resistant linen when you can find it: What you lose in durability, you'll gain in neatness—which always counts.

Wool   A good wool can last you a lifetime, and it only stands to reason that what keeps sheep from turning blue in the cold will keep you nice and cozy, too. But what you might not have considered is that a lightweight wool (like wool challis) can also keep you com-

Going for the Naturals (the natural fibers that mean top-quality fashion)

fortable in the warm. The proof: Caftans worn by desert peoples are made of wool and keep them cool even in temperatures that reach 100 degrees Fahrenheit and over. The secret's in the porousness of the wool fiber and in the looseness of the garment itself. Both allow air to circulate freely around the body.

Silk   It takes six industrious silkworms three days of full-time spinning to make one strand of silk that's finer than a human hair. One good reason the stuff is so incredibly expensive! But oh, the feel of it! The look of it! Even raw silk is deliciously soft, and even fine silk (delicate as it may appear) is strong. Actually, silk is the strongest of all the natural fibers. Depending on the weave, it can be warm or cool, so it's terrific all year round. Silk is also wonderfully absorbent—which makes it great for underwear, shirts, and the type of classic pajamas that Noel Coward characters were always seen tripping around in.

Animal hair fibers   These naturals include camel's hair, mohair, cashmere, alpaca, vicuña, and angora rabbit hair. In their pure, unmarried state, all are on the expensive side. But when mated with other fibers, like wool, they add a lightweight warmth and a luxurious softness that's unbeatable—and more affordable.

Rayon   This one falls into a special category because, although rayon is a natural fiber (we were surprised, too), it's also man-made. Or, to be more precise, rayon is a plant fiber that's been reformed in the manufacturing process. We might have known it, though, because of all the modern fabrics, rayon was one of the few that passed our "feel and comfort" test. In addition, many designers approve of it for its flattering drapability.

4. Lingerie: How It Affects Everything Else You Wear

"I collect lingerie like it's going out of style. I just love satin-and-lace garter belts, hose, camisoles, and teddies and such."

—Actress Morgan Fairchild
(a very petite 5'4")

What you wear under your clothes makes all the difference in the way the clothes themselves look, fit, and feel on. There's no sense in spending a bundle on an elongating knitted dress if you aren't going to do it justice by wearing the right bra. That pale, wheat-colored linen suit with the short jacket and soft skirt may be a knockout, but its polished, professional—and fashionable—look is going to be wasted if the slip you've got on is the wrong cut or the wrong length.

But these aspects are just one side of the story. Because although lingerie has its practical side, today it also has to deliver aesthetically. A bra that gives support and shaping, for example, has to look right: feminine, pretty, and appealing on your particular short body-type. A soft lace camisole with minute panties in sensuous red silk—or tap pants that make your legs look as if they go on for miles on end—are more than just bra-and-brief alternatives. They're attractive, provocative pieces that you'll want as much for the way they make you look—taller, leggier, and sensational—as for their more practical qualities.

This brings us right to the following roundup—the lingerie pieces and styles that make the most of every inch of you—that look best, fit best, and feel best on the smaller woman.

The New Color Rules

If you're anything of a fashion watcher, one of the biggest changes you've probably noticed in recent years, when it comes to under-pieces, is the colors they come in.

Whereas once all you could find was white, black, beige (and occasionally, when you wanted to be a bit daring, a little tea rose!), today there's a range of colors that boggles the senses. Teal, pewter, and platinum. Plum, turquoise, scarlet, and cyclamen. Sounds tempting? It's meant to be—and your height shouldn't keep you away. Because lingerie is one of the fashion areas where short women actually have what amounts to carte blanche when it comes to color choices—meaning there's no such thing as being "too short" to carry off bright red underwear. So indulge!

As to what goes with what, it all comes down to this one maxim: *"When nothing is going to show, anything goes."*

As to the rest of the old color guidelines, here's how they stand, updated:

1. *Under a stark white shirt*, never wear a white bra. It'll show through the shirt and look obtrusive and busy. A bra in one of the new skin colorings is a much better choice.

2. *Under dark tops*, always wear a bra in a dark color like black, navy, Bordeaux, or one in the aforementioned skin colors.

3. *Under tops that are sheer*, wear a flesh-colored or opaque bra, or a nude body stocking. That way, the bra or body stocking outline will be barely visible.

4. *Under white or pale-colored pants and skirts*, never wear dark or patterned panties or slips. The shadow that shows through will detract from the clothes.

5. *Under any fabrics that are sheer or gauzy*, choose skin-color range underpieces: nude, beige, toast, mocha, bronze.

6. *If you are wearing a slip that's going to show a little* (through a slit skirt, for example), wear one in a color that's close to the color of your skirt. That means interesting darks with a dark skirt, pales with a light one.

Getting the right bra fit: The size of your breasts has nothing to do with your height. You may be as well endowed as such legendary petites as Mae West, Jean Harlow, Dolly Parton, or Bette Midler, or you may be, well, more streamlined. But whatever your shape, the right bra is the first step toward establishing the right contour for clothes—and the first step to that is knowing your correct bra size. Most women, we're told, buy the wrong bra size altogether, erring one size too large, rather than too small. So we'd suggest double-checking with the following two-step test:

1. Measure around your ribcage under your bust, snugly, but not too snugly. Then, add five inches to that number for your correct body size. If it's an odd number, like thirty-three, go on to the next highest number, in this case, thirty-four.

2. Now measure around the fullest part of your bust. If that measurement is one inch larger than your body size, you wear an A-cup; 2 inches larger, a B-cup; 3 inches, a C; and 4, a D.

Now that you know your correct bra size, what bra? That depends on your particular figure type, on the clothes you wear most often, and on the look you find most flattering and comfortable.

Choosing the Underpieces That Work Best

The Basic Bra Types
THE NATURAL BRA

A smooth, generally unlined bra that doesn't offer a whole lot of support, is usually very comfortable. Best for the small-busted, firm-busted only.

The lingerie bra is a luxury version of the natural, made in special fabrics like silk, lace, or satin, with unusual ornamentation. Understandably, these are on the expensive side and are usually found in boutiques rather than in standard lingerie departments. But if you really want to indulge yourself, say, to celebrate your next promotion, do buy yourself a few—in silk—with matching bottoms (not so your mother won't be ashamed, if God forbid, you should get hit by a truck and the people at the accident see your unmatching cotton underwear, but simply because nothing is as sexy or luxurious as underwear in silk).

Another version of the natural bra: *the stretch bra*—one made in a stretch fabric. It offers the least support of all bra types and is for small-busted women only. The ones with molded cups offer a bit more support than the others.

UNDERWIRE BRAS　Underwires give support, uplift, and coverage and are great for full-busted, short-waisted, under 5'4" women who need to create the greatest "space" between the bust and the waist. But they can also work for small-busted women who like the more voluptuous cleavage you get with an underwire.

FIBERFILS　There are three types of Fiberfil bras. The first, *a bra with a wafer-thin lining*, adds a minimum of shaping but doesn't add inches. The second type, a *contour bra*, has a slightly thicker lining and is a good choice for women who are between sizes (say, more than an A, not quite a B) or for the very small-busted petite woman who tends to flatten out like the surface of an ironing board when she wears heavier fabrics, like tweeds and thick wools. The third bra type, *the fully padded bra*, archly referred to as a maximizer, adds one full size to your shape and will go a long way toward equalizing pear-shaped proportions.

MINIMIZERS　*If you're short and very full-busted*, a minimizer bra should be an important part of your bra wardrobe (when you're short on height, overly lush proportions can look slightly out of kilter). The minimizer therefore offers the most support and control of all bra types: by gently pressing the breasts to the sides rather than to the front, it reduces the look of the bust by one and a half to two and a half inches. And today modern minimizers are very natural looking—pretty and not massive, appliquéd with ribbons and lace.

Short Chic Shopping Tips for Bras

If you're short and small-busted, you'll be happy to know that the wispy, very feminine-looking, natural bras tend to look better on petite women than on anyone else. Those with a no-show front-closing and/or underwiring add uplift and cleavage, whereas Fiberfils can give you a little more shape under bulkies. We'd suggest taking a look at *Maidenform*'s "Sweet Nothings" line—it tends to cater to an A-cup woman. It also happens to be the best-selling bra line in the country, available in dozens of delectable colors. *Vanity Fair* bras seem to run to the same small scaling. Also check out *Lily of France*'s "Paris Nights" bra—it, too, appears to cater to a small-busted woman.

If you've had particular trouble finding a comfortable and well-fitting small-sized bra, take a look at *Flexnit*'s "A-OK" line as well, which is especially proportioned for the A- and AA-cup figure and allows for the greater separation between the breasts that most smaller-busted women have.

If you're short and full-busted, meaning a full C, D, or more, what you don't want—for obvious proportional reasons—is for your bust to be the focal point of your appearance. To that end, use your bra to create the greatest waist/bust separation possible. Be sure that the bra band is wide enough to be supportive, loose enough to slide two fingers under it (this last for comfort's sake). *John Kloss* bras seem to cater to a more developed figure (although the "Glossies" line, made for *Lily of France*, fits small-busted women nicely). If you're very full-busted, you might consider a minimizer (the ones by *Olga* are among the best—and most attractive—on the market), if only to wear under knits and other form-fitting clothes.

Panties: The Bottom Line

If you think that all panties are alike, then let us introduce you to the subtleties that may have escaped you. Because even within one style category, like the bikini, certain types do more for short women than others.

THE BIKINI

For almost all short women, regardless of figure type, bikini bottoms are the hands-down winners for flattery. The ones with a high-cut French leg will make *your* legs look longer, lengthen a short torso, and even make chunky thighs look longer and slimmer. Bikinis come in all degrees of brevity, and if your figure can take it, we say the briefer, the better.

The basic bikini hits about one to two inches below the midsection and is a good leg-lengthening, body-lengthening look that works on almost all short body types. It comes in all colors and patterns, in special fabrics like silk and satin, even in absorbent terrycloth (which is ideal for sports). Look for bikinis cut high on the thigh that curve right into the hipbone. *Note:* for light control, a stretch bikini is an even better choice. Too, if you intend to buy lace, make it stretch lace because it's flatter and it won't make much of a ridge under clothes. (Added plus: it also adds a little holding-in if you need it.)

The string-tied bikini is the briefest, sexiest, most daring of all bikini styles, body-lengthening, leg-lengthening, too. A winner that does it all! We love it!

THE CLASSIC BRIEF

Not the best choice for the height-conscious, the brief is making a comeback as a bikini-line eliminator under pants. Despite that advantage, it's still a negative-looker to our way of thinking.

Short Chic Shopping Tips for Panties

If you're short and have fairly average proportions, you've probably had very little difficulty finding panties to fit. But if you're *very* petite as well, check out the ones by *D. D. Duds*, *Hanro*, and *Dior*. Sources tell us their size P panties are cut a touch skimpier than the others.

Hip Humps: They're the unattractive little bulges of flesh that some women get when they wear bikini panties—right where the top elastic presses gently into the flesh. Instead of switching to full briefs (which, although they do take care of the problem, are unattractive), we'd suggest a plain, untrimmed bikini that comes about an inch below the midsection, either seamless or with one seam up the back. Another method we've found that works: Buy your regular bikini pants one size larger than usual to eliminate the bumps altogether. Or try the popular nationally advertised cotton-crotch pantyhose with the panty woven right in.

TAP PANTS

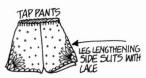

These boxer-cut panties look great on models in fashion magazines, but alas, they are an awkward, choppy length for most short women. But if you're partial to them, here's how to go about it.

First, look for tap pants with side slits or, even better, with side slits visually extended with lace trim. The ones with triangular insets of lace at the sides also work.

A lot of short women tell us they have a hard time finding a half slip that's short enough. If so, consider: Tap pants make a pretty, loose-fitting and comfortable alternative under a lined or nonsee-through skirt or dress. And try a pair under a side or front-slit skirt if you've never been able to get the slit in your slip and the slit in your skirt to match up. Another thing: Tap pants with a matching camisole are good replacements for a full slip. Just look for the shortest ones you can find—that way, they won't ride up.

A variation on the tap pant, these have the most short savvy of all the styles we've seen. They have the charm and appeal of the classic tap pants but with a diagonal slash up the side for a flattering and super-sexy fit. We like them for under wool culottes or a divided skirt or under wool knickers if the knickers are unlined and itchy. When you happen on them, buy them in multiples; the look is worth it.

PETAL PANTS

PETAL PANTS

LEGS CUT ON DIAGONAL

Two questionnaire respondents summed up the slip problem this way:

SLIPS

"Even the shortest ones are always too long. But when I hem them, I lose either the side slits—or the slits wind up in the wrong place—and the beauty of the lace or embroidery trim end up on the cutting room floor."

Rose F., 5', Atlanta, Georgia

"For the life of me, I can't find a full slip to fit me. And I think they're so sexy to run around the house in."

Lois B., 5'1", Bogota, New Jersey

Aside from serving as a substitute nightie (an idea, by the way, that we love and heartily endorse), a full slip and a half slip are necessities for one of two reasons:

1. To avoid the see-through effect you get in bright sunlight with light, unlined wools or gauzy cotton skirts and dresses.
2. To give a smoother, nonstatic, nonclinging line under clothes.

As to this last, consider: If you're at all on the hippy side, a slip is also an absolute necessity for making certain kinds of dresses (like knits and jerseys) pass muster. If you're trying on a skirt or dress that's unlined and "cups" your bottom a bit (but fits everywhere else), a slip can help diminish the cling.

The Half Slip. Standard half slips go from twenty-two to twenty-six inches. And as hemlines inch up and down, slip lengths follow suit. Of course, you already know to look for half slips that are as short as possible, but also keep your eyes peeled for slips with detailing and embroidery on the body of the slip, rather than around the hem, in case you have to shorten. Catherine D., a 5'2" copywriter, told us she found a beautiful half slip by *Diane Von Furstenburg*, with lace insets all around the hip area instead of at the hem, a style that solved the problem perfectly. That's just the kind of

HALF SLIP

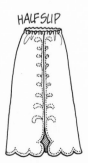

detailing to keep an eye out for! For more slip ideas, see chapter 18, Offbeat Looks and Sources.

Note: In your search for the perfect slip, you may come across a cheapie half slip with a three-tiered lace hem, made to cut to adjust as you please. Most are not real quality items (after all, lace that's disposable isn't going to be top of the line), and lingerie aficionados may sneer, but, in a pinch, it's a handy item to know about. The ones that crossed our paths were made by "Sliperfections" by *Lady Ester Corporation,* and by *Movie Star.*

FULL SLIP
ADJUSTABLE STRAPS
LACE AT THE TOP

The Full Slip. If you've got a knit dress that's the least bit itchy or snug, that's when you'll appreciate a full slip. We always look for ones with adjustable straps, a fitted and deep-veed bodice, and a built-in bra (so that you don't have to wear a slip and a bra at the same time). Also, if you happen to find a full slip with a nice amount of lace and detailing at the top, it won't hurt so much to forgo it around the hem if you have to shorten. Another advantage: You can easily make a full slip shorter by just taking up the straps rather than hemming it around the bottom. And, by the way, if you're short-waisted, a full slip is much sexier-looking than a waist-high half slip any day.

CHEMISES

CHEMISE

One of the most versatile pieces of lingerie, a chemise looks like a full slip cut off at hip length, or a camisole that grew a couple of inches. It's great for a smooth, sleek line under clothes. (But it won't solve the see-through problem you get with unlined or sheer skirts and dresses.) A nude-colored version is the perfect solution under a sheer blouse. You can also wear a chemise under a side- or back-slit skirt if the slits on your standard half slip refuse to match the ones in your skirt.

Short women have also discovered that the chemise is nice to sleep in. ("I find them more sophisticated and less fluffy-looking than your typical baby-doll nightie," writes a 5'4" Minneapolis woman.)

The most flattering chemises for short women are the ones with adjustable or easily shortened spaghetti straps (for tips on alterations see chapter 20); ones with lace insets under the armholes in a lengthening V-shape; and ones with a lace-filled V in the back.

CAMISOLES

"Camisole" refers to any soft, lingerie top that just reaches the waist or drops an inch or two below. It can be scooped, plunging, V-necked, front-buttoned, or ribbon-tied, and, overall, it suits short women especially well. The more elaborate camisole tops (made by designers like *Fernando Sanchez* and *Ora Feder*) can double as outerwear too (and at much less the cost of conventional outerwear camisoles).

CAMISOLE

BIAS CUT

Camisoles that are cut on the bias fit under 5'4" women better than others, and those with appliqué and embroidery at the top are good for peeking out from the neckline of a severely tailored shirt. Other good bets: Pair up a camisole with matching petal pants or side-slit, lace-edged tap pants as a nice alternative to a full slip. One way Anne Marie wears her dressy lingerie camisole: with silk or satin evening pants and a velvet quilted jacket.

Short Chic Shopping Tips for Camisoles, Chemises, and Teddies

A lot of short women—ones who are not necessarily petite by the way—tell us they've had trouble finding these items properly proportioned. Some manufacturers who tend to cut on the smaller side are *Sami*, *Papillon*, *Hanky-Panky*, *Ora Feder*, and *Far West*. And although we can't vouch for the fit *every* time, do check out camisoles and teddies by *Eve Stillman* as well.

TEDDIES AND BODY SUITS

Teddies and body suits admittedly are an iffy fit if you're short-waisted; in which case, you're better off going for a camisole and pant set for the same kind of look. Still, there are many short women who can wear them, which is nice because when they fit, teddies and body suits can be among the best lengtheners around.

TEDDY

Teddies have camisole-styled tops attached to tap-pants or petal-pants bottoms and are loose-fitting and very sexy. But if you're heavier on the top or the bottom, you may want to skip this particular underpiece, opting instead for a two-piece that allows you to mix sizes. Short-waisted? Remember that adjustable or spaghetti straps are easiest to fix and fit.

Bodysuits most resemble pretty, stretchy, form-fitting leotards and are often lace- or ribbon-trimmed. For a sheer, smooth, unbroken line under clothes like knits, they're hard to beat. And, the higher cut the leg, the better. Also lengthening: V-neck, plunging, or scooped-out styles. And underarm-to-hip insets of lace running the length of the body on either side are also elongating, as are veed insets under the armhole and at the leg. Snap crotches don't make much of a difference in terms of looks or fit, but a little shirring around the bust is a good idea if you're small-busted—body suits do tend to flatten. Those in skin-tight, shimmery fabrics are terrific shape-molders if you need it.

BODY SUIT

LONG UNDERWEAR

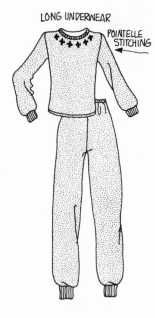

POINTELLE
STITCHING

Long underwear today is warm, cozy, and functional, and it bears very little resemblance to the itchy red long johns your mother might have made you wear as a kid. Today they're a fashion item. Touted as a downright necessity by skiers and other winter-sports enthusiasts, they also appeal to more sedentary types who want an extra layer of warmth under their clothes on subfreezing days.

The especially nice thing about long underwear is that for short women, it becomes casual outerwear, too. Under a flannel shirt, long underwear is close-fitting, snug, and neat, all pluses—and, made up in soft, brushed cotton or flannel, also wonderfully comfortable. Your best bet is to go for the separate tops and bottoms. The tops alone, in soft colors and with pretty pointelle stitching at the edges, look particularly terrific with jeans, with a skirt in denim or corduroy, or peeking out from under a soft flannel or brushed-cotton plaid shirt. They also work under jump suits (and that's still another way to get a great layered look with a minimum of bulk). One more way: Try the tops with jogging pants, tucked into boots. *Tip:* Look for the prettiest long underwear tops under the labels of *Ripcosa*, *Hanro of Switzerland*, and *Lux-Lux*. Small-proportioned women should also check out the young teen and boys departments for buys in long undies. The styling there is just as upbeat and attractive as in the more expensive departments (for more on buys in the boys department, see chapter 18, Offbeat Looks and Sources.

A skivvy, a short-sleeved or scooped-out, lighter-weight version of long underwear, is definitely an item whose time has come. Who can forget how adorable Jill Clayburgh looked in *An Unmarried Woman* going to bed in a skinny skivvy top, bikini panties, and short socks? Besides being awfully cute to sleep in, skivvies have a practical advantage: In summer, they're great for keeping cool (and the ones in cotton absorb perspiration); in winter, they're a warm, cozy alternative to a bra *if*—and only *if*—you wear an AA, A or not-too-full B cup. Try one in summer instead of a T-shirt, worn with a gathered cotton skirt. Another reason we like skivvies: the variety of sizes. Average-proportioned short women can usually get by with a Medium; but if you're very petite, you can find them in size Small, in Petite, and, sometimes, even Extra Petite.

SKIVVY

SKINNY
RIBS

Sleepwear

A lot of sleepwear and robes that are marked Small can be worn by women who aren't small at all. Just buying a night set tagged Petite

—usually the smallest size—is no guarantee on fit either. There was the time when one woman we know (a size 6) brought home a cream-colored satin, size Petite, Christian Dior pajama set, only to discover that the jacket, pants, and camisole appeared to have been designed for a 5′8″ size 12—at least! The moral: Always try on sleep-wear first, to find out which ones are really Small or Petite and which are just pretending.

Short Gowns

If you're on the shorter side of short—like 5′ or under—and especially if you're not into alterations and don't want to shorten a long gown, shortie gowns are your best choice. Even if they skim your knees when they're really meant to fall mid-thigh, they'll still look good.

The fluffy, rather bouffant type of baby-doll gown, however, is *not* your best short-woman choice. Their puffy sleeves and wide, frilly, often stand-out silhouettes are particularly unflattering—unless looking like a coy ten-year-old is your idea of attractive. Fortunately, a lot of the more cutie-pie styles have been retired and been replaced by sleeker-looking short gowns, camisole and tap-pants sets, teddies, and (our choice) terrific-looking chemises.

Sleep Shirts

SLEEPSHIRT

SOFT AND EASY DROP SHOULDER

IN SILK OR SATIN

The sleep shirt is another short-gown style that has its fans—actress Sally Field among them. "My favorite nightshirt is the one that says 'Snoopy Loves Me' across the front," she told us. "I found it in the teen department where you can get a lot of great stuff."

A nightshirt—or sleep shirt—is a nightie made like a man's shirt. It is most often short—hip-length—but sometimes it extends as long as midcalf (both workable, manageable lengths for under 5′4″s). The classic sleep shirt has a rounded, shirttail-styled hem and is seam-slashed at either side (which is very nice for lengthening the look of the legs). And, Snoopy notwithstanding, when the sleep shirt is made of silk or satin, it is a very sexy, attractive, and comfortable garment to sleep in. *Tip:* The ones in cotton or with tiny provincial prints are also nice—they've got a naïve (but not cute) charm that suits short women to a T.

Long Gowns

If your preference runs to long gowns, you may run into trouble as far as length is concerned, no matter what. Even many of the size Smalls and Petites, though appreciably shorter and often smaller-proportioned, may still be on the too-long side. (Remember, these sizes are also meant for very thin, small-boned talls as well.) All things considered, it *is* easier to shorten a hem than to lengthen one. The best advice we can give you is to avoid the nighties with flounced

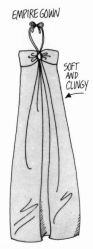

EMPIRE GOWN

SOFT AND CLINGY

BIAS GOWN

SAME TONES OF LACE AND SATIN

FLANNEL GOWN

hems—they're the hardest to fix—and to pick up a pair of wedgie-styled slippers for an extra inch or two. One more thing: Don't discount a gown you like simply because you think it doesn't fit. Sometimes, we've found, a simple inch or two pull-up on the straps is all that's needed to do the trick.

Empire-waist gowns: The empire-waist nightgown is a comfortable, nonconfining classic gown, which has been popular for a long time. It is usually flattering and elongating to short women and is *most* flattering when it's made in a soft, clingy material. The empire-waist gown should always be tried on, however. Although it can look classically elegant on some, it can be matronly on others.

For example, although an empire can never look really bad, if you've got a smallish waist, it certainly won't be doing the most for your particular asset. In this instance, you would do better with a nightie with a slightly raised natural waistline (a modified empire), which will give you the illusion of length but still play up that wasp waist. If you're big-busted, you're better off skipping the empire-waist nightie, too. Since it tends to emphasize the bust, it's best worn by short women who are small-to-medium-busted only.

Bias-cut gowns: Nighties in sensuous, bias-cut styles that gracefully swirl around the body, are worth hunting for. They're out-and-out flatterers to most short women.

"My favorite nightie of all time was a mauve-colored, bias-cut Olga gown," one 5'2" (112 pound) fashion editor recalled. "It was a mass of inset-lace swirls, and no matter what your figure's like, nothing does more for it than a bias-cut gown."

True. If you're thin, a bias-cut gives the illusion of curves; if you're plump, it seems to whittle your own curves into near-perfect proportions. And, of course, its sweeping nature adds height. All in all, when you're looking for a nightgown, a bias cut is a very good choice.

Flannel gowns: The typical flannel granny gown has a high neck, long sleeves, ruffle-trimmed yoke, and a flouncy hem—altogether a trifle much for a petite woman to carry. Still, they're unbeatable for comfort and warmth on cold nights, so look for the ones that don't make you look like a granny.

There are ways to be warm and sexy at the same time—in flannel gowns that are snuggly, comfortable, feminine, and attractive. First off, pick a style that's simple, with delicate embroidery at the cuff and the neck, with a plain hem, please, not hard-to-hem flounces, with gentle smocking and small-scaled ruffles at the bosom. Also good: a "granny-gown" variation with a scooped-out lace-trimmed neck and soft sleeves. Generally, we've learned that short women have a field day with these prettier flannels, whereas most tall women we've spoken to tend to shy away. "No matter how feminine they are, they make me look like a big, motherly *Alp*," one 5'9"-er confided.

Sleepwear Tips: The top part of the gown is where a lot of the styling comes in. Those with snug, rib-fitting camisole-styled bodices can be especially good. Ditto for halter tops—their vertical lines are body-lengthening and slimming besides. Another point: Nighties with separate-cup tops give better shaping and fit than the shirred all-in-ones. Finally, one last tip about length. If you haven't noticed, nightgowns—especially those in cotton (like gowns by *Lanz*) but actually most gowns—shrink, especially in length. "I never even bother with hemming my long gowns," a 5'2" Santa Ana interior decorator told us. "After two or three washings, they shrink up to the proper length anyway."

Short Chic Shopping Tips for Gowns

Some sleepwear manufacturers who tend to cut to size, meaning their size Small and Petite *really are* that: *Hanky Panky* (known for exceptionally pretty styles, all natural fibers, lovely embroidery . . . and a line that starts at size Extra Petite); *Queen Anne's Lace* (tiny rosebuds and baby pinstripes); and *Herbcraft* (small-scale and pretty patterning—and great robes). In general, a pull-up on the straps of their gowns should be all that's needed to make any of these work.

Eve Stillman makes some of the prettiest nighties we've seen. After trying at least a dozen nightgowns on Georgianna, our 5'1¾" volunteer fitting model (who weighs in at 98 pounds, measures 33-24-33), we'd have to say their size Petite *is* Petite. "If I bought this gown, I'd need maybe a half-inch hem—and that's all," she told us, "and the waist and bust are fine." Another Eve Stillman gown she labeled "perfect—perfect length, perfect fit—and I can adjust the length with the drawstring."

Another "perfect" lengther on our model: a size Petite gown, empire waist, by *Givenchy Intimité.* ("It doesn't even need a hem," she said, amazed.)

We love the looks of *Christian Dior* lingerie but found the cut too big every time (on Georgianna and on both of us, as well, by the way). And although we had high hopes for *Mary McFadden's* new line of lingerie—she's small herself—even after lifting the straps to adjust the length, the gowns we tried were overly wide and much too long. ("This one's huge and just hangs on me," Georgianna complained, "and the elastic doesn't even hug in the back.")

Pajamas

When Jean Harlow, 5'2", wore a pair of long, soft, pearl-white lounging pajamas on the movie set, she had her dresser there to see that everything was tailored to perfection. For most of us, however, pajamas—most kinds—pose problems when you're short: the sleeve lengths, the oversized collars, the inevitable hemming and mismatched proportions. Too often, the under 5'4" woman is in for a heavy altering session. Still, pajamas can work—and nicely. One way: Why not try just wearing the tops (the look of a small woman wearing only a too-big man's pajama top is an unbeatably sexy classic by now). As well, the following are other types of pajamas that we've found suit shorter women better than regulation flannels:

Chinese pajamas: These are derived from the work clothes worn by Chinese men and women; we can't endorse them strongly enough as a terrific look for short women. We've had a lot of women complain to us about how hard it is to look elegant when you're short. Well, we can think of few things more graceful, elongating, and elegant than the traditional garb worn by delicate—and often diminutive—Oriental women.

Chinese pajamas consist of a hip-to-thigh-length side-slashed jacket with the familiar high collar, fullish trousers, usually in a silky and embroidered fabric. And depending on how elaborate that fabric is—and sometimes it can be especially rich with embroidery, ornamentation, or brocade—Chinese pajamas can also be worn for entertaining at-home. Keep the jacket on the short side so that you show as much leg as you can (or else you could look short-legged), and taper the pants down (but not too tight or you'll lose the easiness of the look). Another variation: The same kind of Chinese pajamas but with a side-slashed fingertip-length tunic top. If you're on the short-legged (or hippy) side, the longer tunic will "blur" the line where the buttocks start and the legs end, giving you a leaner, leggier

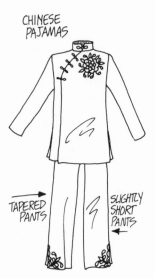

CHINESE
PAJAMAS

TAPERED
PANTS

SLIGHTLY
SHORT
PANTS

look. *Note:* This is a trick than can serve you again and again, with any three-quarter-length top or with a longish jacket or coat.

COSSACK PAJAMAS

Cossack pajamas: These are similar in style and as flattering as the Chinese ones mentioned above. They consist of pants, plus a tunic top with an interesting asymmetrical side-closing. Also along the same lines: karate pajamas. Perfect on short women, they make exceptionally good-looking at-home wear and are nice for casual in-house entertaining, too.

Robes

If a robe needs any alteration other than shortening the hem and the sleeves, you're better off passing it by. Most women refuse to do any more alterations than that anyway, particularly when it comes to robes. Indeed, one retailer told us she wouldn't recommend that a customer buy the robe at all if anything more was needed.

Because robes are designed for comfort—and that means an *un*-close fit—the size Small and Petite do well enough for sizing. What to avoid: big, overquilted, and puffy-looking calico types; any robe with wide lapels; and fluffy "Teddy bear" robes that can overwhelm you. Also keep in mind that unless empire-waist robes are made in soft, shape-clinging fabrics like velour, jersey, or thin challis, they can look dowdy.

On the other hand, robes with self-cuffs, with three-quarter-length sleeves, or with elastic at the cuffs that makes them easy to push up are all good choices; that way you don't have to bother with hemming up sleeves. Another thing: Keep your eyes open for robes in what's known as waltz length—that's just skimming the ankles—which makes it a perfect full-lengther on shorter women, and no alterations needed.

Short Chic Shopping Tips for Robes

Royal Robes (starts their line in a size 2—and it's a real 2: The belt loops are higher, the collars a pinch smaller, the hem and sleeves truly shorter); *Herbcraft* (starts with size Petite, for pretty, unbulky chenille wraps and robes with a higher inset waist); *Queen Anne's Lace* (for small-size "Laura Ashley"-style prints and mini, muted checks and plaids). Fitting model Georgianna was very taken with a

ROBES TERRY CLOTH WRAP ROBE

fine ivory all-wool *Eve Stillman* wrap robe—drop-shouldered, pockets in the right place, proportioned length. Anne Marie's favorite robe —a four-year-old *Vanity Fair*, very simple in style, with a shorter-waist, a three-quarter-length sleeve . . . "needed just a hem." Other good source: An overwhelming number of questionnaire respondents in the New York area, reported a fondness for the neat-looking plaid robes in the boys department at Brooks Brothers. (For more details on Brooks Brothers finds, see chapter 18, Offbeat Looks and Sources.)

CLASSIC KIMONO

Two robes we think are tops. We haven't met the under-5′4″ woman for whom either of these styles isn't a sure thing:

1. the white cotton terrycloth wrap robe
2. the classic kimono.

We have no idea what kind of robes Candice Bergen or Jacqueline Bisset wear when they're relaxing at home, but it wouldn't surprise us one bit if white terry wraps took the honors. (Picture them in the look and you'll know what we mean.) Aside from the color (and white's always a flatterer), there's something very relaxed and unstudied about a robe that's clean and fresh and simple. There's also something indefinably sexy about it, too. As a matter of fact, seven out of ten men we spoke to gave the robe unqualified raves. What we make of the phenomenon: There's something about a white terry robe's "fresh-from-the-shower" look that hints—very gently—that you're naked underneath!

As for the classic kimono, it's designed to flatter small women in wonderful and subtle ways. Like the way it dips gracefully at the back of the neck, wraps, and drapes around the body, then skims down to a very manageable above-the-ankle length. And the sleeves roll up as much as you need them to (there's also the very near-unparalleled prettiness of the traditional colors and patterns). In fact, on two separate occasions we've found men to be very turned on by kimonos, especially when you sash them. (A sashed kimono suggests a geisha look that can be especially seductive on petite women.)

Short Chic Shopping Tip for Kimonos

One of the most beautiful kimonos we've seen is *Ora-Feder*'s one-size-fits-all silk kimono—one of the very few one-size-fits-all items that can work for shorter women. "It looks good on a size two—and on a size eight," said Barbara Wagh, owner of L'Affaire, one of Manhattan's best specialty lingerie shops. Although L'Affaire caters to all sizes (as does Barbara's uptown branch, temptingly called Wife Mistress), it's staffed by three charming 5'3"-and-under women, who—no surprise—know exactly what works and what doesn't work on small women.

At-home Wear

In between what you wear by day and what you wear to sleep in is a whole other category of clothes: at-home wear—the kind of easy dressing that's ideal after a long day, when you want to be relaxed and comfortable but still "dressed."

An especially good turn of events for short women: A lot of at-home wear looks good enough to qualify for out-of-home wear as well. (For some mysterious and wonderful reason, short women can get away with this much easier than tall ones can.) A good example: *Bill Tice*'s beautiful fullish white silk "loungewear" pants—with a high wrapping waist, undefined crotch—that could go out (and did) all summer long. A good friend of ours, who's 5'3", about 110 pounds, bought them in a size 6. They come perfectly scaled down to a size 4 also.

At-home wear can be anything at all, provided that it's comfortable, nonconfining, and flattering. Chinese-style pajamas, kimonos, even velour warm-up suits all qualify. One Connecticut woman we know lives (after-hours) in a pair of black velour pull-on pants topped with a long, side-slit black velour tunic. "There's nothing I own that looks as good and feels as comfortable as that," she told us. Another good look: silky loungewear pants topped with (what else) a short silk or silk look-alike kimono robe—very flattering and very elegant when you're short. *Tip:* One of the very best loungewear pants we've seen, just made for short-woman proportions, we think: loungewear pants in satin moiré by *Fernando Sanchez*. The length and rise are both on the short side and the cut's perfectly proportioned. These are one of those items that can double as evening pants, too, so although they're on the expensive side, we think they're worth it.

Short Chic Shopping Tips for At-home Wear

At-home wear is an area where more and more top-name designers are getting into the act—people like *Geoffrey Beene, Ralph Lauren, Halston, Norma Kamali, Bill Tice,* and *Mary McFadden*—to name just a sampling! The advantage: More variety gives more choices. And if you never could afford to before, this is one way to acquire a Geoffrey Beene at very *un*-Geoffrey prices.

5. Tops: Blouses, Sweaters, Vests, and Tunics That Improve Your Image

Tops are probably the most important staples in your wardrobe, and if you don't believe it, just count the number of tops in your closet as compared with the number of skirts and pants. (See what we mean?) There's a good reason for this phenomenon: Different tops can change the look of any basic bottom—even jeans. The right one can pull an outfit together as surely as the wrong one can break it. And when it comes to workability, a really good top, carefully chosen, can accomplish what accessories do by adding style, impact, and color to everything else you wear.

Lucky for those of us under 5′4″—whether long-waisted or short-waisted, big-boned or small, large-busted or flat—tops are usually among the easiest pieces to wear and shop for. It's the one item of which designers and manufacturers offer a variety of styles, colors, patterns, and fabrics in proportions that fit.

Short Chic Shopping Tips for Tops

The list of quality top-designers and manufacturers runs longer than your arm's length, and we couldn't begin to name them all here. But a few of our favorites would include *Cacharel*, whose collars, pockets, sleeves, and cuffs (as well as patterns) are beautifully scaled for the smaller or shorter woman. Ditto for *Balfores* (they start with size 1), and their pure silk broadcloth shirts are a good buy). *Irka* and *Blassport* are good names to remember when you want a pretty silk blouse with cuffs and shoulders that fit. Another good name for shirts with a scaled-down shoulder fit is *J. G. Hook*. For beautifully, simply styled blouses, there's *Calvin Klein* (on the expensive side) and *Ciao* (in the more moderate-price range). If you're especially small, the unfussy cut makes both of these easy to alter if necessary. And for a neat, slim cut: *Daniel Hechter*. Each year some of the most romantic blouses can be found at *Ralph Lauren* (expensive but worth the splurge). Another source for feminine, romantic blouses that are cut small—those by designer *Maureen Cullinane*. For sweaters, a lot of in-the-know New Yorkers swear by *A. Peter Pushbottom*. (Their cotton-knit turtles and crew necks are especially popular, and sleeve and body lengths tend to run shorter than most.) Another sweater (and top) source: *Perry Ellis*. (His sweaters and blouses are often cut smaller than the rest of his things; check out the sweaters for the yarns alone.) And if you've given up on junior tops as being too poorly made or too juvenile, you should know that there are exceptions to the rule. Among them: *Daisy for Bebé Blond; Fenn, Wright & Manson; French Connection; Mi Bru San*—all good names with more sophisticated styling (and often a cheaper price tag as well!).

Playing the Match Game

There are many women who shop for a top on the "match" theory alone: that is, the stripe of a blouse happens to match the gray of their new gabardine suit. Before plunking down your credit card, ask yourself:

1. Would you buy the blouse (shirt, sweater, vest, or tunic) on its merits alone—even if the gabardine suit wasn't already hanging in your closet?
2. Does it fit well, and, if not, are you prepared to have it altered so that it does?

3. Is it a quality blouse you'd never be ashamed of being seen in?
4. Is it chic, with interesting detailing?

If your answers to any of the above is no, better save your money until the right thing comes along.

And while we're on the subject of buying habits, where is it written that tops have to be bought *after* major pieces like suits and such? Allison, for example, always shops for a beautiful top *first*—whether it goes with anything she owns or not. Then she may hold on to it for months ("a year even,") until it comes out of her closet to be worn. It's an approach worth considering because, when you love a top for itself alone, you know you're going to love it for a long, long time to come.

Blouses and Shirts

The first essential in this department is a classic white or cream blouse in silk, cotton, or crepe. Every woman should have at least one, and when you find the perfect style for you, snap it up on the spot and you'll never be sorry. Because if it's a classic (and most blouses are), it can take you through seasons and seasons of fashion changes—especially when it's made from quality fabric.

TAILORED

Another important thing about blouses and shirts is learning how to use them to achieve the look you want. With the right blouse you can take the curse off a severely tailored suit, give authority to simple trousers and skirts, or turn those same basics into a dressier look for a dinner after work. The truly savvy woman also knows how to use the different collar treatments of blouses to spotlight assets and play down flaws. A good example: If you're lucky enough to catch one of the old Burns and Allen reruns on TV, you'll note that Gracie was very careful about necklines. You see her most often in uncluttered V's and heart-shaped scoops. And even when she wore a collar, it was invariably turned up in the back—an instant neck and body lengthener that's always flattering to a shorter woman. In the following collection of classics, you'll find out which styles to look for and why.

SHAWL COLLAR

TUCKED FRONT

It's one of the most popular perennials, and for some very good reasons: The V-line of the collar creates a vertical line that's especially lengthening for short women. It can make a short neck—or any neck—look slimmer and longer (even more so when you turn up the

The Tailored or Notch-collared Shirt

collar in back à la Gracie). You can dress it up with pearls or a pin, sport it up with an ascot or scarf, or wear it as is under a V-necked sweater. With some suits, the tailored shirt is terrific. But if the suit itself is very tailored or severe, either because of the cut or the fabric, a tailored shirt may be a little much. In that case, try one of the softer classics or a sweater to avoid coming on with too much of a head-mistress look. (It's a common mistake short women make when trying to substitute "authority" clothes for a lack of inches.)

The Shawl-collared Blouse

This one's a hands-down winner for the smaller woman. Like the tailored shirt, it has a flattering and elongating V-neckline and narrow lapels, which are nicely proportioned to your size (or should be). It's also softer looking than the tailored shirt, more feminine, and dressier.

The Stock-tie Blouse

Another blouse that's on the dressier side of classic, the stock-tie is great under suits and blazers (not to mention hacking jackets when riding to the hounds)—and for showing off wonderful little heirloom tie tacks and pins. To look for: a tie that isn't much wider than three inches across. For an even chicer version of the basic cream, white, or pastel solid, look for one in a small rich-looking print.

The Band-collared Blouse

This includes the placket-front shirt—a good sporty classic for jeans, pants, and casual skirts when made from materials like cotton, rayon, or chambray. When it is, it's meant to look easy and comfortable, so don't button it up to the neck like a clerical collar. On the other hand, if the fabric is dressy (silk or crepe), you can go either way: Button it up and add a necklace or leave the top two or three buttons open for a sexier, V-necked look.

The Cossack Shirt

It, too, has a stand-up collar, but the buttons are usually run on the diagonal from neck to armhole, along the shoulder, or top to bottom and a few inches to the side. The Cossack is almost always on the dressy side—especially when made up in crepe or silk. Buttons should always be worn buttoned; sleeves should never be too full. And for a neck that's too long or thick, the higher version of a Cossack collar (say, about two inches high) is the perfect camouflage.

The Square-necked Blouse

It's a classic that can look great on some women, disastrous on others. If you're small and thin with a pair of prominent clavicles, then the square neck is probably not for you. The best ones are usually deeper than they are wide. (Remember, the squared-off line forms a horizontal; if it's too wide, it could make you look the same way.)

We're of two minds about this one: If you have a long slim neck, it could work, but because it creates a horizontal cut-off line of sorts, it may not be the best choice for the short woman. One way to solve that problem: Wear a jewel-necked blouse under the V-line of a blazer so that the vertical of the V negates the horizontal of the blouse neckline. The same thing happens when you add strands of beads, a scarf, or just about any vertical accessory, or when the blouse itself has some vertical detailing like tucks or pleats.

The Jewel-necked Blouse

Reminiscent of big game hunters and PFCs, the rugged-looking safari shirt is a great casual favorite for women. But between the flap pockets and the epaulettes (an optional feature), it can be overwhelming on a small frame unless everything is proportioned to fit. The collar should be small, the pockets scaled down and placed high enough to avoid skimming the waistline, and the whole thing should be made in a supersoft fabric to compensate for all the detailing.

The Safari Shirt

There is nothing more appealing and feminine on a small woman than a frilly blouse in a soft, floaty fabric like silk, cotton, voile, or crepe de Chine. As Cathy G., a 5'1" housewife in upstate New York points out: "We small types have the advantage of looking delicate and feminine in frilly romantic blouses; on a big woman they can look just plain silly." But again, everything has to be kept in proportion if the look is going to work. Make sure ruffles are narrow and confined to the neck, cuffs, and (if not too overstated) the yoke. Although long rows of front ruffles can help to create lengthening verticals, they may also add bulk—especially if you happen to be short-waisted. A better alternative when you want detailing: a blouse that's fronted with tiny pleats, tucks, lace insets, top-stitched seams, or faggoting—flat details instead of bulky ruffles.

The Romantic Blouse

You won't often see this type of shirt in anything but a casual fabric —Oxford cloth, chamois, cotton, or a cotton blend—which gives the shirt itself a casual look. The best ways to wear it: with the first two buttons left open, with or without the addition of a challis scarf or a loosely knotted menswear tie (the way men loosen their ties when they want a breather). Both the opening and the accessories will help create a vertical line—and you've probably gathered by now how

The Button-down Shirt

much we're in favor of vertical lines. If you like the neater look of a buttoned-up button-down, fine, but do dress it up with a ribbon-wide bow tie, a string tie, or an oval pin to keep it from appearing "unfinished."

The Round-collared Shirt

Yes, it's a classic, and on some women it can look great, but . . . we hope you're not especially fond of this style because, for the short woman, it's a real no-no. For one thing, the round collar (what your mother used to call a Peter Pan collar) creates a horizontal. Bad news. And, for another, it suggests a little-girl's-dress look that small woman should avoid like the plague. (If being taken seriously is one of your problems because of stature, dressing like Shirley Temple in her heyday isn't going to help.) "So what do I do with all those round-collared blouses in my closet?" you ask. Our answer: Turn the collar up all around and tie it in place with a loosely knotted scarf. *Voilà*—you've created a vertical high collar instead of a horizontal and added a note of sophistication besides.

The Smock Top

Inspired by the protective outershirt worn by artists, the smock top is loose, easy, and comfortable. But if you're short, you have to be careful about keeping it from making you look dowdy and plump. Look for sleeves that are cut narrower than usual. Same goes for the body. The fabric should be very soft and fluid, the gathers at the yoke not overly bountiful. And whether the smock is worn tucked in or out, it should be chosen to match the color of your skirt or pants (which in turn should be on the narrow side to compensate for the fullness of the blouse). If you wear smocks as a protective covering in your work, go for a knee-length smock instead of a shortie. Reason: You won't always be able to match your bottoms to a smock you wear every day, and a shortie that isn't matched—or even one that is—can have a tendency to make you look pregnant . . . and short.

The Peasant Blouse

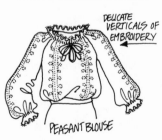

The classic version is usually in a soft handkerchief cotton, scoop-necked, long-sleeved, and often detailed with tucks, embroidery, and smocking. It can be a wonderfully romantic top for a floaty cotton skirt, dress pants, or even jeans. But since the cut is often full, and the neckline does create a horizontal, short women have to be careful about this one, too. The trick is to find one with positive details to counteract the negatives—a narrower cut, verticals of embroidery. Other tips: Make sure the skirt's in a fluid fabric that falls close to the body, and if you have wonderful shoulders, do take advantage of a blouse like this to show them off. The don'ts: Don't wear a peasant blouse if you're on the heavy side or especially short. And never, repeat, *never* be caught in the puffy short-sleeved type—no matter what shape you're in (unless, of course, you happen to be trying out for a part in *The Sound of Music*).

- *Collars* should always be scaled to your size and fit at the neck. Even when larger collars are in style, go for smaller versions of them.
- *Shoulders* should fit perfectly and never droop below your own shoulder line (if you never try on before buying a top, check the neck-to-shoulder length with a tape measure). If your own shoulders tend to slope (or even if they don't), consider adding shoulder pads.
- *Sleeves*, even full sleeves, should never be too full. Many women won't bother to alter a blouse, we know, but you really should consider taking a sleeve seam in when necessary for proportion. Where puffed shoulders are concerned, the smaller your own shoulders, the better. And if you like this style, look for sleeves that puff up rather than out.
- *Sleeveless* blouses (or cap sleeves) spotlight the upper arm. If yours are slim and firm, fine—but even so, you might want to go for a sleeveless style that falls in an inch or so from the shoulder. It will look less little-girlish, more sophisticated.
- *Cuffs* should fit snugly without straining the button. Often, if a long-sleeved, button-cuffed blouse is too long in the arms (a common problem), simply moving the button to make the cuff hug the wrist will do the trick. But if you have to move the button so far over that it destroys the fall of the fabric in the sleeve, you'll either have to alter the blouse or forget it altogether. A good way to check for fit without having to try on: Just slip your wrist through the open end of the cuff.

Perfect to the Last Detail

If you already have a blouse with cuffs that are too long and a button that can't be moved successfully, wear it with the cuffs turned up just once. If necessary, tack the turned-back cuffs in place with a well-concealed stitch or two. Or starch the cuffs so they stay.

Another tip: On small women with slender wrists, a deeper cuff looks sensational and very feminine.

- *French cuffs* must fit perfectly when you buy them (unless you're willing to have them altered). If they fall even a half inch below your wrist, they're too long and loose and will only accentuate your size.

Note: For alteration tips, see chapter 20.

Sweaters

What with the energy crunch becoming an established way of life, sweater dressing has become more popular than ever. But warmth isn't the only reason for the boom; now that designers are turning their creative attentions to the wonderfully flattering textures and patterns of knits, many women want to own collections of them—for summer and winter.

Sweaters in natural fibers always mean good fashion that's comfortable, wearable, and usually timeless. The one drawback for the smaller woman, however, is that knits can't be altered as easily as cloth items—if at all. So your best bet is to make sure you get a perfect fit when you buy.

Another advantage of sweaters is their softness—a special plus for the shorter woman. Depending on the type of sweater, she can look sporty, feminine, sexy, or tailored without looking dwarfed in the process. *Play your cards right and you can even get away with bulky knits*—which many of the women we surveyed put into the "wish I could wear them" category. You can wear them *if* . . .

CREWNECK

- The knit is especially soft.
- The bulk is worn in a single layer.
- The sweater itself isn't oversized.
- You're slim enough to carry extra bulk.
- The bulky's worn only for sport—never in the office.

A rundown of the all-time great sweater classics:

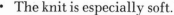

The Crew-neck Sweater

This used to be thought of as a casual sweater, but today it all depends on the knit. Coarser wools in a closely woven knit in classic preppy shades (navy, deep green, red, and so on) are neat top-offs for button-down or band collar blouses. A lacy-stitched crew, on the other hand, can be dressy enough for dinner at your favorite overpriced restaurant—especially if the wool is blended with a wonderfully soft fiber like mohair or cashmere and dyed a delectably soft pastel.

TURTLENECK

A note about the neck, however: Like the jewel-necked blouse, the crew neck creates a horizontal that could be unflattering. To "verticalize": add an appropriate blazer (sporty or dressy), or create a high collar by swathing a thin wool-knit oblong of a scarf around your neck.

A collar that's flattering to most women unless, as one of those we interviewed lamented, you've got a neck like a turtle. Basically, it's a casual look, and because of that you might consider wearing it under a blazer or suit jacket when you want to dress them down a bit. It's also neat under easy, vertical-collared shirts, but make sure the sweater is in a finer knit so that it won't be too heavy for the fabric of the shirt.

The Turtleneck Sweater

The Boat-neck Sweater

We prefer these on their own—no shirt underneath. The observant among you will already have noted the emphatic horizontal line of this style and may have made a mental note to reject it as a short-ener. But this one is worth a rethink: If your shoulders are especially wide, you probably should forget the boatneck, but if you happen to be wider in the hips than you are in the bust, this horizontal may work *for* you to even out the difference by emphasizing width at the top.

The Cowl-neck Sweater

The success of the cowl usually depends on its size. If it's too big, it can swallow you up. Otherwise, it can be a soft, flattering neckline—especially if you pull the front of it down to suggest a V-dip.

The Shawl-neck Sweater

The narrower the square of this sporty kind of shawl neck the better—and the most flattering way to wear it is with the collar up. By the way, this is another style that should go it alone. The collar itself offers enough detail, and a blouse underneath would only add clutter. The same goes for jewelry or scarves.

The V-neck Sweater

It's got the same advantages as the V-neck blouse for adding visual inches to your height. You can wear it over a number of shirt styles (including the open-collared blouse, the button-down, and the band-collared shirt). Or for a dressier (and sexier) look, wear it by itself. Remember: Since sweaters often offer a limited choice of sizes—with S, M, and L the usual designations—you have to make doubly sure that the V is scaled to your size and doesn't soar down below your bra line. If it's a wide V, check to see that it isn't so wide that it threatens to drop off your shoulders. Either situation falls into the kid-sister-wearing-big-sister's-clothes category.

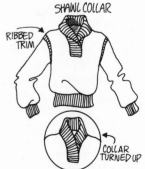

The Cardigan

At its worst, the cardigan sweater puts us in mind of disheveled French landladies. Which is why you have to be careful when choosing one and even more careful about when you wear them. The best cardigans are short and veed at the neck and/or part of a set that's more dressy than casual. When you do don a cardigan, it should be as a premeditated accessory to the clothes you're wearing. Forget the standby cardigan that's stuffed in the back of your desk drawer "in case the office gets chilly"; if you're susceptible to drafts, keep a chic little go-with-everything shawl handy instead.

How to Pick a Knit   When it comes to knit-picking, short women should look for any features that contribute to a lengthening image:

V·NECK

CARDIGAN

CARDIGAN

- *Waist-cropped sweater tops are sensational for short women* because they make the lower half of the body look that much longer. They're also a solution for the sweater-length problem; with a cropped top you avoid the balloon-over-the-hips look you can get with longer ones.
- *A note to the short- or thick-waisted:* Never tuck a sweater into your skirt or pants—even if it's a fine-gauge knit. Blouson sweaters are perfect for you, or when straight styles are in, try them with a thin belt buckled loosely so that it dips in front below the waistline to make it look lower.
- *Super-narrow shoulders?* Opt for raglan or dropped sleeves instead of an inset sleeve. Or check out the teen department in one of the better stores. Classics will always be the same there, quality will be just as available, and proportions and price tags will be smaller.
- *If you're slim*, you might try one of the tunic-length sweaters for tall women as a dress. But only if it's a clean, uncluttered style (front pockets that fall around your knees will be a sure giveaway that you're wearing a tall-girl's tunic).
- *If you're on the heavy side*, the sweater you wear should never be too tight. As a matter of fact, designer Bonnie Cashin (known for her wonderful knitted clothes) feels that a knit like a classic Shetland, when cut to normal dimensions, will make a woman look heavier. But if it's cut slightly oversized, with a deeper armhole for a roomier effect, it can make a woman look slimmer—which usually means taller.

Vests

One popular success-dressing guide for women (written by a man who shall remain nameless) dismisses vests with a cursory nod. "They're too sexy," he decrees, "calling undue attention to a woman's bust." He concludes that if you want to be taken seriously, you shouldn't wear them. To which we say—pure taradiddle! As we see it, few things can add polish to a look so much as a well-chosen vest —especially if you're short. Our reasoning . . .

First of all, a vest is a small piece in itself, which makes it a natural for under-5'4"s. It also has a double-edged versatility that we like a lot: For the office it's more casual than a blazer and can ease up the severity of a shirt and skirt or pants. And for a casual weekend, it can add a finishing chic to jeans and a flannel shirt. And since the best short-chic turnout often calls for simple patterns (or solids) and simple textures, a vest can be a terrific way to add interest by virtue of *its* pattern, texture, or color (as a small top piece, a vest can get away with almost anything).

Vested Interest: Dos & Don'ts

DO look for: fitted vests in tattersall. Thin-ribbed cashmeres, with or without flat cable stitching. Classic Shetlands. Evening vests that are hand-embroidered or shot with glitter. Not to mention classic Argyle-patterned vests that look as great now as they did in the thirties.

DON'T be caught in the vest that comes with a matching suit. Any look that too closely resembles men's three-piece-suit dressing can be the kiss of death on short women. (Instead of looking like an authoritative woman, you'll just come across as a little man.)

DO grab up the vest with a V-neck (always better than a rounded one), a collar or lapel that's narrow (or, better yet, absent altogether), pockets and flaps that are slit or minute (if there at all) and shoulders that cut in an inch or two from the arm.

DON'T wear a sweater vest that's too tight, or it will cheapen your look instead of polishing it.

DO make sure that fitted vests are just that: not too loose and not too snug, but fitted.

The Vest as Proportion-Changer

- *Those women who are thick of waist or ample of hip* will find that a vest can camouflage those bugaboos when it's slightly longer and worn open.
- *For the short-waisted, long-legged woman*, a vest can lengthen your waist if it falls an inch or so below your beltline.
- *Long-waisted and short-legged types* should try a sweater vest or longer straight vest for easing the potential awkwardness

of their proportions when shirts tucked into trousers (or skirts) reveal the natural waistline.

When to Wear a Vest

Sometimes a shirt and pants are better off on their own—if, for example, the top is beautifully detailed with pleats and tucking, with unusual sleeves or a special pattern or print. The same criteria might apply to your bottom half. If either is a real standout, they could probably do without the competition of another piece. But if the best you can say about the top/bottom twosome is that it's neat and subtle—you probably need a vest to turn that subtle to chic. Same principle applies when adding a vest to a simple clean-lined dress.

When to Save, When to Splurge, and Where

Some women who consider themselves short but not small would never think about stepping into the junior department for clothes—they'd never fit. But with vests, it can be a different ball game. Sizing on vests is a funny thing—they are almost never small enough unless you've got a large bust or an unusually large ribcage. (We're talking about fitted vests here.) Johanna B., an average-framed, 5'3" toy store manager from Detroit says that although she buys a 6 or an 8 in most garments, she always searches out vests in the smallest sizes possible ("always a four, and whenever possible, a two—which is rare"). So for her and others like her, the junior department is an ideal place to find inexpensive vests in casual fabrics like denim, khaki, or corduroy that fit across the ribs. Another good alternative is the boys department—especially for classic knitted Fair Isles sleeveless pullovers.

When not to go for cheap: when quality is essential—for vests of suede or leather or for specialty vests (embroidered, crocheted, beaded, or hand-knitted numbers). In other words, for vests you'll want to keep for years and years, splurge a little. The best places—boutiques that specialize in one-of-a-kinds. If the boutique happens to carry French or Italian imports, so much the better—they usually cut smaller than American designers.

Tunics

Somewhere along the line, we got the impression that shorter women tend to regard the tunic as off-limits to them because of their height. *Au contraire*, dear reader! As a matter of fact, a body-skimming tunic could be just the ticket for adding inches to your height—and for lopping a few inches from your width in the process. The key words here are *body-skimming:* By virtue of its straight-from-the-shoulder shape, the tunic creates a long, unbroken, body-lengthening line. And that alone gives it four stars in our book. But, in addition, a tunic—whether it's the long or the short variety—can effectively disguise a large bust; a thick, short, or long waist; and wide hips and a too-rounded stern.

But in order to do all these wonderful things, certain criteria are essential:

1. The best tunics are made from the softest fabrics possible, either knitted or woven from pliable, cushy fibers like wool or silk.
2. The bottom piece below the tunic should always be narrow —that means superskinny pants or a fluid-fabric gathered skirt.
3. This is one top that performs best when it performs solo. But if you do want to wear a shirt underneath, make it a soft one.
4. A belted tunic (especially if it's long) can look great if you're arrow-narrow. If not, take advantage of the unbroken long line and wear it uncinched.

The Short Tunic

With a short tunic, length is all-important, and you may have to experiment a bit before determining the right length. (It should hover in the vicinity of your fingertips—a bit above or a bit below, depending on your figure and what looks best. In any case, if you're going to make any mistake about length, it's better to err on the short side than on the long. (A short tunic that is too long on you becomes an in-between length that is awkward on a short body and destroys all the good that the tunic is meant to accomplish.)

The Long Tunic

The long version of the tunic usually skims above the knee and works best for the shorter figure when the sides are slit. As Margaret H., a 5′11½″ art director told us: "Whenever I'm a few pounds overweight and I need something to make me feel sleek and sexy, I wear my long wool tunic over a pair of wool tights. The slits up the sides of the tunic make my legs look longer, and whenever I wear it, somebody always comments that I look thinner. It's wonderful!" If tights aren't your style, you can get the same effect with a pair of pipe-stem pants.

FOCUS ON: Carol Horn

"Women who are short have to be honest with themselves about what looks good on them and not just copy any style they see," said Carol Horn, the California-based designer whose clothes are known for their young-spirited, easy-going air. "I'm five feet four myself and have a problem because I'm short-waisted, for example. So, I always try to elongate my body image by never wearing anything too fitted and, instead, wearing clothes that just skim the body.

"Of course, women who are short have to be careful about wearing clothes that overpower them too," she continued, "although short women certainly can manage to carry off extremes—women with great personal style. But you'll notice *how* they do it: They usually only go to extremes in one area, like wearing a big bulky top with the rest of the clothes in narrow proportion."

Carol Horn's own fitting model is a size 8, she told us, and her line begins with a size 4 and goes up to a 12. "I do take into consideration that the average woman's height is about five feet four," she said, "and try to make my clothes right for women who are five three to five six.

"There are many things in particular that I'm doing that will work well on shorter women," she said. "Knickers that'll work because of their nice, clean lines, skirts that fit over the hips slimly and then flare out, jackets with a neat shoulder line and seam detail—a slight alteration on your classic—in three styles: a cardigan, a tailored look with an asymmetrical closing, and a tapered effect. And any of the frilly blouses are scaled well for small women and would be terrific."

6. Skirts: Your Most Flattering Shapes and Lengths

If you're short on inches, you have to think tall with regard to skirts for two essential reasons:

1. A skirt covers the waist-to-hem area—that portion of the body with the greatest potential for creating the illusion of height.
2. For the same reason just stated, a skirt is one item that can cut you in half if you don't pay attention to details.

The main thing to remember about a skirt—even the fullest skirt: When it's on you, it should always look longer than it does wide. That doesn't mean you have to wear a skirt to your ankles. It does mean that you have to be careful about length and that the skirt must always fall close to the body.

Short Chic Shopping Tips for Skirts

Unlike other items of clothing, a skirt usually finds its way into a woman's closet because of its color, fabric, and cut alone. Brand names are often an afterthought at best. Even so, you might want to

YOKE WAISTED "A" LINE

BOTTOM CURVES IN, NOT OUT

check out such labels as *Harvé Benard*, *Evan Picone*, and *Jones New York* (in both their regular and petite lines). Also: *Ralph Lauren* for classic good style, *Calvin Klein* for the simplicity of his cuts, *Cacharel* for the fine detailing, and if you're very small, *Adolfo Sport* (the small sizes really are). *Gil Aimbez Genre* is another good bet for quality and class. And again, the junior department might be another valuable skirt source—but always check a junior skirt inside and out for quality. Some are great, some not so great—so you'll have to be sharp when you shop this resource.

The Classic Skirts to Keep in Stock

A-line Skirt

It's a close-to-the-body style that's also easy to wear, and for those reasons the A gets a plus. But there's a minus that can cancel the plus: If the skirt sticks straight out at the bottom like the A of its name, avoid it. A good A-line will be made from fabric that's soft enough to curve in gently at the bottom. Another possibility: Go for a well-made bias cut to accomplish the same thing.

DIRNDL

UNBULKY

IN-SEAM POCKETS

Also to watch for: If you're not detail-conscious, an A-line skirt can come across as dull and matronly. To relieve the boredom, look for cleverly inset pockets, a yoked waist, or a front closing—anything that adds interest without adding bulk. (By the way, if you happen to be a bit broad in the beam, the extra fabric at the bottom can help to balance out the width at your hips. Just make sure the fullness of the skirt starts at the widest part of your hips.)

Dirndl Skirt

The cut of a dirndl can go from slim to medium-wide. It, too, is an easy style to wear, and if you haven't got around to doing your sit-ups lately, the gathers at the waist of a dirndl can help hide a protruding tummy. But be aware that those same gathers are capable of adding bulk at the waistline if the fabric isn't as soft and fluid as it should be (to check, see if it flows through your fingers easily).

Pleated Skirt

This type includes *the classic kilt, fully pleated skirts, and partially pleated skirts* (which can mean just a panel of pleats). Some things to keep in mind about all of them:

- The most common type of pleats—those that overlap one another around the waistline—look best when stitched down from waist to hip. When they are, make sure the hip fit is right; if the skirt's too snug, the pleats will splay out from the hip like a broom fanning out from its stick. The line should always fall straight from the hip so that the pleats fall close to the body.

HIP STITCHED PLEATS

FITS SMOOTH AT HIP

- After the skirt is shortened to the desired length—and you won't want to wear pleated skirts too short—the unstitched section of pleats should be about twice as long as the stitched section, if not longer. If the unstitched section is too short, it could create a horizontal impression that will cut the line of the skirt.

- *Very tiny pleats* or pleats that fan out gradually from the waist (like *crystal pleats* which lie flat around the waist and become deeper as they progress toward the hem) work best when the fabric is extremely fluid and soft.

The last word on pleated skirts is a delightful tip we got from a very genteel Southern lady in her eighties, who told us (with what we suspect was only the merest tongue in cheek): "Whenever a lady wears a pleated skirt, she should swing her hips ever so slightly in order to accentuate the sway of the pleats as she walks." She added with a twinkle: "I've been told that gentlemen find the effect to be very appealing."

CRYSTAL PLEATS

TINY PLEATS MAKE VERTICAL LINES

Straight Skirt

This classic comes and goes in fashion, and we wish it were working full-time for the simple reason that few skirts can give the body such a long line as a well-fitted straight skirt. The key words to note are *well-fitted.* A rich-looking straight skirt will skim the body comfortably without being tight. To check for fit, sit down in it when trying on; if it wrinkles across the top of the legs in front you need a larger size.

STRAIGHT SKIRT

This one should be worn just a bit on the long side rather than just grazing the bottom of the knee. The length will accentuate a longer line and help you avoid the quintessential no-no that some short women are prone to commit: a straight skirt that's so short it looks like a square of fabric instead of a rectangle. Also, if the skirt has a slit or kick pleat (and just about all straight skirts do), you'll avoid making the slit or kick pleat too short in the hemming process. *Hint:* When you expect that a substantial hemming job has to be done, check the inside of the skirt to see if the slit or pleat can be extended a few inches from the top if necessary.

Pull-on Sweater Skirt

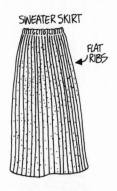

SWEATER SKIRT

FLAT RIBS

This type usually comes as the bottom half of a two-piece sweater dress. It can be straight or gored, flat-knit or textured. Look for the flattest, thinnest knits possible. (It's amazing how a sweater skirt can make even the thinnest woman look like a Weight Watchers candidate if she's not careful.) If the knit has ribs, they should be vertical, not horizonal, and never rounded.

The really great thing about a sweater skirt is that the fabric, because it's a knit, is fluid and can be very flattering to the shorter figure. The bad thing: It's a pain in the neck to alter if it's too long, and if the hem is finished with a knitted border, you can take it up only from the waist. In any case, if you're not a pro at hemming, you'd best leave this one to someone who is because if the hem is not done well, the skirt will look cheap.

Gathered Skirt

It's a full skirt, but for you it should never be too full. And, always, the fabric should be supersoft so that it won't add bulk around the waist and swallow you up everywhere else. As for length, it's better to go a little longer with a gathered skirt—you may need it to balance out all that fabric.

Trouser Skirt

We like the trouser skirt because it has the same chic as a good pair of trousers and can be worn with all the same things you'd normally wear with trousers. It can be an especially neat, tailored look for the office. To make sure of its neatness, check the front zipper closing to be sure it's perfectly stitched and lies flat; there shouldn't be any pull between the top of the zipper and the closing on the waistband when it's fastened.

Tiered Skirt

GATHERED SKIRT

KEEP THE GATHERS SOFT

It's a casual skirt that usually stays in the closet until the warmer months. (But if the fabric is a dark print or if it's made up in a season-less fabric like challis or a soft pinwale corduroy, it can also be a cold-weather skirt to wear with boots.)

Since the tiered skirt is really a series of horizontals, you have to compensate for that with the right fabric and color. The first should always be soft, the second a solid or dark, mini-sized print or at least a single color that graduates from light to dark. If each tier is colored or printed to contrast sharply with the next, you'll only accentuate the horizontal (read body-shortening) lines of the skirt.

Never go for cheap when you buy a wrap skirt. Chances are there won't be enough fabric in it to wrap you properly, and come the first hefty breeze you may open yourself up to an indecent exposure charge. Another way to safeguard against that possibility is to look for fastenings (usually hidden) in all the necessary places—including one around the hip. In general, however, the wrap is another easy figure-skimming skirt that's great for any body type. The best length: a little on the long side.

Wrap Skirt

A true circle skirt is just that—a full circle of fabric. Which means it's probably too much fabric for your height. If you're partial to it, however, keep it soft and fluid and it could work.

Circle Skirt

This trouser/skirt crossbreed used to be relegated to the "casual only" section of fashion, but nowadays you see it showing up in all the best places. Like so many fashion pieces, the culotte's dressiness or sportiness depends mostly on the fabric. In corduroy, it's casual; in a supple wool tweed, it's tailored enough for the office; and in velvet, crepe, or challis, it's dressed up for partying. To look for: interesting details (like stitched pleats, small gathers, or a yoke at the waist) and a narrowish cut that falls straight from the hip. Fuller culottes are fine, too, but only if the fabric is very soft.

Culottes

- *Waistbands*   If you're short-waisted, keep them narrow. If you're long-waisted, look for a wider one that helps cut the length of your waist.
- *Pleats*   Those that open toward the center line of your body are more slimming than those that open toward the hips. If the pleats aren't pressed or stitched, avoid wearing a sweater over them; the multi-layering of fabric is a sure way to add bulk.
- *Pockets*   Most of the better skirts will have them, and the best ones will be inseam (that is, set into the side seams of the skirt), or flat slits at the hipline. If they form diagonals on the front of the skirt, make sure they lie superflat or they'll add inches to your hips quicker than a pan of brownies. Pocket flaps also add bulk (and get in the way if you like to wear your sweaters out). Curved pockets will add roundness and fullness to your figure. Patch pockets? We're not crazy about them, but if you are, keep them on the smallish side

Details that Help Create Illusions

TROUSER-STYLE

TIERED SKIRT

ALWAYS
GRADUATED
COLORS
OR
ALL
ONE
COLOR

WRAP SKIRT

ALWAYS
WEAR
THIS SKIRT
ON THE
LONG
SIDE

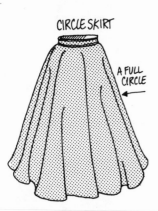

CIRCLE SKIRT

A FULL
CIRCLE

and make sure that they don't fall within calling distance of the hemline.

- *Verticals*   Skirts offer infinite possibilities where these body-lengtheners are concerned. Look for placket or button-down fronts, pleats, vertical seams—they all help to diminish your width, thereby adding to your height.
- *Borders*   Borders are horizontal lines that emphasize width (and cut the body) wherever they fall. If you like border-print skirts, make sure the color or print of the border tones doesn't contrast too noticeably with the rest of the skirt. Also to avoid: bottom frills and short (from mid-thigh down) pleats because these really are just variations on the border-line.

The real problem with borders, however, is a matter of hemming. As Michele M., a 5'1" bookstore manager from Maryland, complains: "I'd love to wear border prints, but when I hem them as much as I have to, the pattern's completely lost. To be short, it seems, is to live in a world without borders!" It was a common theme we heard again and again. One solution: If the border happens to be on a skirt, you might consider taking it up from the waistband instead of from the hem.

- *Bias Cuts*   The advantage of a skirt cut on the bias is that it falls gracefully and wrings the last drop of fluidity from a fabric—even a heavier fabric. But on a cheaper skirt (or even on an expensive one that's not as well made as the price would lead you to expect), the angle of the material can cause the zipper to buckle. That's why you'll often find a good bias-cut skirt using a row of buttons as closings instead of a zipper.
- *Heavy Fabrics*   The heavier the fabric, the less detail the skirt should have. And as we said above, it helps if the heavy stuff is cut on the bias.
- *Width*   If your legs are heavier than you'd like to admit, a skirt with more fabric at the hemline will help to make them seem narrower by contrast. Conversely, if thin legs are your problem, a narrower width at the hem will make the most of what you have.

Hemlines

We know, we know. The fashion hemline seems to rise and fall with as much rapidity (and less predictability) than the Dow Jones average in an election year. But the truth of the matter is that, like most trends, hemlines follow a fairly regular fashion pattern from decade to decade. In the twenties, for instance, chubby little knees began peeking out from under flappery skirts. In the thirties, skirt lengths dropped to the ankle. In the forties they gradually rose up again . . . fifties down, sixties up, seventies down.

Lately, however, there seems to be a heartening trend toward choice. If it continues, it could mean that we'll be free to choose from any number of hem lengths from now on—and still be considered fashionable. Wonderful thought—but where does that leave *you?*

Well, there are some fashion guides that tell you, "If you're short, forget about the vagaries of fashion and wear all your hemlines an inch or so below the knee." We strongly suspect that such statements are written by tall fashion editors who wouldn't dream of doing such a thing themselves. And neither should you. Remember: What tall women can do, you can do—if you keep everything in proportion to your height:

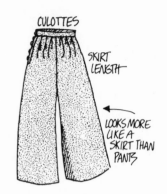

CULOTTES

SKIRT LENGTH

LOOKS MORE LIKE A SKIRT THAN PANTS

- *When the style of a skirt (or the dictates of fashion) calls for a longer hemline*, you'll want a shorter version of what they're showing in the magazines—but a shorter version that's still long on you.
- *When the styles call for shorter lengths*—which can mean anything from just below the knee to knee-topping to thigh-high—trust to your own eye and a little common sense. In this case, just below the knee probably *is* your best bet.

Call us stodgy, call us medieval, but we're still of the opinion that no grown woman in any position of importance should be seen running around in a skirt that exposes her thighs—especially if she happens to be short. If you're young, and if you've got great (and we mean *great*) legs, a supershort skirt over tights or stockings might be a terrific elongating look for sports or evening but never in the daytime at work. Even if everyone else is wearing them above the knee (and chances are "everyone" won't be anyway—too many women are still shuddering at pictures of themselves wearing minis in the sixties), you should opt for knee length. Reason: Aside from the fact that the mini does nothing to help a woman's credibility in the job market, it's also very difficult for a short woman to wear. There just isn't enough material to create anything but a horizontal line . . . and need we explain what that does?

A Few Short Words about Short Skirts

Hems and Legs

Question: Which comes first, the hem or the leg? *Answer:* The leg, of course—because the individual shape of your leg is the most important determining factor when deciding on the right hem length. . . .

- *If your legs are long from the knee down,* you'll probably find you have more options where skirt length is concerned.

- *If your legs are short from the knee down,* chances are that the shorter end of the hemline scale is better for you because it allows more leg to stem out from under the hem. Admittedly, longer skirts should be your *bêtes noires,* but if you love to wear them when they're In, pair them with medium- to high-heeled boots that camouflage the whereabouts of your calves—and you're home free.

- *If your legs are short from the knee up,* you're one of the ones who has to be cautious about straight skirts (remember what we said about opting for a rectangle instead of a square?). Always wear your straight skirts a little longer.

Finding Your PHR (Potential Hemline Range)

There are some women who stick to one hem length for everything. If you're one of them, consider this: Different styles, cuts, and fullnesses of clothes demand shorter or longer hemlines to make them work. And for short women, finding the exact hem length for each is essential. You should never be lazy about taking up a hem—even if the desired difference is only a matter of a half-inch. On you, a half-inch can make all the difference between "not quite" and "just right." Still convinced that only one length looks good on you? Then why not try this little test . . .

- *Slip into a leotard* and nude pantyhose
- *Gather together:* a large square scarf, a tape measure, three pairs of shoes (low-, medium-, and high-heeled), a full-length mirror, pencil and paper, and a willing accomplice.
- *Standing in front of the mirror,* hold one edge of the scarf to your waist, then roll it up from the waist until the bottom

edge hits the lowest point that's most flattering to your leg. Try on your medium and high heels to double-check. When you've decided on the exact length, have your friend measure it from waist to hemline point and note it. This will be the longest you can wear a long skirt.

- *Repeat the same procedure* to determine the most flattering short length. (This time, you may want to try it with low heels, too.) The result will be the highest you can go.

- *Now experiment* with different lengths in between those two points. You may be surprised to discover how much leeway you have—and never took advantage of before!

Note: When dealing with longer skirts worn over boots, your leg shape isn't seen, so you can go even longer than you would normally.

FOCUS ON: Geoffrey Beene

Relaxed, uncomplicated clothes, low-key, *sans* gimmicks—that's what you'll find at Geoffrey Beene. The fabrics are nothing short of wonderful ("I like fabrics that can almost fold up in the palm of your hand," says the designer), and the shapes are comfortable and easy . . . but—we have to say it—on the fullish side.

Still—"No one can tell me my clothes don't fit small women," objected Geoffrey Beene, when we put the question to him. "In fact, I have twelve boutiques in Japan, where women tend to be quite small, and I do one of my biggest businesses there.

"My clothes look very well on short women," Mr. Beene went on to explain. "The key is in selecting what's right." He believes that the biggest fashion mistake petite women make is in defining the waistline. Instead, "They should leave it floating so one never knows exactly where the waistline falls," he said. "In my line, for example, the best bet for a short woman would be my two-piece outfits. My two-piece dresses flow one into the other without cutting the figure. Small women should also not wear too high a heel," he continued. "It exaggerates their shortness and does something terrible to the posture."

One of Geoffrey Beene's ongoing fashion concerns—and one that he continually champions—is *comfort*. "There is no style without it," he declares. "A woman's clothes should move with her body; they shouldn't be constructed, and whatever her size, they shouldn't have any hinderances or bulk."

Although he says he does cut his smallest sizes for a tall thin woman, he offers an exceptionally wide range of sizes—"2 through 14, with special orders for size 16 and 18," he says.

"I like to think of my typical customer as an accomplished working woman contributing to our society," he added. "She is not pampered, and she is of no specific age."

7. Pants: How to Get the Leggiest Looks Around

When asked to name the article of clothing that was hardest to find because of height, the majority of questionnaire respondents said, "Pants." Which is a shame because it's precisely that under 5′4″ woman, who, if she could find the right pair of pants, stands to benefit the most from the long lean lines that pants dressing affords.

Once you find a pair, however (and we'll tell you how in the pages ahead), rest assured that the time spent looking will have been worth it. At their best, a sleek, tailored pair of trousers in a color like gray, black, or plum can provide you with dozens of ways to be well dressed, day or night. A classic example: traditional gray flannels. With a soft jacket and a sweater in almost any color, they can take you through almost any kind of day—working in a casual office, shopping, going to meetings, you name it. A switch to a silk blouse, belted with a suede or leather sash, and you've got an understated dinner look, too.

Sounds good? It is. But the hitch, of course, is finding those good gray flannels to begin with.

The Ins and Outs of Pants Shapes

Remember what we said about sticking to just one skirt length, regardless of fashion dictates? Well the same thing holds true here: because what we're *not* going to be telling you in this chapter is to find your best pants shape and stick with it. We don't have to explain that if you're wearing wide pants while the rest of the world is going straight and narrow, you're going to look dated and dowdy. So what this is going to be about is how to work *with* fashion: how to wear narrow pants when you choose . . . and how to adapt wider ones to fit your height and figure.

Another thing—if you're unsure about whether a particular pants shape is going to last, hear this: A woman in Dallas wrote to us about the wisdom of tapering her fullish trousers to conform with the then-narrow pants trend. Her reasoning: As soon as she got her full pants down to size, fashions would shift—and wide ones would be back again. Well, it doesn't work that way. Because (and this applies to most fashion areas, not just to pants), *almost all fashion changes are gradual*. The evolution from wide-leg pants to narrow ones was slow and took place over a period of several years; the change back will be just as gradual. One tip: a good middle-of-the-road pants shape, which we both keep our very best wool gabardine trousers in, no matter what the current fashion headlines herald: straight-leg, medium-narrow, falling from the hip to the ankle in a clean, straight line. It's a good, always-stylish classic shape that'll hold for a long time to come.

The Ins and Outs of Pants Fit

We might as well be upfront and say, if you're short, there's no use looking for pants in the correct length. Except in very rare cases you won't find them, and that's that. One Florida woman summed up the situation for us this way: "Sometimes I feel I cut off enough pants hem to make a whole other pair of pants."

A small consolation to keep in mind: Even women who are 5'5", 5'6", and 5'7" report that they too have to do a substantial amount of hemming on pants these days. Your guess is as good as ours as to why designers cut pants so long to begin with. (Yes, we know it's easier to shorten than to add-on length, but remember, when you've got to shorten more than three or four inches, you often have to reshape the entire leg as well.)

Beth T., a menswear designer who's 5'2", looked at the situation in practical terms. "My biggest complaint is being charged for excess. Being five foot two, most garments I purchase must be hemmed or altered, particularly when it comes to pants. Why should my size eight Calvin Klein suit, which will have an average of four inches cut off the pants when hemmed, and an inch cut off the cuff, cost the same price as a size twelve that will be purchased by someone five six to five eight most likely, and fit?

"Being in the business, I know what a tremendous savings there could be by the manufacturers if their pattern and yardage markers were gradually scaled down for the shorter figure. This savings could then be passed on to the consumer. At twenty to thirty-five dollars a yard for some wools and cashmeres (and ten to twenty wholesale), why should I pay for a quarter to a half of a yard of material that will be cut off when hemming my pants?"

When it comes to the way pants should fit, shortening the leg is seldom enough. Because when you're cutting off more than four, and sometimes as much as six inches of excess length, often you'll have to readjust the leg shape as well. What's in order: a careful watch on proportions. Meaning: If the current pants fashion demands, say, a 20-inch pants-leg width, translate that as being 20 inches *on a standard 5'7" model*. Then, depending on *your* height, scale the leg width down accordingly, approximately a half inch less for each inch of your height under 5'7".

Your Perfect Fit

What makes the most profound difference in the way pants fit for short women, beyond hemming and tapering, are the way the pants crotch or rise fits, and the fit at the waist and hips.

The rise: The pants rise (crotch) is most often too long on short women whether they happen to be long-waisted, short-waisted, or in-between. But although you can have the crotch of the pants altered to fit, the job is only worth having done if you unquestionably *love* the pants and they're a not-to-be-believed bargain as well. And even then, we'd suggest thinking twice about it. You're really much better off in the long run locating the brand that gives you the correct rise fit in the first place.

The waist and hips: We've found that buying pants that fit comfortably around the hips first is the best bet for most short women. Once you've found the right hip fit, taking in or letting out the waist is comparatively easier than alterations in the hip department, where you'll probably come up against pockets—and most better pants (the only ones worth the trouble of altering) have pockets.

Another important point about pants: To fit properly, no matter what your shape is like, pants should never be too tight. Says one European designer known for innovative pants shapes: "Wearing pants one size larger is always preferable to one size smaller." True. There's an elegance to pants that look comfortably roomy—and *that's* the look to go for. Roomy, mind, not big or bulky, which can be shortening to an already short figure.

When the *ideal* straight leg pants width is 20 inches, your pants width should be scaled this way:

Your Height	Approximate Pants-Leg Width
5'7"	20"
5'6"	19½"
5'5"	19"
5'4"	18½"
5'3"	18"
5'2"	17½"
5'1"	17"
5'	16½"
4'11"	16"
4'10"	15½"
4'9"	15"
4'8"	14½"

Use this chart as a *general* guide, taking into consideration your weight, frame size, and individual proportions. And, of course, your best guide is your own fashion eye.

Two Fashion Tricks That Can Make You Look Taller in Pants

1. Wear your pants with as high a crotch fit as you can possibly find comfortable. Key word here: comfortable (you know you've gone too far when you feel like your eyes are going to pop out of your head). We got this tip from 5'2" Jessica M., a petite and proportion-conscious second-year fashion student at New York's Fashion Institute of Technology. "Jeans that droop in the crotch can shorten your legs by a good few inches," Jessica told us. We found the principle works really well with jeans or jeans-style pants. But with good pants

—in wool, wool gab, or similar fabrics—wearings pants this tight will make them look cheap.

2. Designer Cathy Hardwick (whose clothes, by the way, rank high on our list for good proportion and good style for shorter women) took the opposite tack. Cathy, who's 5′3½″ herself, suggested buying pants with as loose and undefined a crotch fit as possible. That way, she explained, the actual length of the leg is disguised. We tried her theory and found it works very nicely for short-legged, short women—keeping the crotch full and easy in the back makes the leg length hard to pinpoint. Try it with evening pants in soft, silky fabrics like silk charmeuse, thin satin, or crepe de Chine, wearing the pants tapered at the ankle, maybe, and teamed up with a nice high heel.

Although we've thumbed our noses at fashion rules, we think a little rule making is welcome when it comes to pants. Moreover, once you understand the following rules for pants, you've got them for life. They hold fast, year in, year out, regardless of current fashion.

The Hard-and-Fast Pants Rules a Short Woman Can Count on No Matter What

1. *The wider the pants or trouser leg, the softer the fabric.*

This means that leather pants should always be on the leaner side; silk pants or ones in cashmere should have a little more ease. A soft corduroy trouser goes fuller; a stiffer cord is better on the slimmer side. The same holds true for different gradations of wool, gabardine, any fabric.

2. *The wider the pants leg, the longer the length.*

Simply a matter of good proportion here. When you're dealing with extra width and fullness, the shorter woman needs the extra length for balance and to create a longer line. What you've got to be sure of is that the pants *aren't* so long that they drag on the floor. (Nothing will push you into the ground faster than trouser bottoms that droop!) Does this mean that full, shortish pants are *verboten?* Not exactly. Although we don't think they're going to be your most flattering look—and although we do maintain that the style is a difficult one for the under-5′4″ woman to carry—they can work if you're on the taller side of short, and if you scale the width down carefully using the chart we gave you on the preceding pages.

3. *Narrow pants can go short or long, depending.*

Depending on: the shape of the pants leg. Narrow *tapered* trousers, the kind that start out wider at the top and taper at the ankle, look terrific on short women (who often happen to have pretty feet and ankles). And they look tallest when worn with a toned-in stocking and high-heeled shoe. Narrow *straight-leg* trousers—like jeans—should be worn as long as you can possibly wear them without creating any bunchiness at the ankle.

4. *Never buy pants with cuffed bottoms.*

Pants with cuffs will always make you look shorter, no matter what. (The cuff creates one of the more crucial Short Chic horizontals.) We wouldn't wear them on a bet, *no matter how fashionable.* No exceptions.

5. *Always invest in quality pants. Cheap ones look it.*

One tip-off to quality pants (after the fabric, of course)—the existence of pockets. Better pants and trousers almost always have nice side pockets to slide your hands into.

Pants vs. Trousers: Trousers are pants, but not all pants are trousers. The difference: Generally, *pants* refers to the overall category of bottoms; specifically, it means those that are of the tailored, flat-in-the-front variety. Barring fabric extremes, pants are also fairly casual. *Trousers* have little pleats under the waistband and will usually give you a more polished, more "dressed" look.

For example, think of your basic denim jeans. Pants, right? And casual. Now, think of pleat-front jeans, trouser-style. They're still casual, of course, but they're probably the jeans you'll reach for when you want a "dressed-up" jeans look. The same goes for cords. Flat-front pants, casual. Pleated trousers, a little dressier.

The Right Pants for Your Height and Figure

It's often said that short women look dumpy in pants. Not true. If you think that you look dumpy in pants, it's either because of your figure, not your height, or, more likely, that you're wearing the wrong pants for your particular body type. We firmly and steadfastly believe that there are pants styles and cuts that are becoming to nearly every short body type—and you don't have to have proportions like Bo Derek (an unbelievable 5′3″) either. The one exception: If you're short and more than twenty-five pounds over your ideal weight. In that one instance, you'll probably look best and feel most comfortable camouflaging the extra weight in a soft, gathered, narrow-falling skirt, worn with a toned-in stocking and two-to-three-inch-heeled shoes.

Because sizes and cuts vary so much from manufacturer to manufacturer, particularly when it comes to pants, you'll probably have to try on several pairs in several different styles and brand names until you find the pants that work for you. Below, some of the manufacturers we think worth checking out . . .

Short Chic Shopping Tips for Pants

Les Halles ("Their pants fit me perfectly," writes a very petite-figured assistant editor, 5′, 87 pounds, 31-24-32. "Last year I bought five pair! And for nice tight jeans, I like *Fiorucci* and *Adolph Lafont*." Other cuts we think work well: *Yves Saint Laurent* (pricey, but narrowly cut, slim; *Harvé Benard* (another narrowish cut); *Tahari* (a favorite of a lot of fashion-savvy questionnaire respondents —a 5′2½″, 103-pound buyer, 32-23-33 found her size 4 *Tahari* pants "exceptionally well proportioned"); and in the junior department, *H.I.S. for Her* (a nice narrow leg). Allison always gets a good fit from *Calvin Klein* (cut for a small-waisted, rounded-hip figure), from *Finity*, *Albert Nipon Collectibles*, and *Cathy Hardwick*. Others to look for: *Willi Smith for Williwear* (sometimes oversized, but other times just right); *Jones New York*, *Evan-Picone*, and *Liz Claiborne*. For jeans, Anne Marie recommends *Levi's* for their slim cut, *Calvin Klein* and *Gloria Vanderbilt* jeans for a roomier fit.

STRAIGHT-LEG PANTS

FLANNEL

The Basic Pants Shapes

Classically tailored straight-leg pants can go almost anywhere, and their flexibility as a good basic bottom knows no end. How casual or how dressy they are depend on the fabric they're made in and the kind of top you pair them with. The style looks good on most short

Straight-leg Tailored Pants

women (we like them for casual wear best), because it's simple and unfussy. But because they're smooth and snug across the hips, they pretty much show your shape as is.

Pleat-front Trousers

Pleated trousers are one of our favorite pants shapes—they give a little more polish and style to whatever you wear them with. The pleats under the waistband add softness, manage to flatter whatever shape you're in. (If you're rounded in the tummy, for example, pleats will give you just the right amount of coverage without adding bulk; if you're essentially flattish, with a straight up-and-down figure, they'll give you a little more shape.) Pleated trousers can be classic straight-leg or medium-tapered, and they come in single-, double-, or triple-pleated styles. We'd suggest skipping the triples—they're usually too full for a short woman to carry.

Drawstring Pants

The key to wearing drawstring pants is that they should be loose and easy fitting but not too full. As long as you're careful to find a pair that aren't overgathered, there's no reason you shouldn't give them a try. In cotton, they're casual and beachy; in silk or satin, they take on a dressier look. Wear them tapered or medium-straight.

Baggies

PLEAT-FRONT PANTS

We go against popular opinion here. We think a short woman can look wonderful in baggy pants—we've seen it and we've tried it. Dolly M., for example, is a magazine staffer we know who's 4'11" (approximately), who carries off baggie trousers (and almost everything else she wears) with great style. "Too-baggy pants can make a short woman look dumpy," Dolly explained, "but the main reason so many short women have a hard time looking good in baggy pants is that once they shorten the hem, they lose the leg-shape completely."

Baggy pants should fit snugly around the waist and hips, and taper all the way down the leg. They look best on small women when they're hemmed (not cuffed or bunched around the ankle). If you happen to like the style, wear them with low-heeled espadrilles or sporty jazz Oxfords. For a dressier, leggier look (if your baggy pants are in a dressier fabric), try them with a pair of high-heeled sandals. As with any other ankle-tapering pants, don't wear baggies with ankle-strap shoes—the straps will interfere with the pants hem.

How to Stretch a Leg

One of the most important elements of looking taller has to do with looking leggier. So if you're already built that way, consider yourself ten steps ahead of the game. If you're not or even if you are and want to play up what you've got, here's how. . . .

The Pants Shape for Your Shape

If you're short and . . .

short-waisted and long-legged, pants are probably one of your most flattering, elongating looks, and you should look good in almost any style that strikes your fancy. (That's the advantage of those enviable long legs!) What to look for: pants with a small thin waistband, which won't shorten your torso any; pants with a high waist will only shorten your body and exaggerate your proportions.

long-waisted and short-legged, yours is the short body type that really looks tallest in a skirt or dress. But the right pants, chosen with care, can work for you, too. Try pleat-front pants with a high, deep waistband to start. They'll draw the eye upward, the waistband visually lengthening the look of your legs. You may also find that tapered pants, worn with a three-quarter-length sweater-jacket that hits right below the buttocks—and not a half-inch longer—can work very well at lengthening your proportions.

slightly round in the tummy, never wear pants that are tight-fitting. (The same holds true if you're on the hippy side or have big thighs or a wide bottom *for your height*.) The softer and more loose-fitting the pants you wear, the better they skim over bumps and bulges you'd rather not admit to. Flat-front pants, for example, while they add a minimum of bulk, also outline every less-than-perfect ounce. Flat-front jeans are a different story. These, and any jean-style pants, when they fit nice and tight at the top, hold you in a little, which is fine. Pleat-front pants with a certain amount of controlled fullness, will also disguise a round tummy, *if* the pleats lie flat and the waistband is easy fitting. A waistband that's too tight will make the trousers pucker out below.

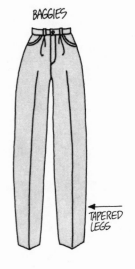

hippy with shortish legs, trousers that stretch tightly across your bottom will only call attention to the problem. What does work: a well-tailored basic cut that falls straight from the hips to the ankles, with soft figure-skimming gathers at the top, or with small unbulky pleats. Smooth fabrics in muted darkish colors are also good (no heavy tweeds or bold plaids). Avoid very full triple-pleated trousers, and large front or back pockets with unnecessary detailing.

- *Almost as important as the cut and fit of your pants are what goes under them.* For the tallest, leggiest look, nothing succeeds like toning-in—that is, wearing pants, stockings, and shoes all in the same color family. If you're wearing pants that are the slightest bit "iffy" for your height, like ankle-length trousers (narrow or full), ones that are pegged or triple-pleated, or any kind of knicker look, it's toning-in that's going to make the difference. For example, Allison wears a favorite pair of loden-green wool pleat-front trousers, hemmed ankle-high—potentially a shortener for her height. But they work because she wears them *toned-in*, with grayish-green sheer stockings and high-heeled dark-green pumps.

- *Another way to handle ankle-length trousers like those, if you want a more daring look:* Add a *contrasting* color in your shoe but not in your stocking. *Navy* pants with *navy* sheer pantyhose and a *red* shoe (or a red-and-white or navy-and-white spectator shoe) would be one way. That way, your leg still looks nice and long, and the eye slides right down the pants leg to a dark toned-in ankle, while the color in the shoe is an unexpected touch. (For more tips and the complete story on shoes, see chapter 14, Accessories.)

- *A good leg-stretching tip if you want to wear pegged or chopped-length fullish pants:* Since these do tend to abbreviate leg length, matching pants to ankles and feet is a must. We're not putting the nix on crazy-colored socks, however. Just have them for pants looks that are easier for short women to carry off. We saw a petite woman on the crosstown bus recently who had the pants-plus-odd-socks look down pat. She wore dark brown wool straight-leg pants and a brown/cream/rust reefer-style wool coat. She looked nice and neat but fairly conventional until she sat down—and we were treated to a flash of hot-orange socks shot with metallic glitter!

Jump Suits

"Lately, I saw a terrific-looking jump suit—if only it would've fit! You wouldn't have believed how baggy it was—in the seat, all the way down the leg, and from the waist to the crotch. But it was the smallest one they made!"

Sherrill R., Display Designer,
5'2", 115 pounds, Houston, Texas

JUMPSUIT

Pants and the Office: We like them but find we're in a distinct minority because, according to top corporate types, no dice. So although women in pants have won acceptance on city streets, in restaurants, and in schools—in the Vatican even—they're still unofficially off-limits in the boardrooms of corporate America.

If you're working for a conservative, rather traditional, organization, in a conservative, rather traditional, field (and these include the likes of law, banking, finance, and such—fields in which a short woman needs all the authority she can muster), you're better off sticking with suits, skirts, and dresses and saving pants-dressing for weekends.

On the other hand, if you work in an industry with a more relaxed dress code—or in any kind of creative field—there's nothing wrong with a pair of well-cut pleat-front trousers for office wear. Never jeans though, even good jeans, beyond a certain level of management. Although your taller co-workers may get away with them occasionally, when you're short you're dressing for a credibility that jeans just don't carry.

We take our cue from one top-level editor who works it this way. A staunch pants advocate, on working-in-the-office days, she shows up in trousers. But for meetings out, conferences in the publisher's office, and industry luncheons, she shows up in a suit or dress every time.

Have you ever worn a jump suit? If the answer is no and you're under 5'4", it's not hard to guess why. Every time you ventured to try one on, you found yourself facing a complete alterations overhaul—pretty much like the situation described above—with the crotch around your knee, a too-long waist, sleeves and leg lengths that border on the ridiculous.

But if you answered "yes" to that first question, you're probably smiling by now. Because you know—and we do, too—that even a total alterations makeover is worth it.

It is beyond our understanding why so many short women have failed to catch onto the proportional magic of a good jump suit. One that fits can make you look taller than you ever thought you could, even out the proportions of almost any short figure type, and make you look thinner, sexier, slinkier besides.

Another thing: Jump suits don't always need a total overhaul anyway. If you're persistent, you'll find jump suits of every type—

zip-front, buttoned-up, collarless, classic, dressy—in styles and sizes that work.

If you're out shopping one day, do yourself a favor and check out the stock. Most better designer jump suits (and we can practically guarantee you'll be seeing more of them in the fashion seasons ahead) are a touch on the long-waisted side. If you are, too, fine. But even if you've found a jump suit that's a wee bit too long-waisted for you, don't bother with alterations. Instead, try adding small shoulder pads. The pads will raise the waist just that needed bit and give you a crisper, neater silhouette in the bargain. Another option if you're short-waisted: the junior department, especially for casual jump suits in colored denims and cords. Look for those without a set-in waist so that you can belt it wherever you please.

If you've never worn a jump suit before, you'll be surprised at how well it will incorporate itself into your wardrobe. It's a lean-looking, easy, and dependable outfit that doesn't need a whole lot of extras, which would only clutter up a small frame. And it's not a just-for-kids-look either. Estelle L., fifty years old and 5'1", finds her black cotton jump suit topped with a beige linen jacket a comfortable look to travel in—and one that makes her long legs look even longer. Account executive Janice J., forty-six, 5'2½", calls her taupe wool drawstring jump suit "a lifesaver." "When I have five minutes to get dressed in the morning, that's what I reach for." With boots, a silk scarf, and a herringbone jacket, she's got a look that's as comfortable as well-worn jeans but polished-looking enough for any situation that could come up in the agency where she works, from seeing clients to meeting someone special for lunch.

Short Chic Shopping Tips for Jump Suits

Allison found several nicely proportioned casual jump suits at the national chainstore for jeans, *The Gap*. The ones that really deserve singling out for under 5'4"s: *Prime Cut* (their tan cotton denim zip-front jump suit, size 5/6, needed just a small hem, all other proportions were A-number one); and *Shanghai'd for Bowman Trading* (their button-front rose-colored cotton jump suit, made in China, size Small, was a trifle on the shortwaisted side, but it didn't even need to be hemmed! The legs were tapered and lean, and the length, with a 1-inch boot heel, was perfect.

Knickers

We've always thought that knickers were tremendous fun. And when they're worn correctly, they will make a short woman look leggier and taller. So if you've got the kind of personal style to carry them off, there's no reason your height should stand in your way.

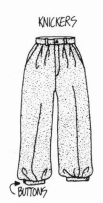

KNICKERS

BUTTONS

Do's and Don'ts

DO wear trim, classic knee-length knickers that are controlled in fullness and scaled down in shape. Regardless of the caprices of fashion, a pair of knickers like that will always receive high marks as a leg lengthener.

DO take care to tie in shoe and stocking colors. Casual cord knickers for example, should be worn with matching color and not contrasting socks. (Otherwise, the knickers will foreshorten the figure.) With evening knickers in black velvet, for instance, the same principle holds true: They look best worn with toned-in black sheer or patterned hose and black pumps.

DON'T wear knickers that are too full and bloomery. *Extreme* knickers and knicker-related looks like exaggerated Zoave pants and jodhpurs are best left to the tallest and lankiest. (Even then, we think they're apt to provoke stares—and not those of the most admiring kind.)

Finally, an informal and wholly unofficial survey of gentlemen we know leads us to believe that many men like narrow, classic knickers on short women for precisely the above-mentioned leg-lengthening assets. Some sample comments:

- "I think knickers look great on all women, short or tall, but not if they've got fat calves."
- "They definitely call attention to the shape of a woman's legs."
- "I like them on short women, especially with boots. Tall women look too overpowering in knickers, while petite women look dashing and French." (It must be noted that this last speaker was 5′8″ and of French descent.)

Shorts . . . Zeroing In On the Length That's Right for You

Come warm weather, shorts have long been a consistent part of the modern fashion picture, in lengths that vary from the briefest and snappiest of short-shorts, to walking shorts, British officer-style to longer clam diggers and pedal pushers. Today, however, shorts aren't only for knocking around the tennis courts or sunning at a resort. In different fabrics (like linen, wool, and gabardine) and with different treatments (with, say, a natty shirt and blazer), they also work for a certain kind of casual city dressing, and, surprisingly, for glamorous evening getups, too. When Lauren Hutton, for example, showed up at an Oscar presentation wearing above-the-knee shorts in glimmering gold lamé, it was clear that the look and the length had come into its own.

SHORT SHORTS

When you go shopping for shorts, be sure that you . . .

DO look for longer shorts that have a comfortably loose and easy-fitting leg, especially if your legs are a little on the heavy side. Whereas loose (but not baggy) shorts legs can camouflage fullish hips and thighs, tight-fitting longer shorts will call attention to them. Short-shorts, on the other hand, look fine if they're snug—and if you've got the legs and the body for them.

MODIFIED
SHORT SHORTS

DO wear shorts with flat-heeled or low-heeled shoes. Comfortable, low wedged-heeled sandals or espadrilles are nice alternatives if you want to add a little height to your stature or length to your leg. A high-heeled shoe with shorts, however, even shorts in a dressy fabric, will quite frankly make you look like The Happy Hooker.

DON'T wear shorts with heavy-looking shoes. And although Bermudas with knee-highs and loafers is a classic country look, it does tend to carry a petite woman back to sixth grade. Instead of flat-heeled loafers, substitute a low-heeled ghillie tie shoe for a little more sophistication. And DO experiment with different shorts lengths. Hemming your Bermudas an inch or two above the knee often results in a more flattering and leggier proportion.

BERMUDAS

DON'T wear shorts with too-full drawstring tops or shorts with blousy pleats. Straight-cut drawstrings or soft-pleated shorts will work as long as the fullness isn't too exaggerated.

Short-shorts expose all of your legs, most of your thighs (which should be trim), and unless you're careful, a little of your bottom as well. Staples on the beach and tennis courts and at resorts, they look terrific on short women with great legs. (And, as designer Bob Mackie pointed out to us, great legs aren't necessarily long legs either.)

Modified short-shorts expose plenty of leg, too, but manage to cover the slight thigh bulge that many women—short or otherwise—develop. This length is more versatile than ultra short-shorts (meaning that you can bend over in them and not worry) and can be worn with great success by most under-5′4″ types.

Bermuda shorts hit just above the knee and function pretty much the way a short skirt does. Put together with the right accessories, they're acceptable street fashion, today even in most restaurants. Still, they're not the easiest length for short women: If you've got short legs or a thick torso, you could find their less-than-leggy proportion awkward. And they do zero the eye right in on your knees, so if yours look like doorknobs or suet pudding, forget it.

Jamaica shorts end around midthigh (three or four inches above your knee) and are shorter than Bermudas but not short-short. We find them the most graceful and attractive "walking shorts" length on short women, whether you wear them for the beach or for the city. Just be careful to measure these carefully to get your own best shorts proportion.

Pedal pushers fall just below the knee, giving you the look of shorts but with a little more coverage (nice if you feel your knees aren't up to the baring or if your thighs are too heavy for total exposure). Women under 5′4″ should wear pedal pushers a touch on the shorter side to show as much leg as possible. Too-full, too-long pedal pushers can be easily tapered in width and shortened in length.

Clam diggers fall to midcalf. (They're called clam diggers because that's the length that clammers used to roll their pants up to, to keep them dry.) These, too, can be shortened and tapered accordingly. They're a good choice for a lot of women because, whereas they can hide less-than-perfect legs, they highlight and flatter pretty feet and ankles. *Tip:* We heard recently that at least one major department store has added a nice short-woman plus to some of their more voluminous summer designer clam diggers: a tiny loop and button so the pants can be worn with more volume or less, depending on whether or not they're buttoned.

Choosing the Shorts Shapes That Won't Shortchange Your Figure

JAMAICAS

PEDAL PUSHERS

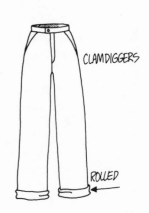

CLAMDIGGERS

ROLLED

FOCUS ON: Cathy Hardwick

"When I was younger, in my early twenties, I made mistakes with clothes," said Cathy Hardwick, the stunning, 5′3½″ Korean-born sportswear designer. "One day I caught a look at myself in a store window and I was shocked—I had a completely different image of myself—what a disappointment! After that, I looked better because I was more careful. Today, I know what I like—what I call *tough* sportswear. I don't feel comfortable in frilly clothes. Not that they are overwhelming but because they don't suit my personality. Still, maybe subconsciously, I don't want to look like a little girl with fussy ribbons and all that.

"I would love to be taller," she went on. "I think I would just look better —more elongated. Right now, I have to be very careful in what I wear so that I look my best."

Cathy takes special care with pants—that they aren't too tight, too wide, or too loose. "Too loose and I can't wear them with a slim jacket," she said. "Even though I don't have big hips, the smallest added bulk will make them look big in comparison. I never wear skirts too long either—but the right length depends on the fashion. When the longer skirt was in, I wore it slightly above midcalf; now I wear them barely covering the knee."

She was wearing flat shoes when we spoke ("comfortable for the office," she said), but generally she looks for shoes that aren't too high or too flat. "I also try to avoid ankle-strap shoes—a pump gives me a longer continuation of leg. I wear monotones, too—the same color up and down, although I will wear a different-colored sock sometimes. Sometimes a shoe just *calls out* for a naughty-colored sock, and then I'll wear one in bright red or blue," she said with a smile.

In addition to wearing her own line where the size 4 is proportioned "perfectly for me," she says, she finds a fit in many European sizes. "European clothes fit me because I have slim hips," she commented. "I find their clothes to be sized much slimmer on the bottoms than on the tops. I often buy separates even though I don't have a short waist, the waists are too long on me."

For evening, she prefers sportswear made in evening fabrics—tailored pants in satin, matte jersey, crepe de Chine. "I wear them with the very bare beaded sweaters I make every fall and sometimes with dressy blouses. Occasionally, I'll wear a simply cut dress with one shoulder, but dressy sportswear is what I feel most comfortable in.

"And I love fur," she continued. "That's because my attitude is different from a lot of people's. I *think* very tall. I can be a size four or a size ten. Why, I try on my sample size eight, and it can fit me better than it fits a lot of size eight women because I just think big. It's what's in my head—it's attitude."

There is something that even thinking "big" couldn't help though, she recalled. "I used to have a lynx coat that was gigantic and came down to my ankles. It really was a bit much on me so I gave it to my daughter."

Cathy has always believed that separates offer the best fit for short women, whether they are long-waisted or short-waisted.

"I do think the shorter woman's main problem is having shorter legs and a longer body. The short woman with a short waist will have an easier time looking longer. She should wear a blouson to deemphasize where her waist falls, never wear wide or tight belts and wear everything a little looser—a blouse pulled over her belt, for example. She has a much easier time than the woman disguising a long-waisted figure.

"I also think a short woman needs to build up a little bit of shoulder, particularly if her shoulders are sloping. A woman who has big shoulders, a small waist, not too much breast, long legs, and no hips—that is the most ideal figure for clothes, in my opinion," she told us. "We don't all look that way, so we have to try and create that.

"Tunics are great proportion-changers for short women," she continued. "Let them end right at the coverage of the crotch so you have the look of two thin legs sticking out—that is best. Women who are short-legged should probably wear narrower rather than wider pants legs, too."

But wearing pants—odd-length pants, like Cathy does often—shouldn't present problems to shorter women if they're in good shape. "Wearing them has to do with proportion and nothing to do with height. Why, I know one tiny, tiny woman who is as perfectly proportioned as if she were in miniature. I don't think she weighs more than eighty-five pounds—and she looks fine no matter what she wears—pants, skirts, high heels."

The Cathy Hardwick line starts with a size 4 and goes up to 14. "I wear the four myself," she said. "I alter the sleeves sometimes when they are too long, and I do cut the pants long because my size eight fitting model is five feet nine, and when the sizes grade down, they are still too long on me. But, otherwise, the proportion of the four fits me perfectly.

"Occasionally, though, I'll buy pants in the size six, depending on the cut because I don't like them to look tight. I don't like myself in tight pants because I don't have the longest legs in the world."

FOCUS ON: Pinky Wolman of Pinky & Dianne
for Private Label

To a devoted coterie of quality-conscious women, clothes by the Coty-award-winning team of Pinky Wolman and Dianne Beaudry are an investment: a combination of wonderful fabrics and whimsical styling. A special attraction of their clothes for us: Pinky herself is short—just 4'11" and one of the best examples of a *small* woman with *big* confidence and a unique sense of style.

"There are no rules because I am short," Pinky began. "I don't consider it at all limiting when it comes to the way I dress. True, I'm small and have short legs, but I wear the kind of clothes I've always wanted to all my life. My whole family is small, so I guess you could say I always thought good things came in small packages."

Pinky's personal style revolves around pants. "I wear exaggerated pants, baggy leather ones one day, jodhpurs or knickers the next. A short woman can wear odd-length pants as long as she gets the proportion right and wears them with the right shoes and stockings," she explained. "The small woman who wants to wear gray flannel cropped pants might try them with white lace stockings and black patent leather shoes with bows, a white silk shirt, and soft cardigan," she advised. "It's a look that's tailored and refined with a level of taste to it.

"People often say they can't believe that I have the nerve to wear the things I do, but I never mind about that. If it works for you, why not wear silk crepe de Chine knickers, a T shirt, and ballet slippers?"

Proportion, of course, and personal flair play a big part in the making of Pinky's kind of style. "When I wear baggy pants," she says, "I might wear them with a skinny shirt and sweater vest to make it all seem longer and taller —a total look. I used to wear very baggy clothing because everything was so big on me. Dianne, who's five feet nine, would wear the same size garment I would, but she'd wear hers long and I'd hike mine up with a belt and it worked." (One designer that she particularly enjoys is Kenzo—often said to be "big" and "hard-to-wear." Says Pinky: "I have many things in my wardrobe that Kenzo did. They're exaggerated, but they suit me and I always wear them.")

"The point is to play with your clothes till you're comfortable with them," she emphasized.

One of the most important assets that can help a small woman carry off clothes is "good shoulders," Pinky continued. "Even though I'm short, my shoulders are broad, and that makes it easier for me to carry clothes. If I were round-shouldered and really skinny and puny-looking. I couldn't wear the sometimes outrageous clothing that I do. How you stand—your posture—is part of it, too." (For Short Chic posture tips, see chapter 17.)

"Often taller women can wear classics somewhat better than shorter women do," Pinky said. "A shorter woman needs something extra. But she should never dress like an antique, fragile doll. She should dress in a more sophisticated way, understated and a little bit severe, I think, accentuating her shape in some ways, the positive points of her dress in another. For evening, for instance, it's always better to be underdressed than over. That's why I wear a lot of black, very tailored evening clothes. Ruffles and organdy don't work on short women."

But what about the short woman who likes ruffles? we asked.

"Get over it," Pinky advised. "Put them on your bed or your curtains or your pillows, but don't wear them."

There is a danger of looking oversevere, however, Pinky felt. "The small woman should be very careful about clothes that give her a too-strong image— her hair pulled back, too many dark and matronly colors. You can't let your clothes take over, whether you're tall or short, and your clothes shouldn't be a barrier between the world and what you really are."

Looking young, Pinky felt, was an advantage. "I think women should leave well enough alone and be happy about that," she said, although she acknowledged that there is a "cute" image that short women have to get beyond. When people call her "cute," she says she "grits her teeth a lot. I act like I don't hear it because I know they don't know what else to say."

Part of the making of Pinky's personal look has to do with her love of accessories. "I always wear them," she commented. "They are what gives punch to the outfit. I particularly like to wear black at night because then I can wear lots of unusual accessories. Last night I wore three-quarter length black pants and a black shell with a sheer black crepe de Chine cardigan with knit trim. And I wore it with black lace stockings, gold jewelry, and leopard-skin shoes. I have to keep my sense of humor," she said of the shoes. "But they were at the very bottom of my feet and not cutting me in the middle or stuck in my hair."

Other details: she prefers bomber jackets instead of coats ("because they fit close to the body and show my legs underneath") and leather instead of fur. ("I wear a padded leather coat with exaggerated shoulders proportioned down to a nine-tenths length so I can layer a skirt underneath a little. It looks well with pants or a skirt and is better on me than a three-quarter length because it's less choppy."

So how does she advise the shorter woman to approach fashion?

"You have to follow the designer and cut that you like," Pinky said.

And, speaking of her own line: "I think it's important for women to know that I'm small and I design the line as if I'm going to wear these clothes myself. I can wear the same kind of clothes than Dianne wears and she's tall."

"I wear our size four, and Dianne the twelve. It's a very small four, which is why we feel no need to cut a size two," she went on. "People on Seventh Avenue who do couturier-type clothes and are dressing an older, more mature woman would cut a larger, 'over-healthy' size four. I am dressing a woman who, though she's anywhere from her twenties to her late fifties, has got an active life and keeps herself in very good shape."

8. Jackets: Investment Dressing That Polishes Your Look

A stunning jacket will probably do more than almost anything else you own to pull your look together. A great jacket is truly investment dressing, whether it is for day, date, or evening wear; as is, or with some periodic remodeling, it can last for years.

A tour through fortyish, 5′2″ Jackie P.'s closet revealed *thirty-four* assorted jackets, all hanging in neat rows. "I'm not afraid of looking as if I'm interested in fashion," the emphatically chic cosmetics executive told us. "I've consciously built my wardrobe around jackets because they get across an image that's businesslike but stylish."

Sara K., also 5′2″, is another jacket collector of a different sort. A vintage-clothes fan, she recently purchased several 1950s jackets at a suburban garage sale. The matching skirts had been hemmed into oblivion ("probably during the mid-sixties"), but the jackets, laundered, and with a nip here and a tuck there, carry on in great style.

It's no news that a jacket-on-the-job conveys its own kind of instant working authority. When Emily B., just 5′1″, landed her first job as an associate traffic coordinator in a large accounting firm just three months out of college, she found her position meant a hurried shopping trip—and the purchase of three "good-quality" jackets to polish up an essentially casual wardrobe.

Paradoxically, however, although a jacket pulls together and polishes a look, the right one also makes everything else you wear seem a little more relaxed and at ease. A tweedy hacking jacket is like that—just think of its relaxed, hands-in-the-pockets quality. But just as surely as the right jacket can work for you on or off the job, the wrong one can undermine your style—fast!

If you're unsure about whether a particular jacket is right for you, glance over the four-point checklist below. If you can't answer "yes" to *all* of the four Short Chic jacket essentials, then the jacket in question is probably wrong for your height and size.

For the shorter woman, the right jacket should have

- *perfectly defined architecture at the shoulder* that anchors the shape of the jacket so that everything else falls into place. If the set of the shoulder line is at all off or not properly defined, the jacket won't work.

- *no excess fabric to it.* Rather just enough to accomplish the style correctly without skimping, and not an iota more.

- *the correct amount of dressmaker detailing.* Enough to be interesting but not so much that it overwhelms your size. A good example: inverted pleat detailing. Not only does it add fashion interest, but the pleats will do for your body what blusher does for your cheeks—create slimness by means of shadowing.

- *a perfectly proportioned length.* This is where you're going to have to be extra careful, extra demanding. As little as a half inch too much in the body-length (or in the sleeve) can foreshorten you and ruin the line of the clothes underneath.

Finding Your Correct Jacket Length

Jacket length is one of the four essential jacket checkpoints for short women; it's all too easy to look stumpy and foreshortened in an overly long but otherwise top-quality jacket. For this reason (aside from the delightful fact they give short women a snappy, racy look), we prefer cropped blazers and short spencer jackets whenever the styles are available. Streets & Co., a New York boutique that caters specifically to professional working women who need conservative but not dowdy clothing, agrees. They, too, say they prefer jackets to be shorter ("to-the-hip"), since long jackets tend to resemble riding coats and are unflattering to many women, especially if they're hippy.

"But I read . . . that shorter women look taller in long jackets," wrote in a 5′ Denver questionnaire respondent. Well, we saw that magazine article, too, and it just doesn't work that way. Because the primary way of adding height comes from extending the appearance of the legs, a longer jacket, which lengthens your torso in relation to leg length, will always make you look shorter.

Your basic jacket length rule: when you are wearing a jacket over a skirt or dress, the length of the jacket (measuring from its neck to its hem) should preferably be *shorter than* (or at least equal to) *the visible length of the skirt.*

The part of the skirt that shows should always appear longer than the length of the jacket whether the skirt is short or long (i.e., the long jacket worn with a *short* skirt foreshortens the under-5′4″ figure drastically; the long jacket paired up with a *long* skirt will be overwhelming to your size and height unless it's a truly long skirt, like a maxi.)

The exception to the above rule: the long, straight-fitting jacket (as opposed to styles that are shaped or fitted). A straight line, which is longish but still narrow and loose, can work very nicely on the shorter woman. It also happens to be one of the best jacket shapes for concealing figure problems like a thick torso or wide-ish hips because it skims over such bugaboos. That's the reason, by the way, that so many matronly looking full-figured dresses traditionally came with straight-fitting overjackets.

So what can you do with your other on-the-long-side jackets?

1. Hem them—preferably have it done by a tailor.
2. Save them to wear with long maxi skirts, where the long length of the skirt balances the length of the jacket.
3. Save them to wear with pants and jeans. Because of the accompanying length of the pants, you can manage to get away with it. *Tip:* When you wear a longish jacket with pants, it should be just long enough to cover your backside, perhaps a teensy bit shorter but never longer.
4. If you're short-legged, try this trick to get more length from waist to floor: Wear your narrow-lapeled longish blazer tapered slightly above your natural waistline, and hem the jacket to the length described in point three.

Height-adding Tips on Shape and Style

DO look for a jacket that fits smoothly and snugly at the neck and shoulder line. Those that dip slightly lower in the back of the neck will make a short neck look longer or highlight the height-adding aspects of a long one.

DON'T buy jackets with wide lapels or distracting breast pocket detailing—both add clutter and will make you look shorter and squatter. Long narrow lapels or a slim shawl collar are graceful and lengthening.

DO look for single-breasted jackets as opposed to double-breasted ones to avoid the bulk-adding flap-over of heavy fabric. A single-buttoned style jacket is also a more flattering and relaxed-looking style for most women than a three-button and is *top* choice in a suit. (For special details on how the jacket combines into a suit look, see chapter 9.)

DO belt your jacket when that's the fashion and if you like the look. It won't subtract height (because it snugs in the look), and it will add style. Thin, unlined wrap jackets belt up best with narrow (half inch to inch-wide) belts in the same or slightly contrasting texture and/or color as the jacket. A blazer, however, never works belted—the look is too tailored and works best open and casual to counteract those tailored qualities. Another thing about belting: A jacket with patch pockets never works belted; the pockets get in the way, look cluttery, and destroy the line.

DO look for jackets in colors and textures that are interesting—not flashy or boring—particularly when you're going for a jacket in a more tailored style, like a blazer. In that instance, instead of thinking beige gabardine, think in terms of a prettier color and texture: like a banana-colored linen weave. That way, the tailoring won't cancel out the charm.

DO add a small, non-exaggerated shoulder pad (such as men always wear in their suit jackets) to your jacket shoulder to bring the look into focus. For some reason it acts as a heightener without adding width.

The Classic Jacket Shapes . . . and How to Wear Them

The Shirt Jacket

Shaped like a shirt with a classic shirt collar, turn-back cuffs, and a straightish narrow cut, the shirt jacket offers a casual and relaxed jacket look that works well on most shorter women. Its simple styling makes it amazingly easy to wear (as long as the collar size is small), and because of its straight line, there's no hassle about where the waist will fall. The shirt jacket looks best worn unbuttoned and over skirts, pants, and dresses. In a fine suede that's soft enough to be tucked in like a heavy top-shirt, it can add a tremendous amount of polish and sophistication to a short woman's wardrobe. (If you can't afford a lot of designer clothes as a rule, one basic piece like a suede shirt jacket, although expensive, can be a good, lasting fashion investment because it adds an immediate aura of quality to your image.)

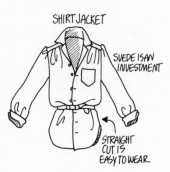

SHIRT JACKET

SUEDE IS AN INVESTMENT

STRAIGHT CUT IS EASY TO WEAR

The Blazer

When most women—short women included—think jackets, they think blazers, and that's where they frequently go astray. Because of its hard-edged tailoring and often overly long shape, a blazer is one of the most difficult of all jacket types to carry off. Even if you're a tailored dresser, a blazer, because of its stiffness, length, and crisp tailoring, runs the risk of looking too constructed and overwhelming on a small frame or of making the wearer appear top-heavy and short-legged.

BLAZER

NARROWER LAPELS

Still, this tried-and-true classic, with its semifitted shape and rounded hem, can give instant polish to a working woman's separates. So how to make it work?

1. Look for single-breasted blazers (to avoid bulk) in the softest fabrics and shortest lengths possible.
2. Look for ones that are unlined (that can immediately relieve its stiffness).
3. Be sure the blazer fits narrowly from neck to shoulders with a waist that's not too nipped in.
4. Don't wear it buttoned up; it'll emphasize the nip-in and cut your height.

When you want to shorten a blazer, unless you're an accomplished seamstress, it's always best to go to a tailor—the rounded corners on most blazers make for a difficult hemming job.

Hacking Jackets

HACKING JACKET

ELBOW PATCHES

TWEEDY

The hacking jacket started life as informal riding gear but was soon adapted as general casual wear because of its overall good looks. It's usually single-breasted, with a straight-across hem, center-back vent, and slanting flap pockets in a wonderfully tweedy menswear fabric or English-style Harris tweed. One in a subtle, multi-colored herringbone tweed mixes with more things than a solid-color and works country to casual city dressing nonstop. (Sometimes the hacking jacket even makes an evening appearance: One of 5'2" Stacy's favorite dressy looks—and an all-time classic no matter what's "in": her five-year-old fitted, English tweed hacking jacket worn with a satin paisley vest and midcalf hunter green velvet skirt.) *Tips on fit:* Wear a hacking jacket hemmed a bit shorter than usual (just stand in front of the mirror and tuck up a few inches and see how much better—and sharper—the whole proportion becomes). The best hacking jackets should also have a narrow but roomy cut so that it can slip easily over heavy shirts and wool sweaters.

Sweater Jackets

SWEATER JACKET

SOFT AND FLATTERING

Like most knitwear, this is a good choice for women under 5'4", because of its soft construction and inherent lack of stiffness. One in a mohair blend in a grayed taupe, mauve, or caramel color, with a shaped shoulder looks wonderful over a silk blouse and a soft skirt and has just the right amount of femininity and businesslike polish to take the place of a basic tan tailored jacket anytime you want a more upbeat look.

Blousons

BLOUSON

SCALED DOWN WIDTH

PLEATING

A blouson (blue-sahn) jacket has a bloused effect at a normal or low waistline, either drawn in by a drawstring or gathered into a wide waistband. The most important consideration for shorter women is that the blouson be extremely narrow, with a minimum of fabric (just enough to achieve a controlled fullness but not enough to "mushroom"). And because even narrowed down, the blouson is a fullish style, it should also compensate by having a slim, probably raglan sleeve, never full or puffy. As for lengths, wear a blouson either short (just over the hips, nicely torso-lengthening if you're a short-waisted type) or just long enough to cover the hips completely. One that falls in between will look awkward and only make you look wide. Another point: On a short woman, a blouson pairs up with narrow bottoms only: a slim skirt or tapered pants, for instance. A blouson worn with a long, bulky dirndl would knock you out of proportion.

The collarless cardigan jacket that buttons up the front and is usually trimmed with Chanel-style braided banding *always* works and is *never* overpowering. "That's because the French understand perfectly how a petite woman should look in a jacket," explained a 5'2½" store fashion director. "When you look at the Chanel cardigan, it's always got a high-cut armhole and a perfectly shaped shoulder, a never overconstructed but set-in sleeve."

Cardigan Jackets

CARDIGAN JACKET

EASY TO WEAR

BRAID TRIM

The Shorties

SPENCER

GREAT LENGTH!

NEAT AND FITTED

This category includes spencer jackets, boleros, and bellboy jackets—all good choices for short women because of their scaled-to-size lengths that range from hipbone long to waist high.

The spencer is a short (hipbone-length), snug-fitting little jacket that resembles an especially pretty and fitted blazer, with a narrow lapel or shawl collar. It looks wonderful on short women because it's fitted, worn with either longish skirts or with pants.

The bolero is collarless, reaches waist-length or above, has rounded corners, no fastenings. It can have a dressy and interesting look when done up in the right kind of dressy fabric.

The bellboy jacket, adapted for women's wear, can also work nicely on women under 5'4", particularly for evening. Seek it out in its classic version: waist length, with a standup collar, and two rows of vertical buttons shaped into an inverted V.

General tip: Unlike the spencer, which is fitted, the bolero and the bellboy have a boxy shape and look tallest when worn with dressy pants that give you the look of continuing length below.

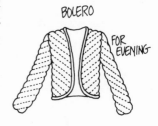

BOLERO

FOR EVENING

Unlined jackets are ideal for layering and great for short women because they're thin, unbulky, and flexible. Even a blazer, remember, loses some of its stiffness but none of its polish in its unlined state. Frequently, unlined jackets are oversized, and you won't always be able to find a made-to-order fit. Too, if you're very small-boned, the look could swallow you up. But if you can carry the unlined jacket through the shoulder line, it makes an extremely attractive seasonless jacket, especially in a textured raw silk. *Tip:* Because of its easy lack of construction, unlined blazers look best with an unexaggerated but somewhat padded shoulder line. If you find one that doesn't work and makes you look like you're dressed up in your brother's clothes, try slipping in a slim shoulder pad to add height and sharpen up the look.

Unlined Jackets

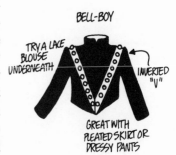

BELL-BOY

TRY A LACE BLOUSE UNDERNEATH

INVERTED "V"

GREAT WITH PLEATED SKIRT OR DRESSY PANTS

Fiddling with a Jacket . . . the Way You Wear It Counts, Too

UNLINED JACKET

SILK

SLIGHTLY OVERSIZED

Call it ease, call it a certain air of insouciance—there are certain things that have to do with the way you wear a jacket (besides the accessories you add) that can make a tremendous difference in the way it appears. It has to do with the small things in the *way* you wear it: going ahead and pushing up the sleeves, turning up the collar, belting it if you like. It's stuffing your hand down in the pockets, tucking a muffler under (or over) the collar. A jacket that adapts to that kind of treatment is the kind of jacket to look for.

For Short Chic shopping tips on jackets, see chapter 9, Suits, which follows.

FOCUS ON: John Anthony

"The reason short women often make mistakes when it comes to fashion is that the garment center does not cater to them," said designer John Anthony. "If a woman is short and well proportioned, though, she is already ahead of the game. But if she is unproportioned and short-waisted, she is probably going to run into trouble.

"A short woman can't just take the clothes she sees on a five-eight or five-nine model and visualize them on herself," he continued. "She needs to have them specially proportioned. She has to be particularly careful about where the waistline stops and where the hemline ends. If she likes ruffles, she shouldn't wear a ten-inch ruffle; it should be minimized down to a three-inch ruffle. If she likes the padded-shoulder look in a jacket, she shouldn't wear a *huge* padded shoulder but must tone it down to her own proportions. She can't wear midlength clothes off the rack but must have them shortened so they are midlength *on her*. Of course, she can be chic, but she must always use her better judgment to see what works for her."

If John Anthony sounds as if he's given the matter a lot of thought, it's because he has. "I'm five feet four myself, and I can really relate to the problems of short women," he told us. "And my wife is only five two and is a superb dresser. She has great flair with clothes, but she also has the most beautiful body. She is all legs—it gives her a head start.

"My wife is a great separates dresser," he explained. "She is in the film business and works as a stylist with clothes. She occasionally wears things from my line but more often wears European clothes—they seem to cater to smaller figures. She hardly ever wears skirts, but she does wear very high heels—although she loves flats, she feels she's too tiny to wear them. She knows just how to wear an oversized men's jacket and look terrific even though she's a size two. She even wears things from *my* own personal wardrobe—my jackets and pants—with a special kind of chic. But few people have that kind of ability."

John Anthony admitted that he, too, cuts for a tall woman. "My size four is a five-foot-seven or five-eight woman and very thin," he said. "But many of my clothes can be worn by short women, especially my suits with medium to short jackets and my chemise dresses. Anything that is less as opposed to more," he emphasized.

9. Suits: What Happens When Jacket and Skirt Go Together

In traditionally male-dominated fields, both young professional women and experienced female business executives alike, have come to depend on the suit as a versatile and appropriate way of dressing for the office (in much the same way that their male counterparts rely on their own three-piece versions). So much is this so that in recent years the suit has become the visible means of separating the up-and-coming and ambitious from the lower-echelon workers.

Because of the overall impression of credibility and "seriousness" it bestows, it makes sense to assume that by wearing a suit, the petite businesswoman will be able to counteract any negative image of "cute little girl" created by her height and to project, instead, one of positive professionalism.

So it could . . . but there's a catch (isn't there always?). Although a lot of women depend on it, the tailored suit on the short woman often backfires because it's much too severe.

A case in point: Susan B., 5'1", a twenty-five-year-old management trainee in a large city brokerage house, had this to say: "I have a very difficult time looking good in a business suit. Most of them look so official on me and somehow *emphasize* the fact that I'm short rather than camouflage it. I tried wearing a lace-trimmed blouse with my navy gabardine [her "interview" suit], but I still think I look like a miniature police officer. But, being *young, female,* and *short,* I feel I have three strikes against me from the start, so I dress for all the authority I can."

The problem here lies in overcoming the almost built-in severity of a suited look. (And it involves more than just going back and reading over chapter 6 on Skirts and chapter 8 on Jackets, although that's the first step.) Because unless carefully orchestrated, a tailored suit, instead of counteracting diminutive stature, will point it up by contrast. It takes more than an assertively feminine blouse, for example, to rescue the look. Rather, it starts with the suit itself.

- *Don't use severity of line to combat lack of height;* it won't work. Instead, the structure of the shorter woman's suit should be markedly *less* severe than standard. The reason: It's a matter of scaling down, not merely in *size* but in *effect* as well. A classically tailored suit that works on a taller woman will come across as too exaggeratedly tailored on a shorter one. A slightly less than tailored version, on the other hand, will appear appropriately businesslike and attractive on the shorter woman and will convey just the right amount of polish and authority.

- *Always watch proportion.* Yes, we know you've heard that before, but when it comes to a suit, we can't emphasize proportion enough. It's all too easy for a suit to overpower the woman under 5′4″, who often ends up in more suit than she can handle—and doesn't know why she feels uncomfortable. Start with the jacket proportions—and notice the tremendous difference even an inch can make in the sleeves, the body shape, and the length.

- *The suit skirts that work best* are usually *slightly* dirndl'd, *slightly* gathered, slim, or soft-pleated, depending on your figure type and preference.

- *The suit jacket that works best* will either be a classic Chanel-style cardigan jacket or a jacket with a combination of the following features: a shorter-than-usual length (preferably hipbone length); narrow, graceful (and lengthening) lapels; shoulders with a small amount of padding for a smart, crisp look; any jacket shaped with vertical pleating; and one-button rather than three-button closings (more flattering to most figure shapes).

Working with the Two Basic Suit Types

The Matched Suit

The matched suit—everyone's idea of a real suit—is simply a combo where the jacket matches the skirt in fabric and color, resulting in a beautifully polished, professional appearance. Although it often tends to look stiff not stylish, it *can* look great if you shop with the following points in mind:

- *Always buy a matched suit with texture interest to the fabric.* (This is a must!—otherwise the suit will look mannish and "suity.")
- *Always look for soft fabrics* like thin wools, wool jersey, or raw silk.
- *Drama in the jacket is a key factor* when it comes to carrying off a matched-suit look with style. By *drama* we mean a chic-looking sleeve, a sophisticated collarless style, an updated length, and so on. Read over chapter 8 on Jackets for more specifics on what works.
- *Color can help substantially*. Although most of the time you're going to be in the market for neutrals, every so often, pick up on an unexpected shade (like teal blue, mauve, or coral). The tailoring of the suit will still provide the polish, and the color will update it. And while we're on the subject, if your favorite color is red, by all means try a red suit; you'll be a refreshingly welcome sight in a sea of navies and grays.

One final point about the matched suit: Be sure not to limit its possibilities. Take it apart and interchange it with the rest of your wardrobe. Wear the skirt with another jacket, and the jacket over pants. It should go a long way without running out of steam.

The Unmatched Suit

Of course, a suit doesn't always have to match. Today, the definition of what a suit is has expanded to include the unmatched variety—coordinated separates that work together and that function as a matching suit functions but with a lot more chic. It's also a lot easier for the shorter woman to carry off unmatched suits because they tend to be softer looking and less overwhelming than matched.

In fact, one of the smartest turnouts we saw during Short Chic interviewing was the unmatched suit worn by Monica M., 5′2½″, a whip-smart tax attorney in her early thirties: a gold tweed short jacket, a cinnamon-colored wool jersey dirndl, a challis blouse in a cinnamon/gold/green print, with a loosely tied black silk scarf under the collar. Proof positive that success dressing takes many forms and doesn't always mean "suited and starched."

The only other thing to keep in mind about the unmatched suit is that the pieces should provide an interesting meld of textures (flat-weave against flat-weave won't work); and that they should be loosely aligned in color rather than highly contrasting and height-cutting, like, say, a black skirt, red blazer, and white blouse.

Although we realize that suit dressing has fast become the working staple for a lot of women, we feel that it's a concept that's been overemphasized and overdone as the newfound ticket to the executive suite. Charlotte Curtis, associate editor and Op Ed Page editor of the *New York Times*, just 5′, 95 pounds, is a prime example of a phenomenally successful petite woman who exudes confidence, authority, and femininity, and who is on record as saying that she's never worn a man-tailored suit or a pants suit in her life.

"There's no more necessity to wear a suit to the office than there is to wear a sweater or a dress, provided whatever you choose is tasteful," Ms. Curtis said in an interview with a major fashion magazine. And although she is certainly not a "frilly" personality, she confessed that she would never go to the office without wearing earrings or a bracelet!

Suit Softeners

We were dismayed to learn that many of the professional women we interviewed felt that by adding a strand of pearls or tying a scarf under their collar (in what could be construed as a subliminal imitation of a man's tie) they were adding "style"—and thereby "feminizing" their indomitably suited images. But style just doesn't come as easy as a strand of pearls. So although any one of the following suit softeners *alone* won't lift a suit from conservative to chic, a careful combination can help.

1. *Try changing one suit piece:* instead of a man-tailored blouse, one with a feminine collar, lace cuffs, pleating or other detailing.

Instead of a solid-color blouse, a printed one; instead of a blouse altogether, a cotton-knit or cashmere crew in a brighter color; instead of a sporty crew, a lacy feminine open-work sweater or knitted tank top. Instead of a jacket, try two matching sweaters (the outer one shaped by subtle shoulder padding); instead of your jacket and skirt, wear your suit jacket over a dress, for the same kind of polish that a suit provides but a softer feeling.

2. *Odd coloring can soften a suit* and lift a basic out of drabdom. One woman we know revived her old reliable navy with a splashy blouse printed in fuchsia and white, added fuchsia and white pumps (and even brought up the color with her makeup).

3. *Neck interest always helps.* By that we mean a casually tied muffler with a lacy texture or a scarf (or two!) in contrasting patterns and textures. When combined with other elements, it's a great suit softener.

4. *Add accessories.* Add suede in a handbag, a shoe, a belt, or a vest. Add a belt that's a woven leather braid instead of one that's stiff. Add jewelry—pearl earrings or necklaces can give a softer impression than the sometimes-hard, glint of gold. For evening, add metallics—a copper-, bronze-, or pewter-colored clutch, belt, or sandals to catch the light.

An example of "suit softening" that combined it all to a T: the suit combo worn by a 5′3″ ad space saleswoman we met on the New York to Washington shuttle. Her jacket and skirt were softened by their warm, coppery color (instead of the usual cool gray); her sweater had two nubbled neck scarves wrapped high over the turtleneck, with a thin leather belt at the waist. The final touch: a bronzy lapel pin. And although the pin alone wouldn't have made a whit of difference, added to the other factors, it's subtle sheen made her look exceptionally polished and well thought out.

Short Chic Shopping Tips for Jackets and Suits

Among the best looking and fitting jackets for women under 5′4″ are those by *Mrs. H. Winter*, and *Cacharel* ("Even when the style is full, like with a smock jacket I own, the sleeve length and shoulders fit perfectly," said Marilyn C., a 5′2″ fashion director). Other top choices: *Harvé Benard* (great for working woman's clothing, like jackets and suits) . . . *Pinky & Dianne for Private Label* (true-to-scale sizing with a witty rather European touch) . . . *Ralph Lauren* (for narrow, very feminine jackets, with a trim, high-cut armhole)

. . . *Finity*, worth a look for style, sensible pricing ("Size 4 Finity jackets—or their size 4 in anything, fit me perfectly," a 5'1", 100-pound art director told us.) . . . *Cathy Hardwick* ("I bought an eggshell-blue Cathy Hardwick jacket last summer that didn't even need alterations," said a 5'2" questionnaire respondent) . . . More: "I adore *Ted Lapidus*. His jackets don't have a breadth of extra fabric in them. And Harvé Benard is the American Ted Lapidus," said a

FOCUS ON: Harvé Benard

For good-looking tailored suits at good prices, for pants that fit and easy-to-wear coats, a lot of women under 5'4" that we spoke to, look to a manufacturer called Harvé Benard. Why? Aside from their newly successful Petites line (started in the fall of 1980), designed and proportioned especially for the petite, 5'3"-and-under figure, the *regular* Harvé Benard line is available in sizes as small as a 2! Another thing: the Harvé Benard fitting model is only 5'6", we learned. "That makes our clothes not a 'tall' line but only a little above average," according to Mark Ellis, the company's chief designer. "Our smaller sizes are even proportioned a little differently from our larger ones," he went on to say. "The waist and hem go up a little, for instance.

"Although we don't necessarily consider our small-size customer to be short, we do attract shorter women for a lot of reasons," Mr. Ellis told us. "One is because we do a lot of shorter blazers that look very good on short women. We also do a large number of suits, which are all in one color and designed with a smooth, slim line. We do two basic suits: one in a banker's gray with a cropped jacket that buttons at the neck and has a dirndl skirt, the other in a wool gabardine."

The typical Harvé Benard customer? "Anyone from twenty-five years and up," Mr. Ellis surmised. Not suprisingly, because of their emphasis on tailored, active working woman's clothes, they sell to a lot of executive women, he said.

Any special advice for the under 5'4" woman? "The most important thing, of course, is to take advantage of what you've got," he said. "That and something I guess any short and fashion-conscious woman already knows—to stay away from large patterns!"

FOCUS ON: Kasper

"My clothes are not cut for the short-waisted woman," said designer Kasper. "But they will fit any short woman who is not short-waisted. I've seen short women put on my clothes, and once you just lift the hem and pin up the sleeves, they become alive on her. But if she's short-waisted, no. Longer-waisted clothes will never fit right or feel right on a short-waisted woman. A good choice for her would be a chemise that is unwaisted and will fit once the sleeves and hem are shortened."

Kasper believes that there are certain things that short women would have some trouble wearing. "A petite woman would have difficulty, for instance, wearing big blousons and big dolman sleeves," he said. "But a tunic would be perfect—it's one of the best examples of how a short woman can adapt clothes to suit her own proportions, and there's no reason in the world a short woman can't wear them well." She should start with the skirt, he explained and proportion it so it's just short enough. (See chapter 6, Skirts.) "It is especially important that a skirt always be proportioned and at the right length when a woman is wearing a two-piece outfit," he told us. "Then, she should take the tunic and see where it best falls in relation to the skirt."

As for his own line, available in sizes 4 to 14 (and a good place to look for very wearable, pretty, almost ladylike clothes with a rather "dressed" quality): "I think many of my clothes would look good on short women," he said, "particularly the little short jacket suits with fuller skirts, my pleated skirts and shirt dresses, and especially the chemise dresses with broader shoulders and thin, narrow bottoms.

"The biggest fashion mistake any woman, short or tall, makes is that she tends to overdo things," Kasper commented. "I call those women the 'fashion freaks'—those who do too many things at once. But with sportswear being so popular, it's much easier for women to dress well than ever before," he added.

"The customer I am interested in likes clothes, but they are not her life," he said. "She is a busy, involved woman, whether working or with her children. Foremost, she is intelligent about her life-style, and my clothes are part of that life-style."

top fashion editor during her Short Chic interview . . . *Calvin Klein*; they fit best if you're on the long-waisted side. . . . *For suits*, we've heard good news about *Tahari* ("I wear their size four right off the rack," boasted a 5'2½", 101-pound display coordinator.) *Kasper* ("I always do very well with his suits, skirts, and blouses," wrote in a 5' public relations senior v.p.) . . . *Nipon* (for their details and flexible fit) . . . *Gloria Sachs* (flattering, conservative suits made for a shorter torso, we've found) . . . *Evan-Picone* (one of the best for short women in the moderate-price range) . . . and *Stanley Blacker* ("Though the skirts need shortening, the tailored jackets and suits fit me just right," says a fifty-one-year-old Minneapolis business executive, 5'3".)

10. Dresses: Your Best Opportunity for Creating the Illusion of Height

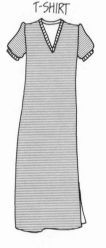

T-SHIRT

SWEATSHIRT DRESS

We're not about to argue with that! The truth is that, aside from their ease, dresses also happen to offer the longest possible line of color and fabric from neck to knee or below. This offers a terriffic opportunity for creating the illusion of height. The irony of it is that, next to jackets and pants, they seem to be the hardest single items for shorter women to find.

The main problem is that with many dress styles the waistline is pretty well fixed, and there's no compromising about where it will fall. If you're short-waisted, that can be one of the chief hurdles, but even for the equally proportioned, it can be a touch-and-go proposition where fit is concerned. (It comes as no surprise to us under-5′4″s that even in their smallest sizes, many designs are cut for the small-framed woman of 5′6″ or so. This means that you're going to have trouble not only with hem length, but also with neck-to-waist length.) The other stumbling block is a matter of excess in design: A dress that looks great on a tall woman can engulf a small one with too much fabric and froufrou.

Given all that, how can you take advantage of the dress's heightening potential? The first thing is to look for designers whose sizing is true (that is, scaled-down proportionately in width and overall length), and/or whose styling is known to work for shorter women.

DRESSY SHIRT-DRESS
PRETTY COLLAR

Short Chic Shopping Tips for Dresses

Albert Nipon was a name that turned up again and again on our questionnaire. Short women love Nipon dresses for their easy construction and pretty, feminine styling. (For more moderately priced dresses, check out the *Nipon Boutique* label.) . . . *Jack Mulqueen*'s silk dresses are another good bet. You'll find simple styling and an easy fit (they make a size 2); *Calvin Klein* doesn't do that many dresses, but they're beautifully cut, and so, usually, the only alteration needed is on the hem. (To note: his dresses are especially worth checking out if you're a bit long-waisted.) . . . *Sonia Rykiel* was a forerunner in knits of all kinds. With this label you can expect to find easy-to-wear flat, simple styling, great sizing for the shorter woman. . . . Also hunt for other European designers; their dresses are almost always cut smaller than the American.

The Basic Dress Shapes

These can be as varied in style as the shirts on which they're based, so you'll find that the same rules that apply for tops in chapter 5 apply here. A review of the classics:

The shirt Dresses

The T-shirt dress is a top that grew. It used to be scoop-necked only (modeled after the original T), but as its popularity grew, so did the neckline choices which include V and crew among others. You'll also find a great choice of fabric—from casual, traditional T-shirt knit to evening-dressy silk. What will always be blessedly consistent, however, is the body-lengthening line of a T-dress. Definitely four stars for shorter women.

The sweatshirt dress, based on the raglan-sleeved design of the original workout top, is another great straight-line dress that comes with a variety of fabric choices. Fern C., 5'2", a New Jersey retailer, has one in a velour with a V-neck and a drawstring waist, and considers it one of her wardrobe basics.

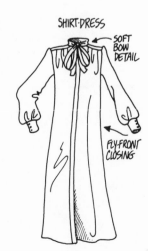

SHIRT-DRESS
SOFT BOW DETAIL
FLY-FRONT CLOSING

The shirt dress is really a dress-length shirt—of any classic style —that may come with a rounded shirttail bottom and side slits (nice for lengthening the legs) or a standard straight hem (easier to take

SHIRT WAIST DRESS

up if needed). Another long, body-skimming line you can wear belted or unbelted.

The shirt-waist dress differs from the other types of shirt dress in construction: It has a shirt top sewn onto a full (preferably not *too* full) or straight skirt. This means a fixed waist line that short-waisted figures may want to avoid unless they're lucky enough to find a perfect fit right off the rack. In addition, you'll want to be mindful of the all-important details that will keep this classic from looking dowdy or dull. For example: Although a shirtwaist in a not-very-extraordinary cotton can evoke images of a soap commercial housewife, the same dress in a fluid jersey, silk, or crepe miniprint can be fabulous. Also look for eye pleasers like shoulder tucks, stitched pleats, and so on.

The Wrap Dress   It's a wrap if the dress is fastened by wrapping half of the double front or back across to the opposite side (or sewn to look as if it were). The best ones are slightly bloused and rich with detailing at the shoulders and/or neckline. We use the word *rich* here advisedly; devoid of detailing, even the most expensive wrap dress has a tendency to look chintzy. Also, like the wrap skirt, the wrap dress should have enough fabric in it not to gap open at your every step or movement.

The A-line Dress   When Christian Dior introduced the A-line in 1955, the less-than-perfect figure found its greatest ally. Flaring gently as it does from under the arms to the hem, it was welcomed by the thick-torsoed, big-busted, wide-hipped, and broad-bottomed alike. Funny thing is that it also happens to be a body-lengthener on short women—with or without figure problems. And the reason for that can be traced back to that flowing uninterrupted line. The important catch: The A-line *must* be made of the most fluid of fabrics to be heightening. If it sticks out stiffly at the bottom, the wearer becomes a walking lamp shade.

The Orientals   If traditional Oriental dress happens to be especially flattering on the short or small woman, it isn't just Occidental (!). Since Asian women themselves are often diminutive, it only makes sense that what's worked for them for centuries will work for you as well. Here are the Westernized versions of two great Eastern classics.

The Mandarin Dress: It took a while for Western designers to catch on to the potential of this side-slashed, waist-skimming dress, but thank goodness they finally did. As we've pointed out, side slits are instant leg-lengtheners (great if you fall into the long-waisted/short-legged category). And note the stand-up collar and diagonal closings: both height-makers that also turn out to be beautifully scaled for the smaller frame. In soft brocade or embossed silk, the Mandarin is a great dress for evening, but you may also spot one done up in a soft tweed or linen for day.

The Kimono Dress: Soft fabric and easy construction make this one a favorite East and West, and the V-neckline is complimentary in any translation. Since the dressiness of the kimono (like the Mandarin) depends on the fabric, this is another look that could work as well from nine to five as it could for after eight.

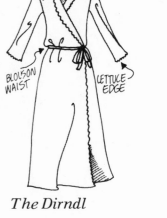

Characteristically, the dirndl is made up of a snugly fitted bodice attached to a gathered skirt. The style of it may vary depending on the neckline, sleeves, and detailing, but one requirement is essential: You should have a narrowish torso and waist to wear it. Do keep it soft—especially if the skirt is full (a dirndl in black wool jersey, say, as opposed to a matronly, stiff linen). And do avoid a dirndl with top and bottom in contrasting colors. To our way of thinking, if you're going to wear a dress in the first place, why detract from its height-adding potential with inch-cutting contrasts?

The Dirndl

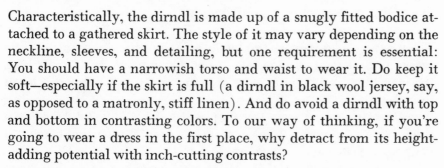

In 1850 the Empress Eugénie of France wore a princess dress by Worth, which pretty well established its credentials as a classic. Aside from the royal endorsement, there's another reason for its reputation: With its curving vertical seams (figure-thinning and therefore height-adding) and absence of a waist seam (no strictures about where *your* waist should fall), the princess is said to look good on just about any figure type.

But, despite its classic status, the princess isn't always in fashion. And when it is, you have to be very careful with it because, frankly, the princess can be a very "iffy" affair. Sometimes it comes across as matronly and old-fashioned; at other times as little girlish and unsophisticated. Here are some general guidelines:

The Princess

- Look for neckline detail to add interest and sophistication (never a jewel neckline).
- Keep the fabric soft to compensate for the matronly multi-seam construction.
- And unless you've found a no-questions-about-it winner, save the princess dress for dressier occasions, and don't take chance with it for the office.

The Sweater Dress

MANDARIN

When you find the perfect one, grab it up in every color it comes in because this one is always surefire on the shorter woman. The two greatest things it has going for it: easy construction that compromises where your figure is concerned and the soft fluidity of the knit. Whether it's in one piece or two, always look for flat thin knits (stay away from bulkies unless you're beanpole thin), and never wear a knit that's too tight.

And here are two more good ways to add to the body-lengthening potential of a sweater dress: Look for V-necklines to make your neck look even longer, or go for a turtleneck that adds to the overall length of the dress itself. (*Note:* What you don't want to stretch, of course, is the dress itself. The best preventative: storing it folded in a drawer rather than hanging it up.)

The Drop-waist Dress

KIMONO DRESS

← OBI TYPE SASH

The twenties made this one a classic, and since then, it seems to have reappeared at regular intervals in one form or another. At its best, the long torso and peplum skirt are cut simply and without a lot of fussy detail.

On the positive side, the drop-waist is good camouflage for a thick torso and waist. It also makes a great proportion-evener if you're big busted and narrow-hipped.

On the negative side: If you're wide-hipped, that peplum skirt will only exaggerate what's already there. Ditto if you're long-waisted. (One solution to the latter problem is to find one with a waist that drops only slightly so you get the style without the exaggeration.

In any case: Do make sure the fabric is fluid and the skirt not overly full so that it falls away from the body instead of skimming it as it should.

The Chemise

PRINCESS LINE

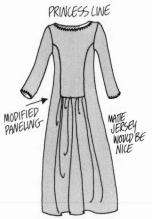

MODIFIED PANELING →

MATTE JERSEY WOULD BE NICE

Through the years the term "chemise" has come to include just about any straight, unwaisted dress, but when we say chemise, we're referring to the sophisticated version with definitive construction and interesting details at the shoulder, tapering slightly to a lean body line that almost always goes beltless. (It's the kind of dress with enough built-in style to be worn as is—without a lot of help from accessories.) The chemise is sensational for the shorter woman because that long, unbroken line is nothing *but* heightening. You can have a large bust or a thick waist and still look great in it, but because of its narrowing bodyline the slimmer you are in the hips, the better.

Details, Details

SWEATER DRESS

- *Dolman sleeves:* Make sure they're modified and don't start too far down near the waist or they'll create a shortening horizontal.
- *Cuffs:* As a rule, a better dress will have a buttoned cuff—not elastic. If you already own a dress with elasticized cuffs, you can push them up out of sight to create a slightly ballooned three-quarter sleeve.
- *Empire waists:* Unless it's designed with great sophistication, a street-length Empire-waist dress will turn you into a twelve-year-old. If you're partial to the style, save it for sundresses worn on the weekend.
- *Blouson waists:* The length fit (shoulder to waist) must be perfect (an overly long blouson pulled up to your waist won't fool anybody). And do keep it as narrow as possible.
- *Drawstring waists:* If you're not wasp-waisted or at least evenly proportioned, these can make you look potato-sackish. Some solutions: Wear the string a little looser, or if it's elasticized, cinch over it with a $1\frac{1}{2}''$ belt or double wrap it with a fabric belt in the same color family as the dress.

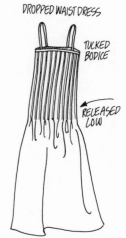

DROPPED WAIST DRESS

TUCKED BODICE

RELEASED LOW

- *Hem length: When a dress has no defined waist*, you have more leeway with length and can usually go shorter or longer depending on which looks best. (If you're going to wear it belted, you'll want to go a little longer to allow for blousing above the waist.) But *when a dress has a defined waist*, treat the bottom half as if it were a skirt, and depending on its shape, hem accordingly following the hemline rules in chapter 6.
- *Jackets:* You have to be careful about dresses that come with jackets—especially if the jacket is in a different fabric. It can sometimes come off as a cheap and/or little-girlish "outfit" that's a bit *too* put-together for our liking. However, if you want to top a dress with a jacket you already own, that's a different matter. A well-proportioned jacket can add as much polish and authority to the simplicity of, say, a silk shirt dress as it does to a skirt or pants and a blouse.

CHEMISE

TALL MAKING TUCKS

FOCUS ON: Adele Simpson

"Nobody is shorter than I," says 4'9" designer Adele Simpson. "I used to have a terrible time finding clothes, and when I was forced to make my own, I turned to designing." It's with that memory in mind, no doubt, that Ms. Simpson cuts her clothes (which run from size 4 up to 14) on a 5'7" model and then proportionately scales them down to the smaller sizes. Her 5'1" daughter is a 4, and she'll sometimes turn to her to check for fit in that size.

The clothes are designed to flatter women of all sizes and heights (and to prove they do, she and her 5'6½", size 14 assistant will wear the same dress when she does a fashion show). "I don't make things with horizontal stripes," she explains. "And I feel it's important to have everything hang from the shoulders and skim over the body. Then it's just a matter of hemming. If I design something with padded shoulders, I scale the padding down for smaller sizes so that it's in proportion with the smaller woman's body. Nothing should be exaggerated."

When it comes to heightening her own image, she says, "First of all, I *think* tall, I'm careful about my posture, and I always try to look well put-together." Beyond that, it's a matter of knowing what will and what won't work for her height. "I never wear anything that cuts me off at the waist, so I'll pair pants with overblouses (if I tuck them in they'll cut me in half). If I do tuck a shirt in, I'll top it with a sweater that goes over my hips. Even with a two-piece dress, I like the overblouse look. Also, I'd never choose an extreme style for myself (for example, an evening dress that's short in front and long in back), or wear something that's too flared. Basically, I like long straight lines."

Because she believes that color and pattern play such an important part in dressing taller, Ms. Simpson makes a point of choosing stockings that match her clothes. "That's an essential. And though I wear any color but green (I'm superstitious about it), I do try to avoid color combinations. If I'm in a beige suit, the blouse will be beige, too. My colors are never shocking. Also, I like small prints and vertical stripes."

What about accessories? we asked. "I never wear too much jewelry—especially earrings because they call attention to my short neck [also the reason she wears her hair short]. My scarves are chiffon only, because they're softer. And I never wear very high heels—first because I'm on my feet a lot and second because they'd only call attention to my short legs."

Although, like most women under 5'4" she's always trying to look taller, Ms. Simpson thinks that being short has worked to her advantage in the business world. She explains, with a laugh, "They think I'm cute!"

FOCUS ON: Pearl Nipon

"List the manufacturers whose clothes work for you," we asked hundreds of shorter women—and the name that turned up most frequently was Albert Nipon. The largest designer dress manufacturer in the country, Nipons are designed by and modeled on Pearl Nipon who is herself 5′3″. The Nipon look, favored by such women as Nancy Reagan, Rosalynn Carter, and Barbara Walters includes dresses, suits, and coats known for such feminine dressmaker details as pleating, tucking, and multistitching, and by the signature lace trim at the hem. They're clothes that have been described as ladylike, elegant, well bred.

"I really don't know why our dresses work on almost every figure," says Pearl, "But they do. When I do a show, a five-foot-two woman will come up to me afterward and say, 'I don't know what I did before you came along.' Then another woman, five-foot-eight, will tell me the same thing. I think it's that the body fits the dress instead of the dress fitting the body. All the clothes are fitted on me. Before I went into this business, it was a nightmare trying to find clothes—I couldn't find smaller sizes anywhere. Even when I was younger and had a well-proportioned body, I was always bigger on the bottom. Not being able to find clothes is what inspired me to go into the business."

Asked why Nipon clothes appeal to the smaller woman, Pearl told us: "It's because they fit well and aren't overwhelming. We try to create an exaggeration that's fashionable but not overly exaggerated. For instance, a blouson would be the perfect kind of blouson—one within reason, not overdone. Our sleeves have special detailing; our ruffles are on a small scale. Really, the major problem short women have is in buying exaggerated clothes. The point is to be attractive, not an attraction. And to be comfortable, because when you feel right, you look right.

"Our clothes fit women of any age," Pearl concludes. "They're always very feminine and fulfill a lot of needs." A final word of advice: "It's difficult to tell any kind of fashion when it's on the hanger. Salespeople in the stores know how well Nipons fit, and once they get a customer to try the clothes on —it's a sure sale."

11. Outerwear: Stalking the Perfect Coat

The first thing to keep in mind about finding the right coat is that coat styling goes through phases. Although basic, classic styles are nearly always available, some years are simply better coat years than others.

But even in a good year coats present special problems for short women: Few items are heavier, bulkier, or more overwhelming to a small frame than a sturdy winter coat. The all-important fabric guidelines for short women—the softness and fluidity of fabric that makes hard-to-carry-off clothing work—are hard to come by in a coat, simply because you're dealing with much heavier fabrics.

Jeanne P., a 5′1″ Boston emigré, now working in a New York art gallery, writes: "Because I'm a size four Petite, I have a terribly hard time finding a coat that looks good and that fits. I once waited five years to luck out on a red cashmere coat, size four, in Filene's basement." (The reason the coat worked so well on Jeanne—the butter-soft, flattering texture of the cashmere knit.)

Attention to detail is also imperative—and another reason that a coat search can be such a time-consuming one for short women. Jane T., a small-framed 5′2″ researcher with a major textbook publisher, searched long and hard before she found her *John Anthony* reefer.

"Because I'm so small I knew I needed a very simply styled coat, with no cuffs or patch pockets or belt in the back," she told us, "But by December—and it was getting cold—I was almost ready to settle for wrapping myself in an Army blanket! Not only were all the styles much too fussy, but they didn't even come near to fitting. On my final shopping Saturday, I was just about to give up; I think I had tried on—and taken off—nearly every coat in town, and nothing fit. But just as I was ready to throw in the towel, the saleswoman turned up a black wool melton coat by John Anthony, size four. And it turned out to be a *real* size four: The sleeves and shoulders fit; the length was even right. I could have walked out of the store with it on just the way it was. Miraculously, it was going on sale—and even though the sale price was steep, it was worth it!"

Short Chic Shopping Tips for Coats

Other manufacturers on whom we've gotten favorable reports are *Luba* (perfectly scaled sleeve and shoulders), *Nipon Coature* (scaled-down feminine detailing), *Harvé Benard*, and *Cuddlecoat*, a better junior line. *Harriet Winter* is also a good bet for coats with well-proportioned shoulders and height-adding signature seaming. (For more on Mrs. Winter and her fashion philosophy, see Focus in this chapter.) Actually, though, when it comes to coats, what works for under 5′4″ women depends more often on style specifics than on individual manufacturers and designers. From time to time, many manufacturers will add a Petite-sized coat to their regular lines, so watch newspaper ads and department store catalogs with care. These additions, by the way, are often of top quality: Bonwit Teller recently advertised a "vanilla-colored cashmere wrap coat," sized down to Petite, that was a real eye-catcher; Saks Fifth Avenue included several good-looking Petite-sized coats in a variety of styles in their last fashion catalog, too. And we're told that when designer *Bonnie Cashin* added a Petite-sized stormcoat to her regular winter coat collection some years ago, it turned out to be one of the best-selling coats in the line!

REEFER

NARROW LAPELS

SIDE SEAM POCKETS

Coats: The Details That Make the Difference

You've probably been told often enough that a simple, classic coat is the one that's going to work best on your short figure. Well, yes and no. Classics came to be classics because they work—and certain ones are the coat styles we think are most flattering for under 5′4″s. But

BALMACAAN

FITS SMOOTH HERE

CHESTERFIELD

BLACK VELVET COLLAR

FLY FRONT CLOSING

BACK BELT DETAIL

just going for a classic is not all there is to it. Take the reefer, for instance. Although it would be hard to make this attractive classic *not* work on a short woman, imagine it in a bold red-and-blue plaid, double-breasted, with a big collar, flap pockets, and shiny oversized brass buttons. See what we mean? This is why, even with tried-and-true classic shapes, it's the attention to details that counts.

1. *Whenever you can, we'd suggest going for a single- rather than a double-breasted coat.* Whether you're short and thin or on the plump side, shorter women seldom have the chest expanse needed to carry off a double-breasted coat. Another reason: The double row of buttons on a double-breasted coat can be responsible for playing some funny visual tricks. Although they can create two vertical lines (which, by all rights, should make you look taller), they can also create a conflicting horizontal as your eyes move from left to right. In addition, the "flap over" of fabric adds bulk. And although the flap-over applies to a classic wrap coat, too, the wrap can work very nicely on a short woman as long as the fabric is thin and the coat fits easily, not tightly.

2. *Watch lapel width carefully.* Even when narrow lapels are "in" and readily available in shirts and jackets, on coats, they may be harder to find. But they are worth watching for. Very wide lapels can make a coat look fussy and overpowering and spoil an otherwise good look. If everything else about the coat works, however, and if the price is right, overly wide lapels don't have to spell disaster. Rosalie M., for example, a 5'1", thirty-two-year-old gymnastics teacher from Arlington, Virginia, wrote us about this find: a classic herringbone tweed coat, marked way way down. Whichever way she looked at it, though, the lapels were too wide. Since she loved everything else about the coat, she bought it anyway and had the lapels altered. And suddenly, all the proportions were in the right place—an iffy find turned into a great buy! This means that if the coat has everything else going for it—why not?

3. *The smaller the coat collar, the better, always.* If you're concerned about warmth, just turn your coat collar up—that way, it not only shields your neck from the cold but gives the coat a stylish and height-making turn, too.

4. *As for cuffs, keep them simple or, better yet, nonexistent.* Not only because it complicates having them shortened but also because elaborate cuffs will make short arms look shorter. If you like cuffs, keep them in the same color or the same color family as the rest of the coat.

5. *Pockets should be in the right place.* One of the most frequent coat complaints short women have is that coat pockets are placed too low. A side pocket that's in danger of getting its bottom clipped when you shorten the coat hem is a tipoff to the fact that the coat isn't proportioned for your shorter body size. In general, slit pockets or slashed pockets (the most unobtrusive kinds) are by far the best choices for short women. Avoid flap pockets; they add width and bulk.

6. *Buttons on a good winter coat are more important than on any other article of clothing.* Although buttons on a blouse or a well-made jacket are usually scaled to size, that doesn't always hold true for a coat. And, on a small woman, very big buttons are just one of the details between a hit and a miss. Sara G., a particularly fastidious fashion editor we know, just 5'1", always makes a point of replacing any oversized, overshiny brass buttons on the rather military-styled coats she buys with miniaturized ones in toned-down metallics. Another way to keep buttons from looking too distracting: replacing offenders with ones in a color that matches the fabric of the coat.

7. *Coat fabrics should be as soft as possible.* Unquestionably, the coat that's going to look best on the under 5'4" women is the one that's in the softest, plushest, finest fibers you can afford. The fabric should drape and fold without looking stiff and move when you move with ease. *Note:* If the fabric is stiff, *any other positive details* that the coat may have (like a small collar or lapel, for instance, or neatly sized buttons) are immediately canceled out. Fabric softness takes priority! (Of course, this has a lot to do with simple quality. In an item like a coat, because it gets a lot of daily wear and because of your height, quality counts even more than ever.)

WRAP COAT

NICE IN CASHMERE OR CAMELS HAIR

The Classic Coat Shapes

The Reefer

If you like them long and lean, then the reefer is your kind of classic. Whether yours is the figure type that tends to get lost in overly big shapes or whether you're on the rounded side, the reefer's slim-fitting simplicity and clean, racy styling make it a natural for short women. It's also the kind of classic that works anytime, anywhere, over jeans or pants, over skirts, over dressy dresses, too. (This means that if you're going to be buying one coat that has to work over everything, this is the one.) Look for a reefer that's single-breasted, with narrow lapels and a small notched or shawl collar. One in a sophisticated neutral color like taupe or chestnut, black, gray, camel, navy, or a small tweed can be especially smart.

The Balmacaan   The balmacaan is a loose-fittting, raglan-sleeved coat with a small collar and button-front that fits neatly at the shoulder and falls from there in a smooth unbroken line. It's a rather sophisticated looking coat style that many short women seem to shy away from because it is loose and, unless it fits perfectly, can be overwhelming on a short figure. But if you find one that sits closely at the shoulders and across the bust, in a soft-enough fabric, the balmacaan can be an unusually chic choice.

The Chesterfield   You may have owned a version of the chesterfield coat when you were a kid. It's a semifitted straight-cut coat, either single- or double-breasted, with distinct classic details: a black velvet collar, small belt in the back, sometimes a fly-front closing. Introduced in the 1840s (by the Earl of Chesterfield, no less), the chesterfield is an enduring classic style with an image that suggests a certain well-bred prim-ness. Because of that, its neat, rather precise look can work very nicely on a precisely put-together short woman. On the other hand, if looking young is your problem, it can accentuate this aspect. If the chesterfield is your choice, take note: It looks especially attractive in a tiny bird's-eye or black-and-white houndstooth check.

The Wrap Coat   Yes and no here. The wrap is a very good-looking style that works on short women only if it's in a very soft and supple fabric like cash-mere, camel's hair, or superfine wool, never anything stiff or bulky. The reason: That wrap-over can give you a double flap of fabric bulk across your body, and who needs that? If the wrap coat is soft, how-ever, and not too tight-fitting (which can make it look cheap), it can be especially sharp in camel, cream color, or pale gray.

The Mandarin Coat   One of the number-one choices for shorter women, the Mandarin-styled coat has straight, slim lines, a stand-up collar that adds height —everyone manages to look a little bit lankier in it. It's got a very feminine, polished look to it that we like on short women a lot.

The Peasant Coat   Lavishly trimmed with fur or embroidery at the cuffs, neck, and hem or with braiding and other opulent trim, peasant coats go in and out of style under a variety of names. Of course, it should never be the only coat you own, but if you get seduced by the substantial romance of these coats, opt for one that's scaled small in a subdued color with vertically worked braiding and trim. But be careful: Since peasant coats often take ornamentation at the hem, shortening can make quick work of their charm. And keep in mind that *too* much decorative work at the hem acts as a border, which can be height-cutting.

An old-fashioned name for another romantic coat that you see now and then, a redingote is a slightly fitted little coat number with a bell-shaped silhouette, which is hard to wear if you are short. The inevitable hemming job tends to spoil the gracefulness of the bell skirt, and unless you're willow-wand-slim, it could make you look dumpy.

The Redingote

A double-breasted coat with large, wide lapels, fitted waist, flared skirt, a cape collar, and big brass buttons! And if you're short, absolutely not!

The Coachman's Coat

The stadium coat is a three-quarter-length coat (really a jacket) with toggle closings, often a shearling collar, and hood. It can be shortening to some under 5'4" bodies; lengthening on others. (For example, if you're short-legged, a stadium coat that comes just over the buttocks, can give you a leggier look for the same reasons that a tunic or three-quarter sweater work as proportion-changers.) Otherwise, if that's not your particular figure problem, and you want a casual coat, you'd be better off with something shorter, like a pea jacket.

The Stadium Coat

MANDARIN COAT

When You're in Doubt about Color

1. *If your coat is going to be* the *coat*—meaning, an all-purpose one that's going to have to look right in a lot of different situations, from jeans to dress, then it's best to go for one of the classics, like a reefer or a wrap, in a basic neutral color. Keep in mind, however, that neutrals aren't only browns and beiges. Black can be a terrific-looking (and authority-making) neutral coat color on a short woman. So can sage green, navy, pale gray, wine, and cranberry red (yes, red's a neutral when it comes to coats—and especially flattering on fair-skinned brunettes). If you prefer to stick to the brown family, then experiment with the range of more interesting tawny colors, like caramel, taupe, russet, and cream. You don't have to stay with just solids either. A small herringbone or tiny tweed are both fine neutral patterns that work over almost anything.

2. *What about brights?* Although we're always in favor of ex-

PEASANT COAT

REDINGOTE

STRUCTURED

perimenting with new colors, we do recommend exercising a little caution when it comes to coats. Because your coat is going to be standing for a lot of service, you're better off saving faddish or offbeat shades for less expensive and easily replaceable accessories, like gloves or scarves. Chances are you'll tire easily of an odd color in a coat. Also, some colors become tremendously popular one year, disappear the next, and because you probably won't be buying a new coat every year, you don't want it to "date" that easily.

3. Finally, when in doubt, keep this in mind: As a rule, the more conservative colors look richest, and will make you look tallest. Unless it's a very expensive and well made coat, a too-bright color will make the coat look cheap.

Short Chic Coat Checklist for Quality and Fit

- Once you've found a coat that appeals to you in terms of style, color, and price, it's time to check out fit. So slip it on. First, it should fit properly—smoothly and neatly, with no wrinkles or bumps around the neck and shoulders (the two very hardest places to alter). If it doesn't, then move on to the next choice.

- If the coat passed step one, see how you feel in it. Consider the body fit: Is it roomy enough (especially around the sleeve and the armhole) to slide over an extra sweater or a suit jacket? Or is it too big altogether (and do you look like a six-year-old who got loose in her mother's closet)? Other points: The coat should button up comfortably and easily; the pockets should fall in the right place. Check the waist, too, while you're at it. It should fall where yours does, not higher or lower.

- Now give the coat a walk-around. See how it moves. If it looks stiff, put it back. Take a turn in front of a three-way mirror and check how the collar falls. (Remember, even in a season of big collars, yours should be a pinch smaller than usual.)

- We've already talked about coat button *size*, but did you know that coat buttons themselves are also a giveaway to quality goods? Look at the coats in different price levels, and you'll soon begin to see the difference between a button that's plastic and one that's horn or bone, between real leather buttons and the molded plastic kind. A really good coat will also have a few extra buttons stitched onto the inside coat flap.

- Coat lengths depend on the lengths of the skirts and dresses you wear under them. But, generally, whatever that length is, your full-length coat should fall at least a half inch and, better, a full inch to two inches longer. Coats that are narrow, like a reefer or a wrap, look fine at any length that's currently fashionable. However, a coat that's fuller, like the fuller skirt you may be wearing under it, should always be a little longer to balance the greater amount of fabric involved. A full coat that's short, like a full smock top and a full dress, will only make you look wide, not tall.

- As for the three-quarter and seven-eighths coats, they can be terrific-looking changes from standard lengths—especially if the standards tend to overwhelm your frame. A three-quarter or seven-eighths coat can also be a nice, rather sophisticated choice for the short woman who usually drenches herself in tried-and-true classics. The key: that the coat be precisely proportioned to fall to a length three-quarters or seven-eighths *on your height*—and that takes careful altering. Another point: the three-quarter or seven-eighths coats work best over pants or over the very slimmest skirts, otherwise they can look choppy.

COACHMAN'S COAT

CAPELET

NOT RECOMMENDED

Lining tips: A good-quality coat should have a finished bottom. This means that the lining should be sewn into the hem with about $1\frac{1}{2}$ to 2 inches turnback. A coat with an unfinished hem (a lining that's just tacked down in three or four places) or one that hangs free isn't a quality coat. The advantages of a finished bottom: Not only is it better looking, but the lining will fall flatter and more neatly—and last longer, too. The best linings are satin, which give more weight and warmth, as opposed to rayon, nylon, or taffeta. (Satin lasts longer, by the way.) While you're checking, you might also want to see if the coat has an interlining, something you'll find in only the very best coats these days. An interlining is simply a second lining, tucked in between the coat fabric and the satin outerlining for a little extra warmth and finish. Another mark of good quality: If the lining starts about an inch and a half to two inches down from the inside of the collar, letting the warmth of the coat fabric rest right against your neck.

STADIUM COAT

PROPORTIONED LENGTH!

Rainwear

Everyone should own a trench coat. A classic, if there ever was one, it evokes memories of Gable and of Garbo, of Bogart, of Katharine Hepburn. A true trench coat (à la *Brooks Brothers* and *Burberry's*, the grand-masters of the style) has certain specific styling details that are musts for authenticity: the long, water-repellant canvas weave trench should be double-breasted (one of the few times *that* works because the traditional fabric is so thin) and have epaulettes; a loose, shoulder yoke; a rain-shield back; and a buckled belt (that you'll knot casually but never buckle).

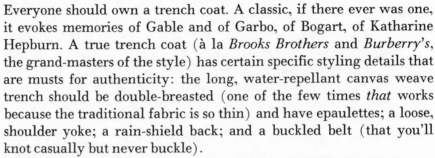

As chic and enduring a style as any, a trench coat is the top choice in rain gear, once you've found one that's perfectly scaled down. *And we do mean perfectly.* With all that wonderful detail going on, it's the rules of scale that are going to see you through. Once you do find one, though, a classic trench goes on forever, which does serve to justify somewhat the rather hefty price tags that the two big B's charge. One with a warm, zip-in lining can layer over sweaters in winter; with the lining zipped out, it can be a light topper in a summer rainstorm. And the trench coat travels well, too.

Of course, a trench coat isn't your only raincoat option. The reefer is another investment classic you might like. Another all-weather coat that looks terrific on short women—the A-shaped balmacaan. As we said before, it's a little trickier to carry because of its swingy shape, but it can work and look especially sophisticated if you can handle it through the shoulders and if the bottom isn't too full.

For casual weekend wear, try a slicker in a bright yellow oilskin or similar rubberized fabric. (The children's and young teen departments are the best places to get this one inexpensively if you're on the petite side of short.) These clip-fastened bad-weather coats (originally worn by sailors) are usually well made and, like most "uniform" goods, have tremendous ongoing style.

Another kind of raincoat you might be tempted by are the very thin, almost whisperweight shells you see in versions of nylon ciré in a variety of colors. These can be a very dressy kind of spring and summer coat, and their thinness and supple lightness are short-woman pluses (as long as you take care to belt them in, perhaps with a pretty scarf, to ward off their natural tendency to billow). One in khaki for day or in black or a bright color like magenta or turquoise at night can be a good choice.

Color note: By the way, except for these shells, classic rainwear should be in classic colors (like beige, khaki, loden, and occasionally black) never in "feminine" colors (like salmon pink, light blue, sea green).

Quilted Coats

Quilted coats, filled with down or polyester Fiberfil, take the honors as one of the warmest, most practical toppers around—also as one of the hardest things to wear if you happen to be short. Look at it this way: With tall women going around looking like overupholstered mattresses, do small women have any chance at all? Actually, yes . . .

The first thing to decide about quilted coats is whether to go for the goosedown variety or those filled with polyester Fiberfil.

Below, a rundown of the pros and cons a short woman should consider:

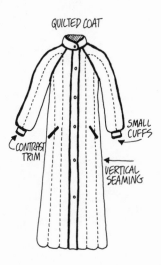

QUILTED COAT

SMALL CUFFS

CONTRAST TRIM

VERTICAL SEAMING

Goosedown

Although a down-filled coat is warmer than one with polyester Fiberfil, and more lightweight, it also tends to be puffy-looking and can make you look like a stand-in for the Pillsbury doughboy. Most are worked in horizontal patterns, very seldom in verticals. And although these patterns are attractive, we all know about what horizontals can do, especially on a coat that's full to begin with. *Note:* The reasons verticals are seldom seen is that down is loose and it's the horizontal patterning that prevents all the stuffing from slipping down to the coat hem.

Fiberfil

Fiberfil, although not as warm or long-lasting as a down, unless you're in for near Arctic winters, is warm and durable enough to do the job, we think. Because the Fiberfil is sliced into long, thin strips, which are then sewn inside the coat, Fiberfils are considerably flatter and more streamlined than downs. And although Fiberfil is heavier and denser than down, it has more maneuverability, allowing it to be worked into attractive, slimming, height-making vertical patterns. And that usually means you can stay toasty-warm, without sacrificing good looks.

- Obviously we're in favor of any coat with vertical quilting. We think it makes a big difference in counteracting the potential bulkiness of a quilted coat. (Amy G., 5'2" owns a Fiberfil

The Details That Make a Quilted Coat Work

quilted coat, which actually looks slim as a result of its long vertical seaming, mandarin collar, and simple, uncluttered lines.)

- Collars should be scaled down and simple. When they are, they go a long way toward making a quilted coat work. A stand-up collar or band, with a snap-front, for instance, eliminates clutter around the face and keeps the neck and shoulder line clean.
- A coat that tapers down to small snap-cuffs or knitted wristlets is another good choice. They will keep your arms from looking like stuffed sausages and keep you warmer by preventing the cold air from rushing in. Raglan sleeves are another important detail to look for to keep your silhouette clean and uncluttered.
- Balance is key when you're wearing a quilted coat. Even with the very slimmest versions, always wear boots to balance the bulky look of the coat.
- The stay-away-froms: horizontal seaming, high-contrast bicolorings that make you look larger, puffy pockets attached to the outside of the coat, any coat that's shorter than a full-lengther.

Sweater Coats

SWEATER COAT

VERY SOFT →

Knitted sweater coats that wrap around you happen to look so terrific on short women that they're worthy of their own category. Soft and clinging and interestingly textured, they meet all the criteria for an A-number one look. Try one long and cabled or worked in stunning, vertical stripes in offbeat colors and patterns. It is, after all, a coat *extra*—for spring, fall, and other in-between weather, and not your all-purpose cold-weather basic. The only negative to sweater coats: Like sweaters, they're difficult to alter by yourself and could need the touch of a professional to get them right.

Capes

Capes convey style. And dash. And short women lust after them, each and every one of us, but because of preconceived notions about what we ought to wear, we often deny ourselves the pleasure. Surely, if you're the swirly, dramatic type, you should own a cape. But what kind? Read on . . .

First of all, we won't deny that a lot of short women simply can't carry off a cape. We think that's often because of a woman's figure and personal style rather than height alone. There are plenty of medium-height (and yes, even *tall*) women who don't have the kind of flair that goes hand-in-hand with cape wearing. And then there are people like petite Gloria Swanson, who's 5', as well as other less flamboyant but equally confident women of style, who could carry off any cape with the ultimate panache.

The most important thing to remember about a cape is that it has to be fluid. "A scarf for the body" is how one fashion writer put it. Jody L., 5'1¾", an artist, craftswoman, and habitual capewearer, told us how she acquired her favorite cape—a soft, hazy blue mohair/wool knit that envelopes her from neck to knee like a soft cobweb.

"I've always liked the special romance of a cape," Jody said, "but knew I couldn't wear one that was very full and sweeping because it would give me the silhouette of a cone! When I found this one, though, in a small shop in Florence, I knew it was right for me immediately. It's hooded and hand-knitted all in one piece—really like a long sweater that clings to my shoulders and falls very, very narrow. Of course, I never wear it with flat shoes, only with boots."

Is there something else she wanted to add about wearing a cape, we asked?

"Yes. There's a certain 'mystery' to wearing a cape. People assume there's something different about you, and you get caught up in that whole thing," she said.

You do. And Jody looks, yes, rather mysterious in her cape . . . and not the least bit short.

Another kind of cape that's a good choice for short women would be almost any cape in very fine cashmere or thin wool. There's a wonderful classic cashmere cape that *Halston* makes in a wide variety of colors (including black, white, and three different beiges) that's been one of his steady sellers year after year, probably because it works so well on so many women of all sizes. The cape is exclusive to his Madison Avenue New York shop, but if you like the look and not the price—and can sew—see Anne Marie's "Halston" cape "recipe," which follows.

One more way to make a cape work for you, not against you— look for what we call a demicape, that is, a cape that's stitched up all along the side to form a rudimentary "sleeve." Allison owns one in a heavy Irish wool tweed. Not only do the stitched-up sides make the cape warmer by preventing cold air from rushing up the sides, but they also tend to curb the cape's voluminousness. Her other favorite cape: a soft chocolate velvet with a ruffled collar. As you might expect, evening capes in velvet or velveteen work because of the gentleness and suppleness of the fabric.

One type of coat-cum-cape we have to put thumbs down on for short women is the Sherlock Holmes style coat with capelet. Ditto for double and triple-tiered capes; any cape that's stiff and that stands out, not in at the hem; any cape in a hard wool gabardine, bulky, inflexible tweed, or big bold plaid.

Anne Marie's "Halston"-styled Cape

If you've got a sewing machine, you can sew up this knock-off of a Halston cape in less than an hour (and save yourself a bundle, too). Because of its construction, one-size-fits-all.

You'll need: 1. a 60″ x 80″ rectangle of good-quality double-knit wool jersey (or other fluid medium-to-heavy-weight wool).
2. 11 yards of matching ½″-wide fold-over knit braid
3. a medium-sized frog closing
4. scissors, thread, a tape measure and straight pins.

The how-to's:

First, fold the 60″ x 80″ rectangle of double-knit wool jersey in half widthwise. Cut front center line on top layer of fabric only. Then cut scoops for the neck to dimensions given below. Finish all edges with the fold-over braid. Sew on front neck frog closings.

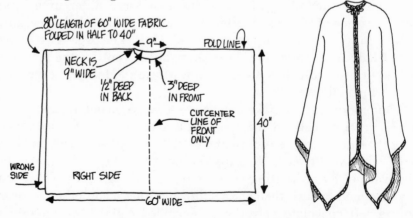

FOCUS ON: Harriet Winter

Harriet Winter, a down-to-earth and exuberant woman, 5′3″, with curly salt-and-pepper hair has a distinct fashion philosophy.

"The reason I love designing is that when I was younger I could buy only what I would call knockoffs of what my mother would wear," she told us. "There was never anything young and great-looking and what I considered mature and sexy and with-it enough. And everything, but everything, had to be picked up and taken in a pinch—long sleeves had to be shortened, every hem had to be redone. So when I started in businees, my ambition was to fit four out of five women, no matter how tall or short they were. Today, my customers range from four feet seven to five feet ten both privately and in the stores.

"We do true sizes," she went on. "We don't do sizes that are very big and soothe the ego; we would rather do sizes that fit. We only go up to a size twelve—that's what I wear—so we are not catering to the big, heavier woman at this point. My daughter who is four feet ten wears our six or eight, and one very little woman we dress who's four feet seven, wears our size four. She has to shorten the sleeves and the hem, but the rest of the garment is in proportion.

"There are really two kinds of short women, I've found," Harriet continued. "One, who I call the 'Lilliputian'—is positively scaled down in size. Her bone structure is birdlike; her tiny proportions are perfect. But she is a rarity.

"The majority of short women—and I've measured a lot of them—are basically normal-size women with slightly shorter legs—or else very short from waist to crotch. And when she's dressed well—she can be as stunning as a woman of any height," she said.

Mrs. Winter feels that all women—and short women especially—look best dressed in a very feminine way.

"I design clothes for a woman's body—a female body," she said. "The woman I design for is not flat-chested—she has, more or less, a bust, and she has a slightly rounded hip. She doesn't have a man's shoulder, she doesn't have a man's measurements, and she can't wear a man's clothes.

"Women have smaller waists, even when they thicken," she explained. "They have soft breasts and soft shoulders. Nine times out of ten, they have a very slight bulge on the upper part of their thighs; they have a slightly rounded butt. They have a little pad below their waists in the back—and that's where you put a little bit of ease in the clothes so no one knows it's there."

But by designing feminine clothes, Harriet Winter is not talking ruffles and frills. Rather, her clothes are characterized by simplicity. Because of their fit and line, she says, they take 3 to 5 to 10 pounds off everybody who wears them.

"There is only one reason to design clothes, and that is to mask all the lumps and bumps you have literally and in your head," she said.

Certain consistent style points make Mrs. Winter's line appealing to shorter women. One point—her specially proportioned shoulder line . . .

"Short women can't wear wide shoulders, which is why I always cut a very narrow shoulder—approximately three inches, ending just below the 'ball' of the shoulder," she said. "Where I add the extra room is in the sleeve, not the shoulder—it makes a difference. This way the bigger sleeve gives the coat or jacket fashion and movement, and you still have the lovely small-shaped shoulder cut," she explained.

Another signature—her visible seaming . . .

"Almost all my clothes—coats, jackets, skirts, pants, have a certain kind of seaming," she said. "Because the visible structure of the garment is very important to me, I put a lot of seams on the outside so I can direct the eye where I want it and draw it away from where I don't.

"And," she added, "when I do skirts, no matter how wide they are, I pull them in closer at the hem. I just start 'caving' it in—which may be 'wrong' design, but I find it pulls the skirt in toward the legs in an attractive way, rather than pushing it out. I prefer that effect, especially if you're small," she said.

The skirt styles she recommends particularly are those with yokes. "A dirndl skirt is an atrocity on a five-foot-four-and-under woman," she commented. "It makes them look dumpy because it 'pots out' right below the waist. With a yoked skirt, you can get smoothness at the hip and a look of soft movement below." Another choice: pleated skirts. "The ones I do are carefully proportioned so they're not bulky at all and fit very closely at the top."

(*Note:* Nine out of ten women, Harriet believes, look better in skirts than in pants, but the same nine, she admits, would *rather* wear pants. "I think a woman looks better with the softness of a skirt surrounding her," she told us. "Women really weren't meant to wear pants—you really need a slim thigh, a tiny bottom, and a little bit of length to carry them off." Her own personal compromise: culottes—which she wears for the flattery of a skirt and the comfort of pants.)

12. Furs: Choosing One That Doesn't Dwarf You

Remember what we said in chapter 2 about scale? Well, here's where it's put to the test. Because despite what you might have been led to believe, you don't have to be 5′9″ to wear a big fur. Big furs, like everything else, come in small sizes, too—and that's where scale—and know-how—count.

Needless to say, going out and buying a fur coat isn't an everyday thing. There's a certain mystique to wearing a fur that's hard to describe. We think it's carryover from those vintage Hollywood films—the ones where Jean Harlow (5′2″) or Joan Crawford (5′4″) appeared in yards of stunning white fox. Today, that glamour still lingers. Put on a fur and you feel special, and you look like a million bucks.

Of course, fur has its practical side, too: If you can afford one, there's nothing warmer and few things more durable. Mink, for example, in addition to being exceptionally lightweight, is one of the warmest and most long-lasting furs going. And because of the warmth that most furs provide, they're starting to be considered as more of a necessity than a luxury, especially in certain parts of the country where the thermostat drops on a regular basis to subfreezing levels.

The first thing that any short woman should know about buying a fur is that everything we said about coats . . . applies to fur coats. To reiterate: When it comes to fur, you're better off skipping any coat

- with round, horizontally worked skins
- that's double-breasted
- with wide, double-notched lapels
- with deep, shawl collars; oversized wraps; wide, roll-back cuffs.

The same details that clutter up a cloth coat, clutter up a fur one. When you're under 5'4", *simplicity counts.*

Which Fur Types Work Best?

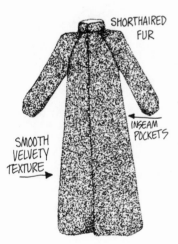

SHORTHAIRED FUR

INSEAM POCKETS

SMOOTH VELVETY TEXTURE →

Let's start with the predictable and admit that, yes, we do think that a short-haired fur is an excellent if obvious choice for the shorter woman who craves fur. It's less bulky and less overwhelming than a long-haired fur, and it's much easier to carry off if you're anything less than model size. And short-haired furs have plenty of positives: Most are exceptionally versatile and extremely warm. (Remember, don't equate bulk with warmth.) Short-haired furs also have a remarkably beautiful luster—all furs do—but it's a lot more noticeable when you're dealing with a flatter surface.

Among our favorite short-haired choices are otter, mole, sheared beaver, muskrat, squirrel, and buronduki (a kind of ground mole), and the different kinds of lamb, like broadtail and Swakara. By the way, if you're still associating lamb with your grandmother's old black Persian, take note: There's an upsurge of interest in that fur these days. In addition to what lamb's always had going for it—unusual warmth and durability (it can last for up to twenty years!) and interesting curly to wavy textures—it's also one of the sleekest, flattest of all furs, which means it styles up slim, sexy, and not overwhelming. Madelon C., 5'3", a Chicago-based fashion consultant says she always considered lamb to be one of the most flattering furs on a short woman—long before the fur began to make it's fashion comeback. "It's as unbulky as my cloth coats," she told us, "only incredibly warmer." For years, her going-to-the-office coat was an extra long ("boot-sweeping"), slim-fitting black lamb wrap, glamorized with a face-framing black-dyed fox collar. (The reason the wrap worked so well is because lamb is so flat.) She wore the coat for *nine years!* And if it hadn't been stolen out of the back seat of her car on its way for its first "face-lift," it would have gone on, she says, for another nine, "easy."

Medium-haired furs, like mink and nutria, are also great options for the under 5'4" woman.

Mink, for many women, is the ultimate luxury fur. Its sterling reputation rests on the fact that it offers the best of everything: looks, warmth, versatility, durability, glamour, at—as far as furs go—a surprisingly affordable price. If you're short (and particularly if you're on the smaller, shorter side of Short Chic) and find that other so-called glamorous long-haired furs, like fox or lynx, are hard to carry, try mink. It will give you the look and feel of a luxurious long-haired fur, and it scales down beautifully for your proportions.

Nutria, a somewhat coarser and less silky-haired fur than mink, is another unbulky fur to try. Natural unsheared nutria with thick, glossy outer hair (called guard hair), is a rich brown color, and is warm and durable, too. Sheared down, it's even less bulky and lighter in weight, offering another option, another look.

And what about sable? Well, sable is considered a semilong-haired fur, which makes it akin to medium hairs but not quite. It is denser than mink but not as long and full as fox and coyote. We queried several New York furriers about the suitability of sable for the under-5'4" woman. Many of them thought it the very fullest fur that a petite woman could go for, although a few dismissed it as being altogether "too much fur" to handle. Our feelings on the subject: If you can afford sable, wear it in good health—*and never mind how tall you are.*

LONGHAIRED FUR

BLOUSON SLEEVE

VERTICALS!

So What about the Long-haired Furs?

Yes, you can. Within limits, that is. Properly proportioned and with an eye to scale, long-haired furs, like raccoon and tanuki, and some but not all varieties of fox and lynx, can be adapted to shorter shapes without losing the element of luxe that makes them so special.

Says David Stypmann, fur buyer at Bendel's: "A short woman can look quite good in a long-haired fur, as long as it's not a fluffy, bulky one. It all depends on the way the long hairs fall. If the hairs are *very* long, they'll fall flat—and not stick out—so the fur won't be bushy or bulky, but still have a luxurious feeling."

He recalled the time that one of his customers—a "very petite and fragile-looking lady"—bought a Russian lynx coat. "The long hairs fell flat, so even though the fur was fluffy, it wasn't bulky at all, and she looked fabulous in it."

Of course, a long-haired fur must be carefully proportioned to a small woman's body, as well. One fur expert told us that when designer Adele Simpson, 4'9", decided she wanted a new fur coat one year, she chose fisher—a potentially bulky fur. But by working out the skins very carefully with her, and keeping an eye on patterning and proportion, she looked great in it . . . "and tall."

Some of the Most Popular Fur Types

Short-haired furs	*Medium-haired furs*	*Long-haired furs*
sheared beaver	mink	raccoon
otter	nutria	tanuki
mole	sable (semilong-	fox
muskrat	haired)	lynx
squirrel	fisher (semilong-	coyote
buronduki	haired)	lamb (Mongolian
ermine		and Tibetan)
lamb (broadtail,		opossum
Persian, Mou-		
ton)		
calf		
kid		
seal		
chinchilla		

The Short Woman's Best Fur Shapes

"When I make a fur coat for a woman who is short, I look at her height, but more importantly, I look at her bone structure and the width of her shoulders because that's where the coat falls from," said one fourth-generation New York fur expert. "It's not just a few inches taken in here or there, but a carefully constructed scaling down. A woman must feel comfortable in a fur. And any coat that weighs heavily on the shoulders will be uncomfortable to wear and is a giveaway to a poorly made coat."

Hear! Hear! Another point we'd like to add to that: *A well-made fur coat shouldn't make you look fat.* If it does—and you're not—it's not the fur shape or the fur for you.

Because fur is one item that looks best when it's lush—and not pencil-slim—go for simple, unexaggerated shapes. They work best,

look classiest, and, with the right detailing, don't have to be boring. *Tip:* How to tell the difference between "roomy" and "too big"? Slip the fur on. You should just be able to move around inside the fur with ease—no tightness, no pull, no skimp.
Keep these points in mind:

- *When you're considering fur styles*, look for narrow but swingy lines, high-cut unadorned sleeves, no cuffs (which will make short arms look shorter), no hoods to clutter up a clean neck and shoulder line.
- *Belts*—unless you're dealing with a slim-fitting wrap coat, a belt can be height-cutting when it comes to fur. If you like the shaping you get with a belt, try a half belt—one that slides inside the coat, ties in the front for shaping, and leaves the back of the coat loose and easy. You can also just slip it off when you want an unbelted look.
- *Set-in sleeves are another detail to watch out for*—and avoid. From the back, the shoulder-to-shoulder expanse they create on a short woman can be broadening.
- *Ditto for nipped-in waists.* Sometimes, they just don't work, particularly if you're medium- to long-waisted. Slip on a raccoon or tanuki coat with a nipped-in waist and see if you don't agree. Most likely, the nipped-in waist on fullish furs like these will give you an awkward top-heavy look (as if you've got most of you're height above the waist and very little below). You'd do better in a fur with a straight-falling back that fits smoothly at the shoulders or with a gently tented balmacaan shape.
- *Nice height-adding trick:* Ask your furrier about a coat with a "sunburst" patterning in the back. This subtle, light-catching detail results from using the slim, darker necks of the skins up near the shoulder line, and it is *very*, *very* flattering.
- *Another nice touch:* a blouson sleeve—one that tapers in to an elasticized wrist. Not only is it practical (warmer), but it eliminates bulk and points up a delicate wrist.
- *A special word about collars:* Although they shouldn't be too big, an overly small collar on a fur is a mistake. Since part of the appeal of fur has to do with it's face-framing-against-the-skin effects, you're selling yourself short if you go for a small collar for proportion's sake. A less-than-luxurious collar can also make your fur coat look . . . well, cheap. So go for a happy medium: a *scaled-down* collar but not one that's

SUNBURST BACK

skimpy. You do want to be able to turn it up against the cold and wind—a look that, besides its practical aspects, feels luxurious and is elongating to boot. (*Tip:* Ask your furrier to "bone" or "wire" your collar so it'll stay in place when you turn it up.)

- *Another collar idea* that we picked up from the helpful folks at Bendel's: a rounded shawl collar (not a traditional shawl) but one that leads right down into the facing of the coat. A stand-up band collar (a mandarin) will do a similar flattering job, and both styles are particularly elegant-looking collar treatments on small women. On a coat like mink, a small notched collar or a mandarin are nice, classic choices. (Bendel's, by the way, is one of the best places for a short, small woman to find scaled-down fur shapes with innovative styling. Their small sizes in furs—as in everything else—are the smallest in town.)

- *To move to the other extreme, what about collarless styles?* We like them. They can look exceptionally well on short types because they keep the shoulder line clean and uncluttered. This is nice compensation, by the way, when you're bending rules elsewhere. Our friend Maria's white fox jacket, for example, could've been too bulky a look for her to carry, at just 5′2″—fox is, almost always, a bulky, fluffy fur. But the jacket's got slim, blouson sleeves, and is collarless and uncluttered. It works. A collarless jacket or coat is also a nice choice if you have a short neck (like a lot of short women) or if you'd just like to play up a graceful long one. Just add an accessory like a fur-tailed muffler before you go out—for warmth—and you're set.

Special Tips On Long-haired Furs

Pay attention to the guidelines mentioned earlier when you're looking for a long-haired fur—and to the way the skins themselves are cut. Vertically worked skins, rather than horizontals, are better for short women in *almost all* situations but especially when you're considering a long hair. Another point: Let-out skins—those sliced in long, narrow sections then sewn together, will give you the slimmest, least bulk-making lines.

The texture of the fur and the degree of fluffiness are also to be considered. Unless you want to look like "a walking ball of cotton," an extremely fluffy fox or lynx can still be too bulky if the fur stands out and not down. As for length, a full-length, long-haired coat usually works better than a shorter one, which can tend to appear choppy.

Although we wouldn't normally advise having your clothing made to order, with fur it's a service worth considering. More often than not, a custom-made coat will look better, fit better, and feel more comfortable than a ready-made, and it shouldn't cost that much more, considering what you're getting. A custom-made fur isn't an uncommon only-for-the-super-rich occurrence either. (If you can afford a fur, you can afford a custom one.) Even in a department store, the fur you choose off the rack will have to be fitted and adjusted to your body shape before you march it out of the store.

Be sure, however, that you're dealing with a furrier or a store that you can trust. The furrier who throws any old fur over your shoulders and exclaims "beautiful" is the furrier to avoid.

Can a Short Woman Wear a Fur Jacket?

A fur jacket requires careful planning to look right when you're short. The basic rule: Any style that falls too low on the thigh doesn't work. Two lengths that do: a waist-length bolero-style and a jacket that's hipbone, not hip-length. (The shorter the jacket, the longer your legs will look.) To carry off a longer jacket, have it stop within a half inch to an inch past your buttocks—no more, no less.

One very important point about jackets, which is almost as important as the shape and the length: what goes under them. *A fur jacket should be worn over pants or trousers only, never over a skirt.* If it is worn over a skirt or dress, a short woman will get a chopped up "three-sectioned" look of jacket, skirt, and legs.

Special Effects

You may have heard about fur being dyed new and unusual colors, like green, aubergine, blue, red, and gold, about it being woven and ribbed and worked in innovative and unusual ways. Although it may have sounded exciting, perhaps you thought "no way." We say: not so!

If you like the look, there's absolutely no reason your height should keep you from a coat that's a collage of fur swatches, velvet, leather, yarn or any of the innovations you may come across. But if it's your first fur and you want it to be an all-around, all-purpose fur, you're better off saving the experimentation till next time.

What if Nothing Works?

If you can't find a fur that looks good on you, try a coat in soft leather or buttery suede, with a fur *trim*—a fluffy fur collar for example. Or try a flattish fur with a long-haired collar. Another option: fur accessories. A muffler made out of soft little fur tails, a jabot in chinchilla, a fox-paw muff, can all give you the feeling and luxury of fur without going all the way.

About Fakes

Although you might think you can get the warmth and style of a fur coat at a fraction of the cost by going for a fake fur, don't. You're really much better off with a good-looking cloth coat and a fur accessory like the ones we mention above. You may think that the fake looks amazingly like the real thing, but take our word for it—it doesn't. Wearing a fake pretending to be real—like wearing fake leather, fake suede, or fake gold jewelry, even—lessens your credi-

---

The one thing that'll help you carry off any fur you try . . . that nearly every fur designer, retailer, and buyer we spoke with mentioned: *attitude.*

One savvy buyer summed it up like this: "For a woman who is small, it's attitude and personality that allows her to carry off the coat with more volume. One customer might come in here and try on a roomy coat and say, "Oh, it's just too much," while another, the same size, but with an attitude that's mobile and lively can carry off the identical coat to perfection. The woman who is petite and who has an *up* personality can carry off any kind of fur she tries on."

bility—something a short woman can't afford. Better to wait till you *can* afford the real thing than to wear fake anything.

As for the so-called fun furs—the frankly fake furs that aren't pretending to be anything else but what they are—we'd suggest skipping those, too. The unspoken message they send is that you're not in league to afford the real goods.

Caring for your fur . . . Even if your fur spends most of its time hanging in your closet, it should have a professional cleaning yearly and always be stored during the warm months with a furrier or in department-store storage where temperature and humidity levels are carefully controlled. In addition, there are other things you can do to extend the life of your fur and make it look better, longer.

1. Always hang your fur on a strong, broad-shouldered hanger in a roomy closet so that it won't get crushed.

2. If you hang your fur in a brightly lit room—like your office—place a cloth over it. Artificial light can oxidize fur and cause a color change.

3. Keep your fur away from heat, like radiators. Those, too, can dry a fur.

4. If your fur gets wet, give it a good shake and hang it up in a dry and well-ventilated place far from any heat source. Never brush or comb a fur—a shake-out is all that's needed to fluff it up.

5. Never spray perfume or any sort of scent directly on your fur.

6. Another negative: flowers and jewelry should be pinned on your clothes, never on fur.

7. Don't carry a shoulder bag when you're wearing fur—the constant rubbing on the shoulder and against the side of the coat can damage the fur and shorten its life.

13. P.M. Dressing

Because clothes say so much about who you are, many short women, even those with an unerring sense of fashion for day, go into a panic at the thought of choosing something to wear at night. Part of the problem, of course, revolves around the uncertainty of the situation. On the job or during the day, you know pretty much what's expected of you. But going-out clothes can mean anything from pants and a dressy sweater to a short dinner dress or a full-length gown. Another part of it: the fact that a lot of short women haven't taken the time to define exactly what dress-up style they most find comfortable.

The Shorter Woman's Two Biggest P.M. Dressing Mistakes

The two most common—and disastrous—mistakes that short women make when it comes to P.M. looks are either overdressing or under-dressing.

Overdressing   This occurs when you start with a show-stopper (for an occasion that only warrants the subtlest bit of dazzle) and then keep piling it on—glittered shoes *and* stockings, still another bracelet. . . . It's a look that's a disaster on a woman of any height but especially so when you're short and more easily overpowered by overdone clothes. We liked what Morgan Fairchild (who's particularly knowledgeable about her own petite good looks) had to say on the subject: "When I walk into a room, I don't want people to look up and say, 'Oh, what a pretty dress.' I want them to say, 'Oh, what a pretty woman.'" And that's the point: *you* should outshine the clothes; *they* shouldn't outshine you.

At the other end of the pole, there's . . .

Underdressing

And we've seen this one brought down to the level of nondressing on a number of occasions. While "less is more" may apply to a certain school of architecture and while it may work fine on the lankier proportions of model types, when you're short, underdressing can often relegate you to wallflowerdom and make you look not understated and elegant but just uninteresting. Consider this questionnaire complaint: "I feel attractive and confident at a party until a good-looking tall woman walks in. Then I feel so overshadowed that I might as well leave." This is just the reason that shorter women have to look especially terrific in cocktail party crowds, if they want to stand-out instead of being swallowed up.

So how can a short woman get away with the subtle art of underdressing and still look good?

Although we admit it's always safer and smarter to underdress rather than to overdress, it works *only* if the pieces you choose are very obviously well made and chic *and* if you don't underdress to the point where you look and feel insignificant. That's why simply cut, understated clothes, for example, should always take a rich-looking fabric or color.

Pinning Down Your P.M. Personality

Your personality will have a lot to do with the evening look you'll find most comfortable to adapt.

Dressing to Type

Designer Bob Mackie, known for dressing dozens of entertainers, from Carol Burnett and Cher to Raquel Welch, in glamorous evening costumes, believes that dressing for evening involves a whole package—your height, your face, your hair, most of all, your personality.

"Bernadette Peters is a good example of dressing to type," he said. "She's short and very voluptuous—not fat, just rounded. You could draw her whole body with circles! She has beautiful shoulders, a full bosom, a small waist, not big hips, and ivory-colored skin; she isn't an ordinary-looking girl at all but looks like a throwback to another period. So it works for her to wear things a little more romantic or a little more dramatic, despite her height. She looks good in pants, but she looks *great* in romantic clothes like corselettes and lacy tops—things that enhance the look she already has. You put clothes like that on her and you think déjà vu—you're in another period. I've always thought of her as the perfect Gibson Girl." (For more on Bob Mackie, see Focus, this chapter.)

Toni G., 5'3", a senior administrator in a large Chicago hospital complex is another example of dressing to type. She describes herself as "very no-nonsense—a sweater-and-pants type of person. It's what I'm most comfortable in and what I know I look best in, too." What makes Toni's sweater-and-pants wardrobe special is that she's adapted the look to work in every area of her life, even for evening. "Especially for evening," she adds. "If I'm going out to a party in clothes I don't feel at ease in, I'm more apt to be nervous and not have a good time." So for a dinner and theater evening, she might wear a beaded sweater and wool crepe pants; for an all-out fund-raising gala, "my knitted red sequin tunic-sweater and matching sequined full pants."

Trying on a New Image On the other hand, you might want to choose an evening style that goes in an entirely different direction from what you usually wear, especially, say, if your job forces you to be tailored and you're really a closet romantic. In that case, P.M.'s the time you may want to indulge your secret soul with feminine, flower-sprinkled prints, lacy blouses, and delicate ruffles.

Your Basic P.M. Pieces

Before you start to plan your P.M. wardrobe, take a good long look at the way you live and consider what your real dressing needs are: dinner and movie clothes may be more in order than floor-sweeping ball gowns. Or theater evening and cocktail party looks may prevail. Once you decide, you'll know how to allocate your spending.

A very basic *minimum* P.M. wardrobe that will work for almost any P.M. situation would consist of the following three different looks: 1. pants and a top; 2. a pretty dress; and 3. a long dress or its equivalent.

Evening pants are an essential in every well dressed woman's wardrobe, particularly if she happens to be short. Why particularly? Because although a short woman can sometimes look overdressed in a dressy dress, she can seldom go wrong in dressy pants. In satin, silk crepe, wool crepe, velvet, or pin-striped metallics, evening pants can be sophisticated, height-adding and flattering. Just follow the rules for your particular figure type detailed in chapter 5.

All of the classic pants styles work beautifully, done up in evening fabrics. A pair in silk, one in glove-soft leather, and one in velvet, for example, can see you through any P.M. situation from casual to dressy. Just remember that . . .

- Flat-front pants are the ones to wear under a tunic top when you'll want an especially smooth line.
- With tuck-in tops, wear pleat fronts—a pair in silk looks good on almost anyone because the fabric is so thin that it adds practically no bulk at all.
- Pull-ons are flattering in satin or silky fabrics. Just remember that the elasticized waist always gets covered with a leather wrap or an ornamental belt or a long top.
- Wide flowing evening pajamas are one look a short woman is better off bypassing. But if you like them, wear them with a soft belted top and taper the pants down a little leaner than everyone else's. If *very* wide evening pants are in—the kind that look like a long skirt when you're standing still—then treat them according to the rules for a long skirt—the softer the fabric, the better.

By evening skirts, we mean either a short, pleated skirt, a short dirndl, a straight skirt of the sort you'd wear to a dinner or a cocktail party, or a long straight or gathered skirt for more dressy occasions.

The short evening skirt: The key to this category is the fabric. If it's velvet, crepe, silk, or something equally luscious, it's dressy enough for your purposes (and nothing is more appealing or says dress-up faster than the subtle shine of satin or velvet). The best and most versatile evening skirts will usually be in a dark or jewel-colored solid to pair up with a wonderful blouse or beaded top.

The long evening skirt: By a long evening skirt, we mean a long skirt that's in a dressy fabric. Just because a skirt is long doesn't mean it's dressy. The points to remember:

- If it's straight, look for a long slit to play up the length of your leg.

- If it's gathered, keep the skirt in a supple fabric and stay away from a too frilly, too blousy top.
- As for a wrap skirt, here's what we have to say about that: Don't. Not for a dressy affair anyway. It will only look like a "just-in-case skirt" (that is, the kind of skirt vacationing women throw in their suitcases at the last minute, "just in case we go someplace fancy"). The wrap skirt is almost always casual, no matter how long it is, so if you have one, save it for entertaining at home.

Evening Tops   Building an absolutely smashing evening wardrobe around a collection of wonderful tops is the fashion secret of a lot of short in-the-know women who realize that although the look can have a lot of sophistication, it's seldom overpowering. And with just one pair of pants and one skirt as basic bottoms—and a lot of tops—there's scarcely an occasion you won't be able to manage. If you want to be smart, you can save money on expensive evening clothes with this system by sticking to fabrics that are seasonless so your wardobe works year round.

The top staples of such a wardrobe might include:

1. A silky kimono-style top.

2. Beaded and/or embroidered sweaters and fluffy angoras that have a dressy look.

3. Bare, spare tank and camisole-styled tops (bareness is all-year-round fare, you know). A bare jersey that works with drawstring pants in the summer, also goes under a special jacket with wool crepe bottoms for winter.

4. Beautiful blouses with extravagant or unusual detailing (extravagant in quality and design, not size), like pleating, lace, asymetrical necklines, and so on.

5. Tunics, indispensable for this kind of wardrobe. Depending on the fabric (one in ivory silk crepe de Chine to wear over hammered satin bottoms for a gala or knitted gray cashmere tunic with beading at the shoulder to slip over pants for a dinner-and-theater evening), they can go anywhere. *Note:* The tunic, remember, is body-lengthening for almost all short figure types. Unbelted, it skims over full breasts and hips, bypasses a short or long waist; belted, it's one evening look a short woman need never risk being overwhelmed by because she can proportion it to fit her own height. The tunic works in all variations too. "My hunch is that Mrs. Reagan likes long tunic dresses because they make a woman look taller," commented Bill

Blass on the emerald green jersey Blass tunic dress that the First Lady wore to several Washington events.

Jump Suits

You know they go for day, but for evening, jump suits couldn't work better for 5′4″ and unders, too: backless, haltered, or just plain, with a few buttons opened down the front. Alexandra K., 5′3″, 109 pounds, a New York fashion merchandising editor told us that one of her favorite, and most versatile evening looks is a long-sleeved silk D.D. Dominick jump suit. "It happens to be perfectly proportioned for my body, except for leg length," she said, "and has an elasticized waist, Mandarin collar, and squared-off shoulders. I really lucked out when the saleswoman convinced me to try it on." When dressing "tall" is a priority, she wears it with a matching black silk belt "so's not to break the line" and a bright scarf wrapped at her neck. Other times, she belts it with a fuchsia-colored kid waist wrap. Then the high collar gets unbuttoned to fall into a skin-baring and neck-lengthening V.

Short Dressy Dresses

A dressy dress, of the kind that used to be called "restaurant" dresses because they had the kind of details that looked attractive *above* the table (a pretty neckline, an edge of bareness, lace, an elegant sleeve), is often one of the harder items to find, but the search is worth it: A dressy dress could be your best look for an afternoon wedding or even meeting someone special for dinner. For winter, look for one in a dark solid color or in a small print on a dark ground; for summer, a paler, gauzier print can be nice. If you're a Petite size, you might check out those by Princess Sumi (designer Princess Sumair herself is but 4′11″). A good alternative to a pretty dinner dress: a soft velvet suit (it'll have the same kind of feminine polish). For specific dress style tips, see chapter 10.

Evening Jackets

A special evening jacket can change the whole look of what you wear, and it can be just the touch a shorter woman needs to add drama and interest to her P.M. wardrobe. Sometimes a smashing evening jacket in a wonderful or unusual fabric can be just the added something needed to liven up basics like plain crepe pants and a silk blouse. Look for jackets in decorative colors, fabrics, and shapes, with pretty sleeves, shined up in satin, hand-embroidered in suede or in multicolored, gilty jacquards. Also nice: an antique jacket (maybe an old-fashioned shawl-collared smoker). What to avoid: anything that smacks of hard edges or stiff, blazer tailoring; the danger is that these will lack the softness and dressiness you want for evening.

Long Dresses　　Black Tie is Black Tie, so when the invitations specify such, there's little question in the minds of the *men* of the party. But for ladies, Black Tie can mean anything from a short cocktail dress to dressy pants and a barish top to a long evening dress. *White* Tie, however, means formal with a capital F—and that's when a long evening dress or its equivalent (a long skirt and top) is definitely in order.

Some shorter women are under the mistaken impression that they can't wear bare sexy, slinky evening clothes or feminine ruffled looks because of their height. Not so. Just be sure that details are scaled down to your size and that the clothes are done in the softest, most feminine fabrics around.

What you *will* have trouble with, however (especially if you're on the shorter side of short):

- Large, stiff, face-framing ruffles in fabrics like organza (frankly they're going to be hard going for anyone under 5'8")!
- Flouncy, peasanty, petticoated looks (best to confine this look to one special piece, not a whole ensemble).
- Puffed sleeves that puff out, not up.
- Tiered skirts that billow.
- Any look so voluminous that it can't be roped in with an ornamental belt or soft, silky sash.

Instead, look for:

- Strapless evening gowns (an elongating choice if you've got the shape for it—which means not height but slim arms, unscrawny neck and shoulders).
- One-shouldered evening gowns can be especially flattering to small women, since the one-shouldered diagonal draws the eye upward, giving the impression of height (which could be the reason why 5'4" Nancy Reagan tends to favor the look). If you find the look appealing, too, see that the body of the gown is figure-skimming and narrow-falling for the tallest possible line.
- Bias-cut gowns (the elegant lines of a well-made bias cut gown can slide right over wide hips, a big bust, or a chunky torso and take a good ten pounds off your appearance). The key to that: *well made.* Cheaply cut bias gowns look it—and never fall correctly.
- Caftans (yes, we mean it; if the lines flow in, not out, these work nicely on the under-5'4"). We admit we didn't think this so at first, but for a very short, chic woman Anne Marie

met at a national hairstylists' convention one year. Dee L. was a plump 4′11″. And the high-necked amethyst lace caftan she wore floated from under her chin to the tips of her toes a wonderful, elongating flow. She looked terrific.

- Ankle-length gowns (an excellent alternative if you feel overpowered by longer looks, and especially feminine-looking on petite women because it shows off dainty feet and ankles).

As with big prints, evening dresses are a tricky thing—you never really know how they're going to look unless you try them on. Occasionally, you run into the case of a dress that breaks *all* the rules—but personality conquers all. Example: One of Allison's favorite evening dresses is a black-and-red check taffeta ball gown, with poufy, off-the-shoulder sleeves, a flounced hem, tight waist with a big candy-box bow (which should, by all rights, *not work* on anyone 5′3″). But it looks bafflingly sensational. Chalk it up to that crucial intangible: chemistry. The dress works so well with the kind of person she is, that height doesn't even come into it. So remember what we said earlier about dressing to suit your personality: If the dress in question suits yours, by all means give it a try.

A great dress-up look doesn't just happen, it's planned. So one of the keys to looking and feeling sensational in evening clothes is planning ahead. You're not going to be able to enjoy yourself at a party if you're bemoaning your peeping bra straps (if only you had made the time to pick up that strapless bra, after all); or if you think that your tunic really *would* look better if you tried it with your gold mesh belt; or if, in your rush, you hadn't grabbed those steep-heeled backless sandals that always make you topple over. So plan it all out ahead of time and give yourself plenty of time to dress. Then, once you're there, forget about your clothes entirely . . . that's how great evenings are made.

P.M. Color Tips

Decide on your own best basic color for evening.

- *Most of us automatically think black when we think of* P.M. *dressing:* It's the sexiest, most tall-making color around. It also happens to work for almost all P.M. occasions. Some folks tell us, however, that they find the color unflattering: honey blondes with beigey coloring; women with sallow complexions. Also, the harshness of matte black gets harder to wear as you get older.

Still, we think black can be such a valuable evening basic that even if it's not your best color, it's worth working out. If you think you don't look well wearing black but can't resist its versatility, then look for:

1. Black fabrics that aren't quite matte but that have an extra dimension to them: shiny black satin, black *lace* that lets the skin show through; textured black velvet.

2. Black pieces that are opened around the neck will give your skin tone a lift. You can wear these bare or filled in with a glittered or bright-colored scarf, a creamy-white collar, a shiny jewel, or other light-catching accessory.

• *White, on the other hand, is madly flattering* to almost all women, especially at night in its cream and ivory tones. And it, too, works year in, year out. There's also something particularly dramatic about a woman dressed in white in the middle of winter that's an instant eye-catcher! And a really memorable look that we like on a small woman is the wearing of something pale and soft, like a pale-tinted angora dress for a look that lets you—not your clothes—stand out.

Other good basic colors, depending on your own taste and coloring; pale caramel, silvery gray, deep wine. But whatever your base color, just be sure its a subtle neutral tone that can be paired easily with different accessories to create different looks. While a knitted dress in black, ivory, or beige can be accessorized to work well in a lot of different situations, you're not likely to be able to do that with one in a bright red or a shiny gold.

• *How to work with vibrant colors:* The P.M. accent colors you choose like scarlet, gold, or sapphire blue will usually be brighter than the colors you might wear for day. The reason: Since night lights subdue color, if you pick shades that are toned-down to begin with, they'll lose all their color impact and look grayed-down and dull. Rich wine-dark velvets, by the way, have two great things going for short women: plushy texture and a depth of rich coloring.

Once you own the basics, here's what to add:

1. *Glitter*   All-out glittery pieces are fine for big holiday looks, but don't underestimate the impact of glitter mixed in with some of your basics—it's one fast way to send across the message that you're

P.M. Checks and Balances

When you're dressing for evening, it's a good idea not to go for the whole show. Instead, try zeroing in on *one great thing* and play it up to the hilt. For instance, if you've got great legs, show them off in a long, side-slit skirt, but then cover up on top. Or if you've got a terrific bust and shoulders, go for strapless and one-shouldered tops and keep everything else simple and understated.

The clothes you wear play a part in another kind of checks and balances, too. "When I dress for evening, I decide on what I want to highlight, then I play down everything else because I know I can't carry it all off," said Francine B., a fashion stylist who also hosts her own half hour TV talk show. "That way, even though I'm only five feet one, I never feel overpowered. If I've got on something in a bright color, like my red silk evening jacket, I keep everything else to a minimum so the bright color has no competition. But when I'm wearing a simple beige dress, I jazz it up with a glittered scarf or interesting jewelry or something else in a bright color."

dressed-up. Just don't overdo. A short woman can get more mileage out of one or two glitter-shot pieces than with the flash of a whole getup. A glittery gunmetal gray turtleneck sweater, worn with pleat-front gray flannel pants, has a quiet elegance that can take you almost anywhere and go a lot further than all-out gold lamé. Another plus: Glittery pieces are seasonless—with enough life of their own to take you through a year of parties.

2. *Special pieces*

The other side of classics are the collectible pieces that make your wardrobe special: standout, ornamental versions of any of the basic pieces you own. One particularly good addition for shorter women: anything antique, particularly jackets and long evening dresses. (See chapter 18 for more on antique clothes.)

Emergency Measures: What Do You Do When . . .

you're unsure of the dressing level of a party?
For times like that, a certain planned underdressing is your best
option. Anne Marie, for example, always wears something very
simple that can go either way—like a well-tailored pair of black
silk pants and a collarless black silk shirt. Then, she says, "I'll
take along two pairs of earrings: one very casual, the other
dressy, and maybe a chain necklace or two, all small enough to
carry in an evening bag. As soon as I see which way the general
dress trend is going, I pop on whichever is most appropriate."

*you're caught unprepared—and need something long and
dressy on just two hours notice?*
For just such a last-minute occasion, Allison, who doesn't
sew (so anything that needed hemming was out of the question), went searching after work for a *midcalf* evening skirt.
She found one in black velvet (the bottom half of an embroidered jacket and skirt suit) that worked perfectly as an *ankle-
length* evening skirt on her, no alterations necessary!

*you haven't a minute to change out of what you've been
wearing for work but have to look special for evening?*
That's when instant "look changers" can come to the
rescue. They include:

1. Anything shiny, metallic, or glittered—in small doses:
   an extra gold cuff, a shiny mesh belt, a coppery metallic leather sash, scarves specked with gold glitter.
2. Anything barer—that manages shows a little skin:
   switching a blouse to a camisole; changing a pump for
   a more open, strappier sandal; even unbuttoning a
   blouse button or two. All can do the trick.
3. Intensifying your daytime makeup—plus adding a touch
   of shimmer.
4. Your hair is an accessory, too. If you've got long hair
   and usually wear it loose, put it up. Or vice versa.

FOCUS ON: Designer Bob Mackie

Best known for his glamorous costume designs, as mentioned earlier in this chapter, Bob Mackie has spent his career dressing women of all heights and figure types. Here, he shares his illusion-making know-how (and some fascinating fashion sidelights) with you.

"First of all, if you're short, the lines you wear can never make you look too tall. Also, if you make yourself look thinner, you're going to look taller. Not that being tall is such a great thing in itself, but as far as clothes are concerned the proportion usually looks better when you try to elongate it.

"A woman should analyze herself to figure out what works for her shape and height. In the old days in Hollywood, leading ladies had the big studios to do that for them, and although many actresses were short (like Liz Taylor, Joan Crawford, and Gloria Swanson), you'd never know it by looking at them on the screen. One reason was that all the clothes they wore were perfectly proportioned and scaled down. Even if a woman played a housewife or a secretary, the clothes were designer-made for her body. Today, the smart actresses know how to analyze themselves. Especially after they've been photographed a few times and see themselves on film, they can point out everything that's wrong or right about them. The audience may see them as perfect, but really they have figure problems like anyone else—it's just that they know how to deal with them.

"With shorter women especially, you have to take figure problems into account. If you're short and perfectly proportioned (Jane Powell is a good example of that), you've got a very easy figure to dress. On the other hand, take someone like the late Judy Garland. She was four feet eleven. Her problem was that she had big shoulders and a big bosom on top of a short waist, narrow hips, and a flat behind. On her, as on many short women, an extra five pounds would look like fifteen. The trouble was, when she was at her thin weight, she looked fine from the waist up, but her legs would be too thin; that's when they dressed her in narrow, floor-length skirts. At her heavy weight (and while her legs were still beautiful), they had to camouflage her bigness on top, so they'd show off her legs with tights and high heels, and play down her bosom with jackets. That's really how it should work for every woman; playing up what's good and camouflaging what isn't.

"Theatrically, even if I'm doing clothes for women who are very tall, like Lynda Carter, who's five ten, I never put anything on them that I wouldn't put on a short woman, because on television, you can never tell how short or tall someone is. Raquel Welch is a beautiful woman who's not really tall—just about five five. She's got small hips, small hands and feet, but because of her bust, she looks bigger. And everyone used to think Cher was a huge, tall woman, but remember, she was standing next to a short man. She's really a tiny size four, but with a size eight shoulder. Although she looks wonderful in clothes, she'd have a hard time finding them to fit because of that. Luckily, she can afford to have them made for her or specially altered.

"Wide shoulders can sometimes be an asset, but if they're too wide, they can push a short woman down. Sloping shoulders are another problem; I always think clothes look a little snappier when the shoulders are straight—especially when you're dealing with something tailored. A padded shoulder makes the hips look smaller, and it makes you look taller by giving your body a little more length. It shouldn't be exaggerated, just enough to square off the figure—the way men have always done it."

Dressing for Night

Since P.M. dressing is a Mackie specialty, we wanted to know: How can a short woman look sexy, romantic, or glamorous without coming across as a little girl playing dress-up?

"The clothes you choose for evening should go with your face, hair, figure—and personality. For example, Sally Field, who's about five two, has a wonderful body but a very young face. She might come across as silly in sexy, sexy things—not because of her height but because of the wholesome image she projects. And by 'sexy,' I mean that bare, trying-to-vamp-the-world look. I've done clothes like that for many different women, but they weren't meant to be worn out in public. Those were costumes for the stage only. Actually, I think some of the sexiest evening clothes aren't necessarily the barest or most revealing.

"Generally, I think that when you buy clothes for evening they should be things you can get a lot of wear from—not just one-time-only things (especially with prices as they are today). Separates are terrific in the evening because it means you can take that top and use it with a shorter skirt or pants or whatever. For heavier women I've found that bias-cut dresses can take off as much as ten pounds. But when I say bias, I mean a loose and easy cut—not hugging the figure. Really, the same rules that go for day go for night. It sounds boring to say things like 'you should always wear stockings to match your shoes if you want to look taller,' but it's the truth."

14. Accessories: Add-ons That Add Up to Short Chic

For several chapters now, we've been telling you about the importance of paying attention to detail, and nowhere does that count more than here. To our way of thinking, accessories don't just finish a look, they *define* it by adding character and interest to everything else you're wearing. With accessories, you can turn the most basic clothes into a look that's unique, exciting, and fun. You can experiment with new ways of using standard add-ons. (Wear a necklace as a bracelet? A scarf as a belt? Earrings as pins? Go ahead!) Let your imagination run wild among all the different colors, textures, patterns, and shapes. Because when you come right down to it, accessories are the "toys" of fashion, and toys are meant to be played with. But since every game has its rules, let's go over a few basic ones that apply to all accessory categories.

RULE 1: *When you choose any accessory, your foremost consideration should be the quality of the materials, the uniqueness of the design, and the richness of color and texture.* One good test: Does the item itself give you pleasure when you look at it or touch it? If the answer is yes, chances are you've picked yourself a winner.

RULE 2: *Scale everything down to size.* That doesn't mean you have to wear ditzy little pieces that can be seen only with the aid of a microscope. It does mean that the pieces shouldn't be so big that they make you seem small and/or short by comparison.

RULE 3: *Keep your accessories consistent with the season.* For example, gold and silver bangles and chokers are great for the cold-weather months, but come spring and summer, you'll want something lighter to go with the lighter fabrics of your clothes—naturals like wooden beads, straw bangles, and so on. Another idea: Use accessories to enforce the character of "seasonless" pieces. To winterize a tiered challis skirt, say, just switch from summer sandals to leather boots. Or to summerize a crepe dress, turn in your dark winter pumps for bright little sling-backs.

RULE 4: *Opt for multiples.* One lone skinny bangle is too timid to merit anyone's attention (you might as well not wear any at all). The better way: Wear two or three thin-to-medium-sized bangles at a time. Same goes for scarves. Pins. Necklaces. It's a matter of adding impact. (Remember the one about strength in numbers? It's true!) The only exception: If the piece itself is strong enough to stand on its own. In that case let it be the star.

RULE 5: *Make use of accessories to add color, pattern, and texture*—especially if you've gone in for the "safe, solid, and basic" look in your clothes. As a matter of fact, the more understated the clothes, the more drama you can use in the pieces you accessorize them with. Another important point: When accessories like hats, shoes, gloves, and neck scarves are spiked with bright color, it allows you to add color impact to your look without breaking up the body line.

RULE 6: *Every now and then, do invest in a trendy accessory to update clothes you already own.* In the long run, it will be a lot kinder to your bank account than buying new clothes to keep up with every new trend.

Chic Add-ons from Top to Toe

Hats A man's opinion: "I think tall women in hats look like they're going to topple over, while a short woman who wears them can look so appealing. I like to see a woman who respects her femininity. (After all, there's no reason a woman can't be intelligent, good at her job, *and* feminine—and hats are very feminine.)" Hear, hear! But we should point out that hats can be "iffy" things. The trick to wearing a hat is to look polished in it without looking studiously put-together (as if you tried too hard). But if you're comfortable in them, and they suit you, they can be the ultimate height of chic. Some tips to hang your hat on.

- *If your head is small and hard to fit*, check out the teen department for brimmies, berets, and such, the boys department for driver's caps, and the men's department for caps, fedoras, and other finds. (Unlike most women's hats, men's are sized and some are quite small.)
- *When trying the hat on, study yourself from all angles* as you would when checking a new haircut. The hat you wear should be flattering coming *and* going.
- *If you like wide-brimmed hats, go ahead and wear them.* But exercise moderation and don't make it too wide lest (as one wag put it) the effect be one of "an elf standing under a mushroom."
- *To add inches to your height*, go for a hat with a crown. Often, flat-topped hats "press" you down making you look even shorter.
- *Train your eye to compare the crown of the hat with the face underneath*. If the crown itself is longer or wider than your face, the hat's too big.

Scarves

Tie them on for the quickest way to add pattern and color! The best scarves are soft and flowy—and that goes for everything from silk oblongs to gaily patterned challis squares to long wind-around mufflers. One friend of ours, a confirmed scarf collector, confesses she can hardly walk by a store without buying another. "I wear them in twos and threes, and my favorite has raccoon tails hanging from it." Some good scarf tricks to try:

- *A skinny-knit muffler* wrapped around your neck is one way to soften a tailored suit.
- *Try wrapping a long, nubbly scarf* around the collar of a thin-gauge knit turtleneck to add interest to that basic sweater style.
- *Menswear scarves*—whether in silk or wool—are a super find for shorter women. Menswear patterns are usually scaled down and classic (dapper foulards, tiny paisleys, and skinny-stripe knits, to name a few examples). Also to check out in menswear: knitted ties and silk ascots.
- *If you're big-busted*, you can deemphasize that area by wearing a dark top and a bright neck-tied scarf. The flash of color at the neck coaxes the eye upward and away from the bust.

· *If the color of the top you're wearing isn't as flattering as it should be, swathe your neck with a scarf that is.* Good choices are white, ivory, peach, coral, and pink—complexion flatterers all.

· *An oblong scarf* worn loose with the ends hanging down is a good way to add body-thinning/heightening vertical lines.

Jewelry   Always go for the real thing when you can, and by real we don't necessarily mean gold, silver, or precious stones—though, of course, these are first choices if you can afford them. But real can also include other naturals like wood, stone (semiprecious or otherwise), straw, copper, coral, and the like. Other good bets: quality costume jewelry to wear by itself or mix in with better pieces. For example, if you've got two 14K gold neck chains and one quality imitation gold pin, the latter will bask in the pedigree of the former and look like the real thing, too (and you won't have to tell anyone differently). Look for antique pieces, too—Victorian hanging earrings, Art Deco pins, and such. And do investigate the arty section of town for one-of a-kinds that are works of art in themselves. More pearls of wisdom . . .

· *Earrings* that tilt upward from the lobe or length-adding drop earrings are always a good choice for shorter women. Not good choices: hanging earrings that hang *too* low or any earring that looks outsized next to your face. Another tip: If you have a short neck, overly long hanging earrings will only call attention to it.

· *The watch you wear* should be a good one—it can say a lot about your credibility. And the same goes for the watchband. As alternatives to the usual gold and silver, you may also want to look for a lizard-skin strap or a fine-grain leather or suede.

· *Bangle bracelets* are often a problem for smaller wrists. Some solutions: Scout out the teen department for smaller versions or look for the kind with a hinge and/or snap-on closing. (These are usually made smaller, which is why they need a hinge and snap-on in the first place.) Preferably, the shape of the bangle should be flat against the wrist; rounded versions may look too bulky on you. You could also go for an oval shape, which seems to fit better because it conforms more naturally to the shape of the wrist.

And what about loading up your arms with wonderful large-sized wide bangles and big cuffs? Go ahead. But when you do, let them be your one-and-only accessory statement. Wearing a big three-inch cuff or bangle is all the accessory you can carry when you're short. If you're very petite and find even one three-inch cuff over-powering, create a similar look by wearing *three inches worth of skinny bangles* or two medium-sized cuffs instead of a wide one. This is still fashion but not at the sacrifice of your petite proportions.

• *Long necklaces* can help elongate a petite figure, provided they're not arbitrarily piled on. "A few strands of beads in different sizes worn together can be fine on a petite woman," says Siri Vail, fashion coordinator for accessories at Filenes, "especially when the petite woman wears them with a simple crepe de Chine chemise that has a thin vertical pin-striped line (which is making her look taller anyway). And pendants are an excellent way for a small woman to lengthen her look. On a blouse with a full-cut sleeve like a blouson or a dolman, a pendant hanging below the bustline can make a short woman look taller by deemphasizing the boxy shape of the blouse." (For more accessories tips from Siri, see Focus, this chapter.)

• *Short pendants*, made up of two or three objects vertically hung underneath one another, can also help elongate the look of a

Jewelry is one of the best ways the shorter woman can make a fashion impression without cutting her height. The reason: Jewelry directs the eye where the petite woman wants it to go—upward toward the neck and shoulders (which is why a drop earring or necklace always lengthens your look).

There are generally two kinds of jewelry looks: hard (chunky necklaces, geometric pins, bold cuffs) and soft (feminine pearls, antique pendants, delicate drop earrings). The Short Chic guidelines: With soft looks, you can afford to wear more accessories on any given outfit. With bolder pieces, follow the principle of making just one statement. A large choker, for example, should get tiny stud earrings (or none at all), no hair ornament, a belt in the same color as your clothing so you don't draw attention to both your neck and your waist (that's cutting you off twice!).

The same principle applies to a big, free-form pin, an oversized bracelet, or any belt that's wider than two inches—go for just one at a time. *Special tip:* When you do go for bold accessories, a higher-heeled shoe will give you a little added height to help carry them off.

high-collared blouse or big-sleeved shirt. As for pearls—they're an accessory basic, and for the shorter woman, we think the graduated strand (as opposed to the matched) works better because it's more graceful and delicate-looking.

• *Pins are especially impressive* when you wear a collection of them. When you do, keep them in the same mood (you would not, for example, stick a plastic Mickey Mouse pin next to a diamond-topped gold lapel pin. If it comes to that, you shouldn't even *own* a Mickey Mouse pin or any jewelry that's even questionably cutesy). Terrific look: one smashing pin stuck onto a saucy beret.

Belts   The two main reasons for wearing a belt are to add texture and polish and to control the volume or shape of a dress or top. (These days the purpose of keeping one's pants up doesn't even enter into it.) In some cases, a belt can also help to shorten the length of a too-long knitted dress. But that's not all a belt can do for you . . .

• *If you're short-waisted*, a skinny belt's your best bet—but you already knew that. What you mightn't have known: A skinny belt that's loosely buckled so it vees slightly in the front can also make a short waist look longer.
• *If you're long-waisted*, your belt can go wider—even so, don't go too wide or it may accentuate short legs.
• *Color tricks to play at your waist:* To make a short waist look longer, match the belt to your top. To make a long waist look shorter, match the belt to your bottoms. And to make a thickish waist look thinner, go for a dark belt.
• *Another way to shrink a thick waist:* Wrap it twice around with a medium-wide fabric belt with a slight stiffness to it. It will work like a cincher.
• *A sash that hangs down from its knot* is another easy way to add a width-cutting vertical line.
• *If you've got hips*, don't ever cinch a belt too tightly—especially important if you're belting a jacket.
• *If you're wearing a large-buckled belt*, don't wear it in conjunction with a large bracelet or watch. During the day your hands are usually in the vicinity of your waist area, and you don't want anything "fighting" the belt. Instead, go with a bold clip earring—your ears are far enough away from your waist to make the look work.

Gloves   Need we tell you that mittens are not a good choice if you're trying to live down a little-girl image? (No, we didn't think so.) But aside from that, anything goes for gloves. As one woman we talked to put it: "I've got a pair of bright, multicolored knitted gloves that were hand-made in Uruguay. And when I wear my black Calvin Klein reefer and black boots and look all polished and professional, I wear those gloves to show I'm *me*—and not just a recruiting poster for the working woman." Some other gloves to love . . .

- *Cashmere gloves* are superwarm, less expensive than leather, and usually fit small hands well.
- *When you do go for leather gloves* (lined or unlined), opt for the pointy-fingered kind to make hands look longer, more graceful, and delicate.
- *If you have small hands* that mean a difficult fit, always shop at the beginning of the season (and never settle for a size too big that looks it).
- *If you can only afford one pair of good leather gloves*, try to find them in go-with-everything mahogany or burgundy.
- *If you like to own a collection of gloves*, don't be afraid to experiment with colors like bright fuchsia, yellow, or emerald green. They're one way to add a splash of interest without breaking up the body line because gloves are on the extremity of the body.
- *For in-between seasons*, you may want to get a pair of string knit and leather gloves which look great on a smaller hand.

Hosiery

Funny thing about stockings: The only time some women pay them any mind is when they run. If you're shorter than average, however, you can't afford to be so blasé. Especially when you consider how much the right stockings, tights, or socks can add to your height . . .

- *The best way to stretch your legs*—by matching your stockings to your shoes. (Translation of "matching": anything from a stocking that's faintly tinted the same color as the shoe to heavier tights or socks that exactly match the shoe in shade and color intensity). This trick works even if the shoe and stocking don't match the skirt. And by matching stockings and shoes to pants, you create the longest possible line of color from waist to toe.
- *When you wear evening sandals in a bright color*, stockings should echo the color in a tint or be in a shoe-complementing natural.
- *A black skirt always takes a black- or gray-tinted stocking.*

Skin-toned legs between a dark skirt and a dark shoe are too body-cutting.

- *Contrary to what some short women believe, you can wear patterned stockings*—as long as the colorings are subdued, most patterns work fine. The best choices: small-scale patterns, of course, like tiny diamonds or dots, or herringbone V's. Other pattern tips: A dark vertical stripe that's not too wide will help make a leg look thinner, whereas light horizontals or wide diamond patterns will help add weight.

- *About what to wear with what:* The sportier the shoe and the lower the heel, the thicker or more opaque the stocking should be. The dressier and higher the shoe, the sheerer the stocking. *Note:* Be particularly careful of ribbed wool tights and leg warmers. If you like to wear them, pick a thin, vertical-ribbed stripe or plain no-texture color; stay away from bulky knits and exceptionally bold patterns that draw the eye down.

- *Short socks or knee-highs* should be kept in reserve for casual skirts only or for under pants. Even if the whole outfit rates an A for spiffy, socks and a skirt aren't going to help your credibility in a conservative office. You say you've got a pair of Argyle knee-highs that you love? Wear them under a longer skirt and they'll look like tights instead of girls' prep school knee-barers. Or save them to liven up the look of tailored wool trousers.

- *The best way to test for true stocking color* when buying is to hold the stocking against your inner forearm. Testing against the back of the hand won't give you an accurate reading because, for most of the year at least, your hands will be darker than your legs.

Shoes Although many women may not realize it, the right shoe can carry its own in the inch-adding department—and we're not just talking about the height of the heel. (For foot notes on that, see box.) There's also a lot that can be accomplished with shape and color.

- *We've already said that shoes matched to stockings will extend the length of your leg.* And that same principle applies to those women who wear beige and taupe stocking shades more often than not. If you're one of them, opt for shoes in beiges, taupes, banana, or light tan.

- *If your legs are thin,* light, natural shoe shades will help make them look heavier. So will delicate, unclunky shoes.

- *If your legs are heavy*, stay away from delicate shoes; your legs will look only heavier by contrast.
- *A shoe with a vamp that dips* into a V or scoops low and narrow will also help lengthen the leg, whereas a horizontal or high vamp will do just the opposite.
- *Ankle straps or T-straps* are instant leg-shorteners—avoid them unless shoes and stockings are both in the same shade and have the same intensity of color.
- *To make a foot look longer and narrower*, go for a tapered (as opposed to rounded) toe. It doesn't have to be needle-sharp or narrow enough to make you feel as if you've got two toes too many, just so it suggests a point.
- *Shoes, like clothes, should be divided by the season:* A dark leather pump with a gauzy summer dress will look as out of place as Christmas pudding at a July Fourth clambake.
- *Always keep shoes polished and in good repair.* A shoe that's scuffed or run-down at the heel is a poor reflection on you—and it won't do very much for the clothes you wear it with either.
- *If you wear a small size*, always shop at the beginning of the season—and we mean the *very day* the new styles come into the stores. As many tiny-footed women have discovered, small sizes are the least well stocked and the first to move off the shelves.
- *Another tip for the small of foot:* If you haven't done so already, do investigate the designer shoe department. Yes, we know designer shoes cost the earth, but you'll be getting softer, more supple leathers, better workmanship, and sleeker styling that really know how to flatter a small foot. Anne Marie, who has always been an insatiable shoe buyer, recalls the first time she discovered the designer shoe salon at Bergdorf's: "I thought I had died and gone to heaven! Instead of asking for a five and then waiting until the salesman came back to tell me that the only size he had was a seven, there were shelves and shelves of fives—all in scaled-down, delicate styles that looked great on me."
- *In the boot department:* Boots are one of your best bets for creating a leggy lengthening line from skirt to toe, particularly when you're wearing longer skirt lengths. (The high boot balances the look of *more* skirt above.) If you're very petite and find boots are often *too* high for you, look for a medium-high boot—on you it will be high without covering

The Great Heel Controversy

When you talk about the height-making potential of a shoe, the first thing most women think about is the height of the heel—and what a lot of controversy that subject sets off! Fashion editors will tell you that "a short woman shouldn't wear too high a heel; it keels her body forward and makes her look ridiculous." The health-conscious will tell you that any high heel will throw your back out of whack and cause a number of unpleasant things to happen to your insides. And short women themselves have always been divided between the "I'll never give up my three-inch heels" school on the one side and the "forget height, I want to be comfortable" school on the other. Well, here's our view of the matter. . . .

Your choice of heel height shouldn't depend so much on your height as on the length of your foot. The heel itself should never be so high for your foot that it pitches you forward. If you wear an average size 7, your foot can better accommodate a higher heel. But if you're a size 5, anything higher than a 2½-inch heel (measuring the inside of the heel facing the sole) is going to cause you abject misery, if it doesn't actually put you in traction. Even then, you'll probably want to save the 2½-incher for evening wear only.

A good alternative for women who want to look taller and *be comfortable:* a shoe with a medium-high heel that's slim and tapered. The slim shape of the heel itself will make the shoe (and you) look taller and more graceful, and it will be adding substantial inches to your height without etching lines of agony on your face.

As for flats, no shoe you wear should ever be pancake flat. Even a 1-inch elevation helps add to your height, and that certainly won't interfere with your comfort. In this category, you'll find wedge-heeled sandals, espadrilles, ghillies, low-heeled Oxfords, and so on. The point is that you should always avail yourself of an inch-adding opportunity, and heels are one of the best around.

A final word about heel height: As a general fashion rule, the shorter the skirt, the lower the heel; the longer the skirt, the higher the heel. Pants worn on the long side, whether wide or narrow, can take a lower or higher heel depending on your preference. Short wide pants, however, will usually look better with a medium-to-low heel, and short (ankle-high) tapered pants will work better with a high heel.

the knee. Short boots? They're a terrific fashion look and great for tucking pants into (a neat trick for controlling the volume of wide pants). Short boots won't necessarily make you look taller (especially if your boot contrasts with the pants tucked into it), but in this case it would be a matter of chic overriding short. If you like the look, by all means have fun with it.

You know all those fashion articles that tell small women not to carry big bags? Well, for the most part they're right. A small woman can look weighted down carrying a bag designed for a woman 5'8". Trouble is, small women have as much assorted paraphernalia to tote as tall women. So how can you cope?

Bags

- *If a shoulder bag is what you're after*, look for one that's scaled to your size but soft-sided. You'll be amazed at how expandable those soft sides can be.
- *Don't make do with a shoulder bag strap that's too long.* If the length can't be adjusted by a buckle, take it to the shoemaker and have a few inches chopped off as needed.
- *When buying a bag, always check your image in a mirror* to see how the two of you look together. Forget what the saleslady tells you, if it looks outsized to you—even a little—start looking for another bag.
- *A clutch bag should always look neat and flat*—not like a stuffed flounder. It, too, should be scaled to size, and if you have the small-bag problem that comes from attempting to defy a basic law of physics (i.e., no two things can occupy the same space at the same time), try double bagging. How it works: Use a big carryall type bag (in leather or something equally attractive and chic) to hold all your gear, and also carry a small, neat clutch for absolute essentials (wallet, keys, and so on). To and from work, you can stow the clutch in the carryall and remove the clutch when you go out to lunch and don't want to cart the whole shebang.
- *The style of a bag* should be as individual as the woman who buys it. So do experiment with interesting shapes (as long as you don't get too cute about it). One good rule, however: Do avoid a bag that's too wide. It will make a figure-cutting horizontal.
- *Where color is concerned*, you might want to avoid what one editor we once knew called "the matchy-matchy look." A bag doesn't have to match your shoes. Just make sure that it's

the same color family (say a taupe bag with dark brown shoes) or that it doesn't clash outright. Also, you may want to use your bag as a source of splashy color. A little leather clutch in a parrot-bright yellow or green can be a marvelous focus of interest for underplayed dressing.

- *For evening, you'll need a small collection of bags* to cover every occasion. Say a black suede and leather clutch, a multi-toned snakeskin, and, for very special, a hard gold metal minaudière.

- *A word about luggage:* As far as your height is concerned, the only requirement is that you don't have to lean over to one side to keep your suitcase from dragging on the ground. If you really need the space of a very large piece, you can either buy two smaller pieces (one could have a shoulder strap for easier carrying) or save your back and call a porter!

FOCUS ON: Siri Vail

Siri Vail, at 5'1½" has a special eye for accessories. A former Vogue accessories editor, now fashion coordinator for accessories at Filene's in Boston, she gave us these special tips on how to wear shoes, belts, bags, hose, and jewelry—and make them work for your height.

"Generally, the neck is one of the best areas that the shorter woman can play with where accessories are concerned," Siri told us. "It won't cut your figure at all to wear a large necklace or pin, as long as you wear them properly. A scarf or pin on a high-necked blouse (which is already elongating your figure) worn with a simple, narrow belt (or no belt at all), plus a one-and-a-half to two-inch heel, can give the shorter woman a very tall look. When the neck is the focal point, though, don't wear large earrings. They're best when you're wearing an interesting belt because the waist and ear are far enough away from each other so the accessories won't compete with each other, or overwhelm you.

"Chokers look best worn with a solid or small-printed or striped blouse," Siri continued. "One with a bold center can work nicely on a blouse with a stripe, providing the stripes are thin verticals. The only necklace I wouldn't suggest for shorter women are the wide (three inches) Victorian-type neck collars. They tend to shorten the neck, which is what a tall woman may want to do, but a short woman shouldn't.

"With a high-collared blouse," she added, "a petite woman can make herself look taller by wearing her hair up, and adding drop earrings and a discreet belt. In this case, she could also afford to wear an interesting shoe or a sock with more detail to it (like a textured pattern or metallic) because the earring is far from the shoe and won't cut her look in half like a belt would."

Generally, Siri recommends that belts be kept as simple as possible. If a petite woman wants to wear a wide or an ornamented belt or a gutsy rope, she should wear them with separates in the same color family so that the waist becomes the sole focal point.

"A belt should be used to add color or textural interest to an otherwise plain look," she advised. "Mixing coordinated separates of different colors with striped or textured belts should be left to the taller woman who can carry that look off. The exception: If the separates are very close in color tone, like an ivory blouse with a pale peach skirt. That could take an ornamented belt with the same two colors in it—in this case, the accessory could actually help to pull the two colors together and lengthen the total look."

Most short women find very wide cummerbund belts difficult to wear because they tend to shorten and cut the figure. "If the wide belt were in the same color as the separates, a petite woman could get away with this look *if* she also wore a higher-heeled shoe," Siri commented. Another effective way: "Try a monochromatic look—a wine silk blouse with matching pants, for example, and a wide wine-colored cummerbund sash but with a surface texture or the slight hint of another color. And a belt that is larger in the front and tapers off to thin strips that tie in the back is better and more flattering than a belt that is three to four inches all around."

As for big buckles ("like the ones by Barry Kieselstein-Cord"): "Everyone loves this look no matter how tall they are because it is dramatic," Siri said. "Petite women can wear them, too, if the buckle is large, but the belt is only an inch wide or less. A skinny quarter-inch leather belt with three large hammered brass discs laced throughout the belt would be one style that a petite woman can carry off successfully."

More special pointers . . .

• If you love shawls, pick one with a small print (or if the print is large, wear it with solid-color separates or dresses). Tie it neatly, knotted on one side of your shoulder, so you shorten it by the way you tie—that way, it will look cleaner and not overpower you.

• Interesting hair ornaments, like cascading gold leaves and flower combs, are fine on the shorter woman but not worn with a big necklace and earrings. When you wear noticeable hair ornaments, any other accessories you wear should be at the waist or below (like a belt, a shoe, or a bracelet), and not in the proximity of the hair ornament.

15. Wedding Gowns: Elongating Tips for the Bride

What goes into a beautiful wedding? Lots of things, and a beautiful wedding dress is a classic ingredient. However you picture your ideal bridal look to be—romantic and old-fashioned, elegant and sophisticated, or as traditional as the proverbial "something old, something new"—finding it is a piece of cake . . . *if* you know what to look for.

The most important thing to know about wedding dresses, first off, is that most are custom-ordered. (Many, in fact, are beaded and embellished with the kind of hand-detailing you'll find only in couture!) Then they are carefully fitted on you to conform *to your own specific measurements—which means you don't have to worry about fit*. Not only are sleeve lengths and hems adjusted to size with loving care, but more painstaking alterations are performed as a matter of course: necklines can be lowered or raised, depending on what you find most flattering; bodices carefully tapered so they fit with nary a wrinkle; even sleeve treatments can be changed (a dress *sans* sleeves, for example, can be ordered with sleeves).

Taking It Step by Step

Before you go hunting for the perfect dress, read over the Short Chic concepts in the previous chapters and note what applies: the most flattering necklines, the most body-lengthening dress shapes, the prettiest sleeve treatments, the fabrics that best add to the illusion of height. Then incorporate those facts with your own four wedding day essentials.

1. The time and day of your wedding (a Saturday afternoon affair is apt to be more formal than a Sunday midday event).
2. The season (satin can be lovely in November, but hot and heavy in May).
3. The degree of formality and general mood of your ceremony and reception.
4. How much money you want to spend.

Next, leaf through some of the current issues of the top bridal magazines. Because of the tremendous variety of styles available, whatever your height, weight, and figure type, one dress is bound to strike you as "something special." *Note:* Since bridals are custom-ordered, do start shopping early—*at least six months before the big day* if you're planning a formal wedding with all the trimmings. This will give you plenty of time for alterations, plus ample time for the dress to be ready for formal portraits, and for bridesmaids' gowns to be delivered and altered.

Height-adding Guidelines Here are some inch-adding tips that both we and the fashion editors at *Brides* magazine recommended for the under 5'4" bride.

- *Look for fabrics that are soft*, supple, and that won't overwhelm you. Lace—flat, delicate, and feminine—is ideal; so is sheer silk chiffon. Creamy-colored satin can be sensuously soft and fluid if it is of very fine quality. Taffeta, however, can be iffy if you're short, as any fabric that tends toward stiffness can be. "Petites in taffeta tend to look very young," commented one bridal consultant whom we spoke with. "The fairy princess look, you know."
- *Look for details that lure the eye upward* (special interest around the neck and shoulders, an intricate beaded lace bodice, a high Victorian neckline) rather than details around the hem that draw the eye downward.
- *Some of the most lengthening dress shapes* are those with neat

seams (the princess or A-line, for example), long vertical appliqués, and narrow body-tracing lines. A slim skirt with vertical lines, like those created by pleating, can also add the illusion of height.

- *If you've always dreamed of a luxurious full-skirted bridal look*, go ahead—just keep the skirt in a wonderful, soft flowing fabric and add additional length with a graceful train.

- *Empire-waist gowns* are known for adding the illusion of height—and are one of the most frequently suggested styles for under 5′4″ brides. Combined with a high Victorian neckline, an Empire waist can be especially height-stretching and torso-lengthening for a short-waisted petite bride. Most bridal consultants advise against a low-necked Empire, however. As one explained, "The look of the bust, squeezed between the neckline and the skirt can be terribly foreshortening." Since Empires go in and out of bridal vogue, a slightly raised natural waistline can be a chic alternative that still allows you the gracefulness of a long, sweeping skirt.

- *Natural-waist gowns* with fullish "ballroom" skirts aren't out of the question. But they do work best if you're on the taller side of short, with a little middle, and as long as you keep the skirt very soft and fluid.

- *About necklines:* The charm of a high-necked wedding gown is ideal for continuing the line of the dress upward (and best for short-waisted types) but it is by no means your only option. You can also add height by lengthening the look of your neck with a discreetly veed bodice or with a sculptured and seductive Queen Anne neckline that hugs the nape of the neck in the back and falls into a low-scooped or scalloped sweetheart neckline in the front. An off-the-shoulder scoop that provides a hint of cleavage is another way to stand tall because it lets your torso rise beautifully above your gown.

- *What about sleeves?* Broad puffed sleeves, elaborate leg-o'-mutton styles and such are apt to be overpowering, but fullness can work when you confine it to the lower part of your arm rather than cluttered up near your neck and shoulders. Tiny, puffed, short sleeves or caps, although demure and pretty, can be oversweet on a petite bride—so if sweet and innocent isn't the look you're going for, you would do better to avoid them.

- *Your headpiece and veil* are two of the best ways to add to your tall image at the altar because they lift and draw the eye's focus upward. The most flattering styles: anything that's high-crowned—an inch-adding floral circlet, a jewel-encrusted tiara, a crowned style (called a Camelot), even a Juliet cap when it's set back on your head and "lifted" with a mass of carefully draped tulle. As for hats, small-brimmed ones add more height than others do. What doesn't work: a wide-brimmed floppy hat (pretty but stunting to a petite bride) and a mantilla because it drapes downward and closes in on your face rather than opening it.

Note: Remember, the veil itself should be carefully proportioned to your height. Since a full-length veil is often overpowering even on a taller bride, we'd suggest trying a sheer fingertip style—it's a particularly graceful length with all the elegance of a longer veil but more delicate, less overwhelming.

Figure Flatterers

Your height won't be your only consideration when shopping for a wedding dress. You also want one that'll do the most for your particular figure type. Some pointers:

- *To balance wide hips and a big bottom*, try a gently flaring skirt combined with a full-sleeved top.
- *To deemphasize a wide waist*, try a pretty tucked bodice or slenderizing peplumed style. Avoid tight cummerbunds that only bring it under scrutiny.
- *To make less of a big bust*, avoid Empire waists that come up high under your bosom. Stay away from too-clingy fabrics like jersey, and keep bodice details centered, not out to the sides.
- *To show off a pretty bust*, a sweetheart neckline or deep scalloped scoop can be particularly flattering.
- *Narrow shoulders look well* when draped with capelets or cape collars.
- *For an overall slimming effect*, try a slightly lifted waistline and an A-shaped figure-skimming skirt.

Short Chic Shopping Tips for Bridal Gowns

Although most of the styles designed for the bride of average height and figure will look lovely on the shorter-than-average bride when adjusted to size, many bridal salons carry entire lines of petite bridal dresses, which, for the short-waisted bride with a petite body build, offer an excellent fit. For the most part, these gowns run along

Junior Petite lines (sizes 1, 3, 5, and so on) rather than Regular Petite measurements (sizes 2, 4, 6, and so on).

One of the best among the petite bridals is *Priscilla of Boston's Teeny* line, where you can find the same kind of exquisite detailing the Priscilla gowns are known for, but scaled down to size. Priscilla is also the only house that does a scaled-to-size veil as well. Other choices: A limited selection of Petite styles at the *House of Bianchi*; then there's *William Cahill*, *Brides Choice*, *Bridallure* (a division of Alfred Angelo), *Petite Place*, and *Miniatures*.

Keep in mind that although these Petite lines offer excellent proportions, there's no reason to limit your selection to them, since all bridal gowns are altered to fit anyway.

16. Maternity Dressing: Looking Tall When You're Dressing for Two

"I resent being treated like a fashion dropout just because I'm pregnant. I have to see clients and go to business meetings, and I can't afford not to look polished and pulled together. And I'm *not* going to wear baby blue smock tops with little animals printed on them."

Phyllis K., 5′2¼″, San Diego, California

We won't deny that taller women seem to carry their pregnancies with more ease; we worked with one 5′9″ editor on a day-to-day basis and didn't realize she was pregnant till she was well into her seventh month. The fact is that the twenty-five pounds or so gained in the course of your pregnancy represents a much smaller percentage of a taller woman's total body weight—so the change in shape isn't so drastic. But ah, if you're short, it's a whole other ball game—those twenty pounds can make an enormous difference—short women look proportionately bigger and bulkier.

At the same time, fashion expectations don't just up and disappear when you're pregnant, especially if you're working. But the fashion guidelines that have served you up until this point now need a little revising. This time—for the next few months at least—you're dressing for a different body, with a different shape—not taller but wider—and the clothes you'll want will have different demands placed on them as well.

In your first trimester, you'll look pretty much the way you usually do, only a little thicker around the middle. If that bothers you, don't let it. In just a few short weeks, there'll be no mistaking the condition you're in. The advantage: you can get by with most of your regular clothes, and if you're slim to begin with (and, of course, depending on how you carry), they may even hold into your fourth, fifth, and sixth months. Another point, and one we feel strongly about: the fact that you'll look best and feel happiest and most comfortable in clothes that most resemble your prepregnancy style. If you always liked dressing tailored, or tweedy, or *very* feminine, you still will. Just because you're pregnant doesn't mean your personal style will have undergone a sudden transformation.

One good example of keeping your style though pregnant: Sandy J., twenty-eight years old, 5'3", a display designer for a major department store (who just so happened on our questionnaire while pregnant). She writes: "Right now, I'm pregnant—six months—feel great and, I think, look great. For work I am living in leggings and big sweaters or big sweaters worn as minidresses with thick, patterned hose and flats. For dress-up occasions I wear elastic-waist pants and a long smock top or silk tunic, capes, and unconstructed jackets."

Very modern, very interesting. And although not for everyone certainly, in Sandy's line of work where what she wears has to express a sure grasp of trends, an up-to-the-minute creativity, it's right. And not far off the mark from her prepregnancy style.

The word on color . . . Your best colors will still be your best colors, although you might find yourself reaching for them in their darker, more toned-down versions. (Darker shades, being more elongating, will give you sleeker line.) Another reason that many women, short or otherwise, go for deeper colors while pregnant, aside from the slimming effects is the fact that maternity clothes get worn over and over again, and you probably don't want to call attention to the fact. Also for practical reasons: It's a good idea to color-coordinate your pregnancy wardrobe so that you'll get the most use out of each item—a shirt that will work with both a jumper and with pants; a jacket that goes over pants *and* over a dress.

As your pregnancy advances, there is one overall rule to stick with: that you'll probably look most attractive and least cumbersome in clothes that are close to the body . . . somewhere.

For example, although a top may be sort of wide or blousoned through the body, it should fit you nice and neat through the neck and shoulders. The same thing goes for pants—tapered ones will be better looking than those that are wide or baggy because they'll emphasize the areas where you haven't gained weight.

Another thing, fabrics. Yes, there are lots of less-than-good-looking synthetics out there. And yes, we know that synthetics are easy to care for. But when you're pregnant, your body temperature tends to go up a few notches, so whatever the weather, you're going to be a little warmer than everyone else. This is why clothes that are loose and unconstricting, that keep your body cool and aerated, are a must. And, as we said before, generally that means natural fibers. Whenever you can (and we *know* it's not easy) seek out cottons and thin wool jersey, cotton flannel, pinwale corduroy, silk, and the kind of wool challis that falls close to the body. Your best warm-weather choices: airy cotton muslins and voiles, non-see-through gauzes, and the like. Try to avoid heavy wools and bulky tweeds, of course, "layered-look" clothing, and any synthetics that won't breathe. Sweaters and knitted sweatery-type dresses, usually a short-woman plus, will be itchy and uncomfortable now and should be bypassed for the "duration."

One advantage to being short and pregnant when it comes to fashion—that if you're normally within ten pounds or so of your ideal weight (which means if you're under 5'4" and wear anywhere from a size 2 to a size 10), you can probably get away with buying regular clothes in a size or two larger than you usually would for much of your pregnancy. In your very last months, however, you will want to check out the maternity selection, at least when it comes to pants.

As for specifics, the following list can help in planning your pregnancy wardrobe . . .

• *Tops:* Short tops are best avoided. They'll make you look shorter and wider. Since many regulation maternity tops are cut to fall about crotch-length on women of average height, short women shouldn't have much trouble finding ones that are long enough. The most attractive styles are those that are yoked, falling from the shoulder line and not from under the bust. These will make you look slimmer and less bulky. Tunics, no surprise, are an A-1 choice. At one wedding we attended recently, the bride's best friend, 5'2", was pregnant—and sensational-looking—in a long, glamorous red silk tunic ("Lady Madonna," she said) over narrow, pull-on pants. A tunic like that (in silk or any thin dressy fabric), cut on the bias so the fullness flows *in* and not *out*, for dressy wear, and one in a more casual fabric for every day, could turn out to be your pregnancy mainstays. As for sleeves, full ones are okay, but only if the fullness falls near your wrist, not up near the shoulder.

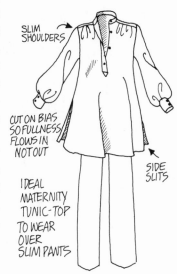

SLIM SHOULDERS

CUT ON BIAS SO FULLNESS FLOWS IN NOT OUT

SIDE SLITS

IDEAL MATERNITY TUNIC-TOP TO WEAR OVER SLIM PANTS

• *Skirts:* In the early months of pregnancy, you can rely on any of your regular drawstring waist and elastic-waist pull-on skirts to be indispensable. But, later, you'll probably find you won't look that good in skirts anymore or feel that comfortable. Reason: Skirts and other two-piece maternity outfits are binding and height-chopping, particularly on short women, and they will only make you look wider (especially if the skirt and top are in two different colors). Keep those skirts in easy reach, however—they'll be perfect right after delivery.

If you're addicted to dressing in skirts, there are ways to go about it naturally. First, do buy only those skirts that come with a top to match and take special care to tie in your shoe and stocking colors. As for skirt length, we'd suggest going a little *longer* than your ideal, to balance your weight above. *Note:* If you think the hem on your maternity skirt or dress is falling unevenly in the front, it's not. Maternity garments are usually cut a little longer in the front—the extra length will be taken up as the baby grows.

• *Pants:* Pants can certainly give you a lean, slimmer line, especially when you wear them with a longish tunic, as suggested earlier, or with an unconstructed wrap jacket worn open. We'd suggest sticking with bottoms in basic dark colors and bringing in the brights for the accessories. One woman we know, 5'3", conducted business as usual while pregnant in this getup, and she looked stylish and comfortable: narrow black drawstring pants ("I wore them at least three times a week," she said); a stretchy black shell with a thin black wool jersey kimono wrapped over it; sheer, black knee-high socks; and bright raspberry low-heeled sandals.

Another nice pants option, for weekends or after-hours: overalls —the oversized men's kind, dyed maybe a bright color like lilac or red. Worn over a striped or plaid shirt, overalls can look great and are "expandable." (When you've lost your waistline, your sense

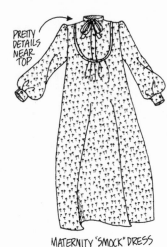

PRETTY DETAILS NEAR TOP

MATERNITY "SMOCK" DRESS

A GREAT BASIC

MATERNITY WRAP DRESS

of humor doesn't automatically go with it.)

• *Dresses:* A tried-and-true favorite because they're exceptionally easy to look good in and require little fussing. Look for dresses in small patterns, with pretty detailing like pleats or tucks, interesting collar treatments, and soft, attractive colors or with thin vertical stripes. Deborah G., 5′2½″, found that a terrific rust-brown French cotton flannel smock dress was one item she wore constantly while pregnant. High-necked and close-to-the-shoulder, it worked for business with medium-heeled, rust-colored pumps and on weekends with tooled cowboy boots.

Loose roomy ethnic-style dresses and Indian-print dresses are also alternatives to traditional maternity garb *if* you work in a casual office (or for weekends) and *if* you like the style to begin with. Another tip: For casual wear in the summer, search out the full, bare cotton sundresses. In warm weather, a petite pregnant woman can carry off a bare, cotton-printed dress better than a tall woman can (especially if she's got slim, pretty arms) without looking "massive."

A note about hemming: If you're buying nonmaternity dresses, remember to have them hemmed longer in the front than in the back. (The excess fabric gets "lifted" up, as your pregnancy advances.) Before measuring, you might want to tuck a small pillow underneath the dress to "guesstimate" your eighth-month size.

• *Jumpers:* Jumpers got gold-medal accolades from nearly every woman we spoke with. They look neat over a T-shirt in the summer, and one in pinwale corduroy over a roomy Oxford-cloth man's shirt or a stretchy cotton-knit turtleneck can be terrific when it's cooler.

Linda P., 5′1″, a Washington D.C.-based finance officer, built her working pregnancy wardrobe around three jumpers last year: one in dark green wool, one in a light gray pin-striped wool ("like men's suit material," she said), and one in burgundy velvet. "I wore the jumpers over different blouses, most with self-ties, in different colors—white, pink, pearl-gray, pin-striped, and with a long strand of pearls or gold chains. Sometimes, I added my regular tweed blazer worn open. It worked just fine, and I always felt professional-looking."

• *Jackets and coats:* Granted a jacket will be hard to find—and to look good in—in your last few months. But for a time, you can count on getting away with wearing your own jacket or blazer worn open, as Linda and a lot of other women found themselves doing. Another—very chic—option that we're especially fond of: the look of a hip-length kimono-style jacket. (Not only is it unconstructed, which means you won't look or feel "upholstered" as a lot of pregnant women complain, but it can be worn again, belted, right after delivery.) We like the look of a kimono jacket so much and think it's so versatile during pregnancy that if you can't find one in your local stores, we'd suggest sewing one yourself or having one made. One four-months pregnant friend of ours brought in a few yards of rose-colored cashmere knit and an ordinary short cotton kimono robe ("the kind you can buy in Azuma") to her tailor, who copied the kimono in the knit, line for line.

Because you'll be warmer than usual, you may not need to invest in a special winter coat. A bought or borrowed cape and plenty of wrapping shawls and scarves, plus your own winter coat, may do just fine. As for rainwear, slick ponchos are water-repellent and inexpensive, and they look the same on everyone, regardless of height.

• *Shoes:* You'll want to trade in your higher heels for lower ones (and for shoes about a half size larger, by the way), since your feet are carrying around more than they're used to. Still, you can use fancy footwork to add to your style. An assistant buyer from Seattle, 5'1½", pregnant with her first child, wrote to us saying she's planned her pregnancy wardrobe around a very limited color scheme—navy and white—but added color with about half a dozen flat-heeled shoes—in red, blue, green, lavender, yellow, and rose.

• *Accessories:* You may find that, for the first time, you can carry off a fashion you never could before. Like a cape. Or a broad-brimmed hat. Bolder and chunkier jewelry. So do experiment . . .

• Try long bright-patterned scarves worn looped around your neck—they're elongating color-adders.

• Any accessory worn at the neck raises the eye upward and draws attention away from your waist. To try: scarves, unusual necklaces, especially pretty earrings, even hair combs or hair ornaments can do the trick.

• In all cases, the way you look from the neck up becomes even more important when you're pregnant, so you may also want to try different ways with your hair and your makeup. One makeup pointer: Your skin tone (as well as the degree of oiliness or dryness) is apt to change during pregnancy. Your complexion could be rosier or more sallow, so be sure to adjust your foundation makeup accordingly. In the latter case, you might also try adding skin-brightening accessories for a pickup of color.

Two Personal Viewpoints

Gail Malles, 5'2", is a fashion merchandising editor who has two small children. Lois Letz, also 5'2", is a fashion editor who covers the junior sportswear market. At the time we spoke with her, she was five months pregnant with her first baby. Both women worked out two different approaches to an on-the-job pregnancy wardrobe.

GAIL: "Without question, shorter women have a bigger problem looking good while pregnant—being shorter accentuates the fact. I gained twenty pounds, and when you're shorter, the weight gain is much more noticeable. My stomach was enormous—it was like I had put a football under my clothes. So to compensate, I felt I had to be exceptionally well groomed and pulled together.

"I never wore pants, except at home; they just weren't flattering on me. I also avoided two-piece outfits and stayed strictly with dresses. I found those by Laura Ashley worked really well for me, but they wouldn't if you have a large bust. I also favored clothes with smaller patterns and made sure they were narrow at the shoulders and avoided sweatery tops or anything too bright. I wore things that were fitted but not too full, and that had sleeves that were a little puffed or slightly tapered.

"My favorite items were two Laura Ashley dresses, which I still wear, by the way. One was a bluish gray; the other a pinky color. (I found I needed a little color.) I think if you wear black all the time it's sort of obvious what you're trying to do, and it will make people notice even more that you're pregnant. I was very fussy that the dress lengths were perfect and was constantly going to the dressmaker so that my dresses wouldn't be shorter in the front.

"I stayed away from most accessories but bought things with interesting details—the two dresses had self-tie bows. Sometimes I would wear little blouses underneath the dresses, too. But my shoes had to be comfortable, as my feet were quite sore. I wore basically low-to-medium heels—no flats.

"For a coat, I wore a cape: a lightweight camel-colored cape with a matching scarf. I couldn't bear anything too heavy, and the cape was perfect.

"My advice to other short pregnant women: Stay away from two-piece outfits and large patterns, very bright colors, and any knitted fabrics. Wear pretty little things at the neckline, like pretty bows, pretty shirts, or cotton turtlenecks underneath dresses to vary the look and to draw attention away from your stomach."

* * *

LOIS: "Short women *absolutely* have a harder time looking good while pregnant. If you're taller, you can carry more weight. I'm almost five months pregnant now, and at this point it's hard not to look dumpy. I wear a lot of dresses. So far, I just buy a size or two larger than I normally wear. I buy clothes from two junior manufacturers that I've found to be particularly good: Panache and Partridge. These clothes are nicer than those of many junior manufacturers and are cut very roomy. And they're not too expensive—about fifty-five to

---

Lady Madonna is a maternity store with more than ninety-six locations around the country. It was started by Richard Teifer, who first became aware of the need for attractive and fashionable maternity clothes when his wife, who was pregnant for the first time, couldn't find anything to wear.

The Lady Madonna people, who have given a lot of thought to the matter of looking good while pregnant, came up with these tips for pregnant Short Chic.

DO WEAR: princess and A-line dresses; belted, button-up-the-front shirt dresses (all Lady Madonna dresses have belts, by the way, to wear in the first few months of pregnancy and, then again, after delivery); two-piece dresses only if the top and bottom match; slightly tapered sleeves, elongating scarves, and chain necklaces; V-necks and shawl collars; lightweight unbulky sweaters; jackets that aren't too boxy or too short (you can wear slightly padded shoulders, if you like, but generally keep the silhouette as close to the body as possible); narrow tapered pants; lightweight layering in cold weather; A-line coats.

DON'T WEAR: contrasting color tops and skirts; wide or baggy pants; big bold stripes and patterns; double-breasted looks (if you like, you can start out with a double-breasted jacket and then tailor it down to single-breasted as your pregnancy advances); bulky sweaters and short jackets; quilted coats.

seventy-five dollars for dresses. They show them belted, but I just take off the belts and cut off the loops.

"I've also bought some pants at Lady Madonna and find I wear one pair of corduroys a lot. A friend of mine gave me a pair of jeans, too. They're not maternity but are much larger than my normal size.

"I shop a lot at thrift shops, looking for tops that are cut full. I just bought several at Encore (a shop on Madison and Eighty-fourth Street in New York City). I don't worry much about colors or patterns yet either, but just buy what I like. I have some big plaid shirts that I wear, and I think that whatever is nice is still nice when you're pregnant. But I do wear prettier colors as opposed to drab ones that make me look washed out. As far as accessories go, I'm not much for scarves or things at the neck, but I do wear nice earrings and things in my hair. And I wear flatter heels since I'm pregnant. I just don't seem to be able to wear the high heels I'm used to.

"For winter I'm planning to wear my white wrap coat and to move the buttons over on another warmer coat, which should see me through several months.

"My advice to short pregnant women: Shop around at thrift shops, Loehmann's (or any discount-designer store), Lady Madonna for things like pants, and wear hand-me-downs. That's the best way."

17. Petites: The Big News about Small-scale Sizing

Used to be, we'd ask a shorter woman what she thought about clothing for Petites—and then duck. Typical are the answers from our earliest questionnaire returns:

"I may be short, but I'm not tiny!"
                    Barbara D., 5′2″, 120 pounds, New York, New York

"I wouldn't wear them on a bet! They're usually poorly made from cheap fabric and badly designed. Most seem to be styled for teeny boppers or great grandmothers—and I am neither."
                    Pamela G., 5′1″, 100 pounds, San Francisco, California

On the "positive" side:

"I might wear then if I could find out which department the stores hide them in—I just don't see that many around."
                    Hazel N., 5′1½″, 113 pounds, Washington, D.C.

And from one woman who did wear them on a regular basis, this apologetic explanation:

"They're not top quality, and the styles aren't very attractive, but Petites are the only clothes that fit me."

Name withheld, 4'10", 96 pounds, Englewood, New Jersey

All in all, a pretty poor report.

But as we said, that's the way it used to be, and as the latest incoming questionnaires indicate, some welcome rays of hope are beginning to warm up the bleak horizon of Petite sizing. A case in point is this reply from Marianne de S., a 5'2", 103-pound computer systems analyst from New York City:

"Lately, I'm finding that some Petites are perfect for me. And the quality seems to be improving. For instance, I discovered an Evan-Picone Petite blazer that I could wear right off the rack—no alterations needed!"

The chief reason for the about-face, oddly enough, can be traced back to the recession (which only goes to show that every cloud does have a silver lining). The fashion industry scuttlebutt tells it like this: Reacting to the economy's discouraging effect on business, some manufacturers decided to increase their sales volume by pursuing new, previously untapped markets, and the middle-income Petite-sized woman was one of them.

Budget dress manufacturers had taken the plunge long ago, but now better-quality dress names were getting their feet wet, and eventually the separates people began to follow. But here's the really important development: Some of the name designers, who were previously cutting clothes in regular sizes only, are now turning *their* creative attentions to the shorter woman as well. All this within the last two years or so. What it promises to mean for you: quality fabrics and good design in sizes that actually fit—with little or no altering.

Are Petites for You?

According to the new definition:

- Petite sizing is for the woman who measures from 4'8" to 5'4" tall and weighs from about 85 to 125 pounds.
- Necklines, shoulders, bust, waist, and hips will be cut narrower; sleeves, pants, and skirt lengths will be shorter; waist-

lines and armholes higher; pants more tapered, and all details (pockets, collars, ruffles, and such) scaled to size.

- Sizes run from 2 or 4 to 12 or 14 (and sometimes even 16, which disproves the theory you have to be Dresden-doll-delicate to wear a Petite).

- Finally, if the item is a designer Petite, you can also expect to find some professional understanding of the shorter woman's needs in terms of softer fabrics, scaled-down patterns, more sophisticated styling, and a moderate-to-expensive (as opposed to budget) price tag with improved quality and workmanship to match.

If you're still unsure about whether you fit into the Petite-size category, compare your body measurements with those in the U.S. Department of Commerce chart below, which was designed to act as a guide for Petites manufacturers and designers.

The New Petites Sizing

SIZES IN INCHES	2P	4P	6P	8P	10P	12P	14P	16P
Bust	30–31	31½–32	32½–33	33½–34	34½–35½	36–37	37½–38½	39–40½
Waist	20–22	22½–23	23½–24	24½–25	25½–26½	27–28	28½–29½	30–31½
Hips	31–33	33½–34	34½–35	35½–36	36½–37½	38–39	39½–40½	41–42½
Back (Neck to Waist)	14	14¼	14¼	14½	14¾	15	15¼	15½
Inseam Pants Length	24⅝	24⅞	25⅝	26⅝	27⅛	27⅞	28⅝	29⅝

Short Chic Shopping Tips for Petites

As of this writing, quality labels available in this category include: *Jack Mulqueen Petites*, with dresses in silk or crepe de Chine . . . *Princess Sumi* and *Francesca Damon for Starington Ltd.*, for dresses with simple, graceful styling, pretty details. . . . And for conservatively classic Petite dresses, there's *Ciao* and *Abe Schrader*. . . .

In the sportswear market, check out *Evan-Picone Petites*, *Jones New York Petites*, and *Liz Claiborne Petites*, some reliable names that were among the first in the designer sportswear field to think small. . . . For tailored suits and coats: *Harvé Benard Petites* and *Betty Hanson's Petites* . . . Also for suits and coats: *Reflections for Petites*, *Prestige*, and *Young Impressions*—all three offer quality fabrics at affordable prices. . . . For Petite-sized jeans, try *Calvin Klein* (the first major jean-designer to scale down). . . . Other names to investigate: *The Petite Body Engineering Co.* (silk blouses, better dresses, evening dresses, pants—the works) and *PTP Prime Time Petites* (moderately priced related separates, including two-piece dresses, dressier skirts/jackets, nice jeans, casual tops).

Note: Right now, the Petites market is going through its growing pains, and by the time you read this, you may find that some labels have discontinued production whereas others have entered the field. Our advice: Buy with discretion because there are still plenty of Petites-label items that *are* the way they used to be: poorly made and badly designed. You'll just have to check out the fabric and workmanship, try on, and use your own judgment. And if it isn't what you're after, keep on looking because the good ones are out there!

The Tale of Retail

Does the Petites outlook sound encouraging? You bet your charge card it does! And as more quality stores give over more floor space to Petites departments, the news gets even better. In New York City, for example, *Saks Fifth Avenue* was one of the first stores to feature a section of quality Petites dresses.

According to their buyer, Nancy Rogers: "Our timing for opening the section was based on the fact that better-priced lines were starting to be available. There's obviously a customer there and it's a very viable market."

At the time of our interview, Ms. Rogers talked about the store's plans to expand the department to include suits and, when they became more available, separates. Saks isn't just an isolated example, either; these days we're seeing the trend catching on in other better department stores as well. Places like *Altman's* and *Macy's in New York City* . . . *Filene's in Boston* . . . *All branches of Jordan Marsh* and *Marshall Field* . . . *Gimbels in Philadelphia* . . . and *Macy's in San Francisco*.

If you haven't already found a Petites department in a better department store near you, ask if they have plans for one. You'll probably be pleasantly surprised by the answer.

Also be on the lookout for smaller shops and boutiques that specialize in better-quality Petites and small regular sizes—places like *Piaffe in New York City* (see Focus, this chapter) and *Especially Petites in San Francisco's Bay Area* (1398 Grant at Green), to name two of the better ones.

FOCUS ON: Ellis Oppenheim, Founder and Co-owner of Piaffe

In 1978, after fifteen years' experience in retailing, Ellis Oppenheim, along with his partner Fred Rosenfeld, opened the doors of Piaffe (841 Madison Avenue, New York City)—a small shop that features a complete wardrobe of designer-quality ready-to-wear for the smaller, shorter woman. Since then, Piaffe has been attracting people like actresses Marlo Thomas (not short but small-framed) and Anita Gillette, jazz flautist Bobbi Humphries, and several dancers from New York City's ballet companies, as well as a number of professional businesswomen.

Why a store for smalls? "My sister happens to be tiny," Oppenheim explains, "and I have an aunt who's very small. So after hearing the problems they had trying to find clothes, I did some research and discovered that there was a big gap in the market waiting to be filled. When I started this business, no one was making quality Petite pants and blouses. Finally, we had our own patterns made for us and now our own Piaffe label constitutes about twenty-five percent of our merchandise." Today the store also features many other Petite labels, as well as regular-sized lines that cut true-scale 2s and 4s (Piaffe's overall size range runs from 0 to 8). "Sometimes," Oppenheim told us, "a designer who doesn't normally cut small sizes will make a two and four especially for us."

Size isn't the only consideration, however. "We look for things that are flattering to the shorter woman. Cropped jackets with scaled-down details.

Dresses with a long, unbroken line. Two-piece silk dresses that can be bought in separate pieces to accommodate, say, a woman whose hips are larger than her bust (which is a common figure type among American women). I'll reject outsized prints, split-color breakups, and costumy kids' looks. That's not what our customer is after.

"One reason for Piaffe's success, I think, is that we take statistics on the women who come into the store, and then we sort everything out by computer. We find out what women want and need and then we give it to them. For example, we offer free alterations (with express service for out-of-town visitors), as well as a personalized executive shopping service for busy women with little time to look for clothes."

In 1979 Piaffe opened a sister store in Philadelphia (at 1700 Sansom Street), and plans are in the works for other branches throughout the country. In the meanwhile, if you can't make it to either of the two existing branches, you can order their free catalog. Just send your name, address, and request to Piaffe, Mail Order Department #70, 1500 Broadway, New York, New York 10036, or call (212) 744-9911.

18. Offbeat Looks and Sources: Shopping for Finds in Unexpected Places

Looking great for less $$$ . . . what you can find in the boys, girls and teen departments . . .

One of the fashion advantages of being short is the chance to make the most of unusual fashion resources—ones that offer classic pieces that are up to par as far as quality is concerned and that also offer, in many cases, a better fit and, in all cases, a better buy.

In order to check out what really works and what doesn't in the departments listed above, we recruited two volunteers to shop the market with us. They measure up as follows:

	Dorothy	Nancy
Height:	5'1¾" (5'3½" in shoes)	5'3" (5'5" in shoes)
Weight:	98 pounds	112 pounds
Bust:	33	35
Waist:	24	23
Hips:	34	36
Figure type:	long-legged/short-waisted, small-framed	long-waisted/short-legged average framed

After instructing both of them to wear comfortable clothes that are easy to get in and out of, we then dragged them all over town, from store to store, department to department, trying on everything that caught our eye. Here, a rundown of the top "finds" . . .

The Boys Department

Yes, there's a gold mine in his closets, something savvy fashion folks have known for years and responded to by ransacking the wardrobes of countless husbands, fathers, uncles, boyfriends, and brothers. The Short Chic advantage: You can shop the *boys* department for the same kind of sporty merchandise you find in the menswear department and get it for a lot less money.

Sizing Up: If you're full-busted, you'd be better off skipping this stop. But if you happen to be boyishly built to begin with, i.e., narrow-hipped, small-busted, and slim, you're in real luck!

What to Look For

- *Terrific wool crew-neck sweaters* in pink, red, green, camel, navy, light-blue, and beige, nice tops to punch up the look of a starkly classic suit. The size 14 was Dorothy's best fit—and an incredible buy to boot.
- *Wonderful sport sweaters.* The standout, a gray wool, made like a *knitted sweatshirt*, also in a size 14 on both models.
- *All-wool ski sweaters by Izod:* cabled wool pullovers in oatmeal-color and in navy, again at not-to-be-believed prices ("I just spent over twice that much for a sweater like that," moaned Nancy.)
- Good weekend wear—*boys down vests*, size 14 on Dorothy, 16 on Nancy.
- Boys *navy blazers*. The ones we found were by Pierre Cardin, with monogramed buttons and a signature lining. Nancy felt they were cut too much on the straight side for her; the size 17/18, however, looked casual and campy on Dorothy, who liked the look of a slightly oversized jacket. Another: boys blazers by Ralph Lauren for Polo. They're not cheap, but they don't come near to approaching the price of a Ralph Lauren jacket in the women's department. So, if the fit is right on you, you're in luck.
- Boys *Lacoste polo shirts*, in the same popular colors you find in the men's department, but a good ten to twelve dollars cheaper at this writing. They're shorter-waisted than the

men's versions (good if you are), and you won't be stuck with superlong shirttails either. The size 12 looked skimpy to us, so check out 14s and 16s.

- Boys *flannel pajamas* in pale yellow or light blue. Real classics (à la Katharine Hepburn) and incredibly *cheap*. An assistant professor at Cornell University, 5′2″, swears by them but recommends buying them one size larger than you really need. ("They really do shrink up," she told us.)

The most famous boys department is at the one-and-only Brooks Brothers in New York, where under 5′4″ women regularly pick up staples like classic Oxford-cloth button-down dress shirts in pink, light blue, white and yellow. Says Kenneth Shields, manager of the department, "Since the women's and boys departments are on the same floor [the fourth], there's a full circulation of customers coming in. Women who intend to go to their own department end up walking around the entire floor and spotting merchandise appropriate to their own needs.

"Boys clothes fit small women well because smallness is not unusual in the boys department but average," he continued. "Most short women buy size fourteen or sixteen in boys tops; in trousers, they usually buy one size larger in the waist to compensate for hip needs."

The most popular items? "Oxford-cloth dress shirts, tweed blazers, sports coats, basic Shetlands, and turtlenecks, with some interest in pajamas and cord trousers.

"Actually, there's far greater value in buying boys' as opposed to women's apparel," Mr. Shields added. "Women's clothes are thirty percent higher in cost. While a basic herringbone sports coat in the boys department may cost eighty dollars, in the women's department, it's over one hundred dollars."

The Girls Department

Girls clothing, sizes 7 to 14, doesn't offer much in the way of sophisticated styling and we wouldn't suggest putting it on your regular shopping route. But for basic practical pieces needed to fill in wardrobe gaps and for playful and inexpensive accessories, it offers good savings.

Sizing Up: You may think that unless you're very small-framed, this department is off-limits. Well, not so! Nancy was surprised to find that, except for tops ("too short-waisted and too snug across the bust"), everything else—skirts, jackets, etc.—worked fine and, in some cases, were even too big!

What to Look For

- Rediscover *children's sneakers,* not the new, monster running/jogging/tennis shoes but honest-to-goodness, old-fashioned *sneakers,* in red, white, or navy, with rubber toes. If you've got small feet, size 5½ maximum), they make great-looking casual and beachwear. When Anne Marie wore hers this summer, everyone wanted to know where she got them.
- White Indian-styled *beaded moccasins* with fringed flaps are another summer shoe find. With soles or without, they're a couple of dollars cheaper in the children's department.
- Gorgeously crafted *cowboy boots,* the kind you find at Western specialty shops are a pricey item. But at New York's Tee-pee Town, once you get past the women's boots at *well* upward of one hundred dollars a pair, there are kiddie models, less ornate and shorter, but then just twenty-five dollars, too.
- Children's *rubber rain boots.* Remember the funny rubber boots that pull over shoes in rainy weather? Well, if you're a size 5½ or less, they still fit. Allison dashed into Alexander's during a slushy rain one day, picked up a pair, and she's been hooked ever since.
- *Shiny yellow oilskin slickers,* a nice find in the girls or boys departments. Like most gear of navy origin, it's classic, functional, and good-looking—and you can't beat its bright yellow cheer on a gray day. On both Dorothy and Nancy, the sleeves didn't need a lick of shortening; the length worked fine over casual pants like jeans.
- Other weather beaters: *pile-lined taupe suede gloves* (four dollars cheaper than identicals in the women's department—and a much, much better fit all-around). *Knitted children's gloves and mittens,* also an easy fit (the ones we liked best were bright green with knitted yellow ribbed cuffs).
- *Felt berets in gray and in plum-colored wool,* a find in the girls department. Dorothy said the ones she's always bought before were invariably too big; these, a perfect fit.
- *Fisherman knit, Fair Isles, and crew-neck sweaters,* in as-

sorted girls sizes, depending on manufacturers, all make very nice collectibles.

- *A black/red/white full-length tartan plaid kilt* with real leather side buckles, elastic inset at the waist, nice detailing. This one was a real surprise—it fit both models smoothly at the hip and the waist, hit about midcalf to ankle-high in boots. The kilt was in an acrylic/polyester blend that could pass for wool and cost next to nothing (and could make a nice at-home extra for winter parties, worn with high-collared blouse, and, instead of a velvet blazer, a soft paisley shawl).

- An autumn-colored *plaid blouse with a lace collar and gros-grain ribbon tie*, by Gloria Vanderbilt for Murjani. It's tapered through the body, with darts and a perfect sleeve length; Dorothy purchased it on the spot. "It's just what I need," she explained, "and because it's short-waisted, it fits me better than most adult blouses do." *Note:* Buying children's fashions by top-name designers is a good way to get good fashion at a good price (and if you're short-waisted and small-framed, often an excellent fit).

- Leather goods—a *glove-soft jumper in chestnut-colored leather*, lined in satin with adjustable, buckled, shoulder straps. A touch on the short side for our models wearing heels, but with the buckles taken down a notch, do-able. A nice rustic look to wear with a textured sweater and boots—and a comparable leather garment in the women's department would be at least two and a half times the price.

- *Half slips* in the girls lingerie department looked *short, short, short*—so if you've always had problems with slip lengths, you're in luck. In white with a bit of minute lace edging, the size to look for if you're small-framed is 12. Other finds for the 5'-or-under: woolly tight long johns.

- *Down parkas*, again, cheaper than women's. Size 12 worked on Dorothy; size 14 was a little roomy on Nancy.

- *Children's 14K gold jewelry*. If you're small-boned, you can carry these off to a T. The jewelry cases in all the children's departments we surveyed were filled with delicate-looking rings, necklaces, earrings, chains. The best of the lot: tiny gold bracelets studded with seed pearls, baby rings (nice to wear two and three at a time on one finger), thin chains, heart-shaped, on-the-lobe pierced earrings. And while you're at the counter, check out the tortoiseshell barrettes and hair combs, too (no sense paying a dollar more downstairs for the identical stuff).

The Preteen and Teen Departments

The things that passed our standards in the preteen departments were trouser-style corduroy skirts that were inexpensive, sized well, and good for casual wear; basic sweaters; and one wool-blend reefer coat, which although not exactly fantastic, certainly could work. Generally, however, the pickings in this area were slim, and high-quality items with sophisticated styling were few and far between.

But the lingerie department was a different story—and a good source for short women seeking nighties, robes, and at-home wear at less than top-of-the-line prices. If you pass over the blatantly ingenue looks and go for simple styling and classic lines, you can find some very nice buys and an excellent fit, especially if you're on the short-waisted side. Look for nighties by well-known women's manufacturers who also make junior lines (*Vassarette Juniors*, for example). And if terry-cloth robes in the women's department are becoming too expensive, the preteen and teen departments offer nice alternatives.

European Clothing

It's no secret that French and Italian designers tend, on the whole, to cut their clothes smaller and leaner than the Americans do. So it's a good way for the shorter, petite-framed woman to find sophisticated and innovative fashions that fit and that are designed to set off

European Size Comparison Chart					
When you see a European size:	42	40	38	36	34
Translate it as an American:	12	10	8	6	4

Note: But remember that you won't always find the proper fit in your size equivalent. The European size 38 is slimmer and leaner than the American size 8.

their own smaller proportions. (A good example of the European cut —Yves Saint Laurent. His pants are cut incredibly slim and his skirts are "practically hipless," reports one of our scouts.) If you usually buy an American size 8, you'll probably find yourself riffling through the European 10s, even though you haven't gained an ounce. Waists are sized smaller, too. One woman we know who always has the waistbands of size 6 American designed pants taken in, never has any trouble when it comes to European cuts.

Antique Clothing

There's no question that the antique clothing craze is growing in popularity—and that thrift shops and better antique specialty stores, even flea markets, are good places to pick up interesting clothing extras for your wardrobe. But did you know that under-5′4″ women have a better chance of finding things to fit than tall women have?

"It's true," pointed out Harriet Love, who owns one of Soho's best-known antique clothing emporiums, "particularly in clothing from the Victorian and Edwardian periods when clothes had smaller and shorter waists, a petite woman can pick up some real finds. Sally Struthers [5′1″] came into my store a few years ago. She has a round face, short torso, big bust, and small shoulders. She found beautiful Victorian clothes—white blouses, petticoats, jackets. They were beautiful pieces and the blouses and jackets looked terrific, even with jeans. Small women can also be lucky with antique shoes," she continued, "often they have wonderfully shaped heels and interesting designs, usually in small sizes." (For more of Harriet's tips on antique clothing for 5′4″-and-unders, see the Focus interview in this chapter.)

One of the most important things about antique clothing is not to take it at face value. Kelly T, a small-framed 5′4″ illustrator and fashion watcher, had long been a fan of turning somewhat questionable thrift shop pieces into finds that work with her own unique style. "I like to wear things like little boys vests and T-shirts, men's baggy boxer shorts wrapped at the waist (nice on the beach instead of shorts). And I like to try clothing backward, inside out and upside down. I might take the red pleated skirt off a drop-waisted twenties chemise with a damaged top and then wear it as a miniskirt. Or a fifties bolero worn backward, buttoned only at the top, with nothing underneath, instead of an evening top.

Kelly likes seeking out antique shoes, too. "They're often smaller and narrower," she says. "They can look like early Maud Frizon."

FOCUS ON: Harriet Love

For some special insight on the antique clothing market, we spoke to antique clothing expert and boutique owner Harriet Love, who explained its special appeal to under-5′4″ women.

"The major advantage of shopping in antique clothing stores for women of any height is the endless variety potential. Until the late 1940s and 50s, when fashion moved into ready-to-wear, clothes were mostly custom-made. And because fashion in the old days didn't dictate what women wore as much as it did in later years, seamstresses designed clothes individually for clients, resulting in an enormous choice of styles and details. But since women were shorter one hundred years ago, there is a *particular* likelihood that the petite woman will be especially lucky in finding something in an antique clothing store that fits.

"A lot of the clothing we're finding today from the Victorian and Edwardian periods—periods that definitely cater to the smaller woman—are teenage clothes, which is one reason they're so perfect on small women. During those times teenage girls were treated and dressed as mature married women, so shorter women can find a good fit. Another reason I think the shorter woman may very well find her niche in the antique clothing store is that she won't see all blouson or all short or long styles, but rather fifty years of fashion. Three months ago, for example, I found a collection of clothing that belonged to an actress who was 5′2½″. Every dress was custom-made, and the collection included all of her clothes from the time she was twenty-eight to age fifty. She was a rather slender short-waisted woman, and the collection included sweaters that were fitted at the waist, coats out of crepe wools trimmed with furs, blouses with puffed sleeves. Francine Scherer, an owner of the Soho Charcuterie, who is 5′4″, slender, and extremely well dressed, bought three or four items from the collection. Generally, I wouldn't recommend that short women wear forties and fifties dresses—these often have a lot of shoulder padding, sweeping 'fishtails' in the back, sweeps in the front, peplums, and some in big prints. They're not easy for anyone to carry. I would also discourage twenties clothes for women who are short and short-legged—they accentuate a low hipline and short legs. But of course, there are always exceptions. Some women just have a terrific sense of fashion and look good in almost anything. One of my customers, a 5′1″ woman from Seventh Avenue, who is a manufacturer of bathing suits, changes her hair style, hair color, and general 'look' often. She buys an enormous variety of clothes from me. She wraps big sweaters in with a belt and wears them over slender pants and looks terrific. Alexandra Penney, who writes for the *New York Times*, is 5′3″ and knows how to make clothes work for her own figure. She always buys twenties clothes—the straightest shifts—and belts them at the waist. About three years ago Debbie Reynolds bought loads of twenties clothing—lingerie and beaded shifts. Her daughter, Carrie Fisher, who's also petite, bought lots of Victorian clothing. . . . Overall, good bets for short women are Victorian and Edwardian blouses, forties and fifties fitted suit jackets, soft thirties blouses (they have no padded shoulders), and Kimberly-knit jackets."

Ethnic Finds

Ethnic finds of all sorts can be an especially good source for the under-5′4″ woman. Why? Because whereas a taller woman can add style by the sheer dramatic size and scope of the clothing and accessories she chooses (like a flat, shiny, oversized copper choker or a dramatically flaring coat), a small woman doesn't have that option. Instead, she's got to go for effect through the uniqueness, not the size, of the items she wears.

Hillary L., an artist we know, often wears a black cotton jacket ("made years ago in Afghanistan"), embroidered with rose-colored silk flowers, with her basic jeans tucked into high fur-topped, low-heeled boots. She's 5′2″. "I always try to wear at least one odd, personal piece," she told us, "otherwise I just don't feel as if I stand out. I think it's harder, generally, for smaller women to be noticed at all, so dressed this way, I feel who I really am distinctly comes across."

When you're buying ethnic garb, look for the best—the unusual, the hand-crafted, the one-of-a-kinds, otherwise, the look comes across as just plain cheap. Some great examples we've seen worn with smashing success by under-5′4″ women: a sweeping Russian quilted coat, hand-embroidered shawls, unusual jewelry in carnelian, cinnabar, and ivory. Felice T., 5′1¾″ is a producer whose job takes her traveling from home base in California to places like South America, Japan, and Thailand. She has brought back such finds as real coolie pants, handsome cloisonné bracelets, harem trousers, and exotic wraps. "The Japanese hand-painted robe I found last year is an art form in itself," she commented.

One tip: If you're in doubt about whether or not a particular ethnic item is suited to you, look to the country of its origin. If the people tend to be on the shorter side, then the traditional native garb is probably designed to set off the attributes of shorter women at their best—and would be equally fetching on you.

19. The Beauty Part: Uplifting Thoughts on Makeup, Hair, and Posture

How Your Face and Hair Can Be Your Fortune

Admittedly, your clothes will be doing most of the work when it comes to creating a taller, more powerful image, but the beauty part has an extremely important role, too. The way you apply your makeup, the way you wear your hair, the way you walk, stand, *move*—all are going to add the final elements to the image you create. These aren't "extra touches" we're talking about; on the contrary, they're indispensable if you're short, and want to be taken seriously in the job market.

Do we detect some skepticism? Then consider this: When a woman is tall, she can get away with more than her shorter sister. In the working world, for instance, a taller woman may be able to ignore the "little" things—like attractive makeup and a flattering hairstyle—and still be successful. She has her height to establish a sense of presence for her. But since a short woman starts without that advantage, she *has* to be careful about the way she looks to avoid being put into the "young/inexperienced" category by those who (perhaps because of limited contact with her) are forced to make judgments on appearance alone

A case in point: We personally know of one delicately made, under-5'3" woman who had been blessed—or cursed, depending on how you look at it—with a very young face. To be precise, at twenty-eight, she looked like a sweet sixteen, and she did very little to alter that impression. Her clothes were pretty much the same skirts and blouses she'd worn in college, her hair was cut in a girlish style, and, as for makeup, if she wore any at all, no one knew it. Now this young woman had for several years worked as an assistant to a series of bosses in the creative department of a magazine. She was talented (in one case, more talented than the boss she worked for), extremely competent, knowledgeable about the running of the department, and pleasant to work with in the bargain. So when the third boss left for parts unknown, we all assumed that Sally would be given the long-deserved raise and promotion she was asking for. But it was not to be. Word came down through the grapevine that the reason she didn't get the job was because the ruling powers (who didn't know her as well as we did) thought she wasn't capable of handling the job. But more than a few of us were willing to bet on the real reason: Because of Sally's girlish looks, they thought she was too young and inexperienced to handle it.

An unfair way to think, yes. But unreasonable? No. Not when you stop to think. *First, or casual, impressions are often formed on the most elemental levels which have nothing to do with logic.* Put syllogistically, the ruling powers' reaction to our friend Sally probably went something like this:

> Most young girls do not wear makeup.
> Sally looks young and does not wear makeup.
> Therefore, Sally is a young girl.

The conclusion that follows from that, of course, is that young girls should not be trusted with responsible jobs. Any student of philosophy could point out the fallacies in our silly syllogism, but remember: gut reactions don't tend to work on the principles of Aristotelean logic. And because they don't, you will have to cater to that kind of thinking if you want to make the kind of impression that's going to elicit confidence.

Makeup

For some reason, many short women tend to look younger than their years. Cute is nice, but if it's getting in the way of your career, better cash it in for something more suitable. Like chic, polished, or sophisticated. Polished makeup is Essential No. 1 for creating a favorable impression in the business world—and just about everywhere else for that matter. Aside from helping you to establish that "capable-adult" image, it will also help you look your prettiest—a definite plus.

Now chances are that you've already discovered the right makeup for you, and you don't need any help from us. But if you suspect that you may have an image problem where your cosmetics are concerned, then read on.

Playing It Down the Middle

If the shorter woman has any particular problems with makeup because of her height, it's usually a matter of going to extremes. Either she underplays (or goes without makeup altogether), which tends to make her look adolescent and contributes to her not being taken seriously as an adult, or she overplays it in an attempt to look more sophisticated and to compensate for lack of inches. Here's some good advice for both types:

The shorter woman who underplays her makeup (or goes without) often does so because

1. she doesn't think makeup is important, or
2. she's afraid of looking garish, or
3. she simply can't be bothered with a complicated makeup routine.

To answer these reasons in order:

1. Makeup is as important to your career as every other effort you've put into it, and it should be considered as such.
2. If more makeup looks too garish to your eye, it's probably because you're not used to seeing yourself that way. Better leave the final judgment to a friend whose taste and opinions you trust. Beautifully done makeup—whether a little or a lot —will never look garish. And
3. If you don't like to spend a lot of time at your makeup mirror (or don't have the time to spend), you might try these easy minimum-makeup routine suggestions from the pros:

Minimum Makeup Routine I: From New York makeup artist Mark Nahmias, this quick, ease-into-makeup how-to for the woman who never wears makeup or who has very little time to spare for a makeup routine.

1. Choose a powder blush in a shade that's suitable for your skin type (softer if you're fair-skinned, darker if you are).

2. Lightly brush the blush onto the upper eyelids. "By doing that," Mark explains, "you've suddenly created a bit of warmth there, and the eye doesn't look so naked."
3. Apply mascara.
4. Brush the same blush you used for your eyes onto your cheeks, following the natural contour of the bone.
5. Finish with lipstick.

Minimum Makeup Routine II: When you feel more comfortable with makeup or on those mornings when you do have a little more time, follow the same procedure as above but concentrate a little more on the eyes by doing these two steps between steps 2 and 3 described above.

2a. Accent the eye hollow by using a powdered shadow along the face of the eyebone. *Tip:* The powder will stay on longer if you apply a cream base first.
2b. Use an eye pencil to line along the upper and lower lash lines, then smudge the lines slightly with a cotton swab to keep the lines soft and natural-looking.

Says cosmetic expert Sandy Linter: "I think the eyes are very, very important, even for the woman who wears very little makeup. It's the eyes that can give the face a more forceful, intelligent look. It doesn't have to be a complicated process either. You can take one great pencil—in a soft gray, for example—and do your whole eye with it if you know how to contour the eye. You can underline with it, line the top of the eye, bring out the hollow—and then you can blend all that with a shadow brush."

A final word to the "minimalist":

Once you see how great you look in makeup, you'll want to develop your expertise. The best ways include studying the better fashion/beauty magazines for how-tos and to find out about the latest trends.

Or you might go to a professional salon to have them make you up and teach you as they go. (But before you make an appointment, you might just want to check out the place to see if they turn out the kind of look you can be comfortable with. What you don't want is a makeover from someone who doesn't take the time to consider your needs and tastes or who's just out to sell you a lot of cosmetics.)

Or look around your office and among your friends. If you see a woman whose makeup you admire, ask her for pointers.

The shorter woman who overdoes her makeup is another common phenomenon. Even a pro like Sandy Linter (who's a tiny 5'2½" tall) admits: "When I first started in the makeup business, I remember thinking that I would be overlooked and lost in the crowd if I didn't wear a lot of makeup, so I did go a little loud with it at one point in my life. But when I was ready to get serious, I went for a chic, elegant look. And everything was coordinated—my makeup, my hair, my clothes. And it worked for me."

The woman who overdoes usually knows how to work with cosmetics; the only problem is in not knowing when she's gone too far. So much, of course, depends on your personality, your clothes, and the type of job you're in. As Mark Nahmias explains, "It all comes down to a sense of balance. The face has to be balanced with the entire look. There are times you *can* get away with a lot of makeup—if you're wearing, say, some kind of gypsy thing with gold threads and lots of color in it. But if you're in a gray flannel suit, and you're wearing bright pinks and blues all over your face, you're going to look like a clown." So with those ideas in mind, here are some Dos and Don'ts:

DO wear makeup that relates to the colors and types of clothing you are wearing. When you don tennis whites, for example, it's not the time to dip into every makeup pot on your dressing table. Same goes for the office. Your makeup doesn't have to look natural necessarily (that is, as if you weren't wearing *any*), but it should be sophisticated and elegant.

DON'T overplay the eyes. Eyes are important, and if yours are great, you'll want to play them up. But go easy on dark shadows and heavy liners (which make the eyes seem heavy and serve to draw an imaginary line across that part of your face), and don't exaggerate the shape of your eyes with corner lines that wing out to *there*. For evening that may look great but not for day.

DO remember that neatness counts—especially if you wear a lot of makeup or enjoy using dramatic colors. Bright pink lipstick, for example, looks pretty only if it's impeccably lined to define the mouth. (*Good tip:* To keep lip color neat, apply foundation so it falls slightly into the mouth line; powder, then line lips with lipstick-matching pencil. This way color won't "bleed" into the surrounding area.

DO make up in adequate light. If the light is dim when you apply makeup, you'll use more of it to look good. But then, outdoors or in bright office light, that same makeup could make you look like a neon sign. This rule especially applies to cheek color. All the pros we talked to were unanimously thumbs-down on what one of them described as "an ugly gash of dark color under the cheekbone."

DON'T underestimate the importance of blending, blending, blending. Color isn't meant to stand out in spots, slashes, and dots on the face. It's used to enhance your features, and in order to do that, it has to fade gradually into nothingness—that goes for eye shadows, liner, foundation, *and* blusher.

Pretty for Evening   The universal rule for evening makeup: Do everything that you would do for day, only exaggerate it more. Because evening light is dimmer, you have to compensate for that by using darker liner, more mascara, perhaps brighter mouth and cheek color. But, in addition to that, you may also want to try these special tricks for instant glamour.

- When "dressing for dinner" means five minutes of doing a presto-change-o act in the company ladies' room, you can add a shimmery evening glow to your day makeup if you had the presence of mind to stash a loose, bronzy metallic powder in your desk emergency drawer. Just dust a bit of it on your lids over your blusher—you can even mix a smidgeon of it with your lip color.
- Or you could try some glimmery gold highlighter just under the browbone and/or on the lid so that it extends a little around the outer eye corners. You might even use that same gold on the tips of your lashes to add a sparkly effect every time you flutter them.

Makeup and Proportion   Besides giving you a prettier, more adult image, makeup can also help to even out your overall proportions. Here's how . . .

SMALL FACE/TINY FEATURES   Delicate features can be a real asset but only if you play them up so that they'll be noticed. To bring them to light and to make your face "balanced" in proportion to the rest of you, try this advice from New York City makeup pro Leonard Weitz:

"Before you apply your foundation, you should use an underbase highlighter cream that's one or two shades lighter than your foundation. Highlighting is an essential step for giving definition to the face. It's like doing a portrait: If the painter doesn't work with light and color to add depth, the completed canvas is going to look flat and unanimated."

Using the tip of your little finger, pat the highlighter onto the areas you want to emphasize

1. On the forehead, make a V-shape from inner brows to hair-line.
2. On the nose, down the flat front surface to the tip.
3. To strengthen a weak jawline, use highlighter to make a thin wedge-shape from the corner of the chin to the bottom of the ear.

Note: Don't blend the highlighter in; you'll be doing that automatically as you apply your foundation. Also, highlighter can be used to camouflage under-eye circles, folds next to the mouth, or to "bring up" the tip of a nose that drops down (just apply on the underside of the nose itself and along the outer edges of the nostrils).

For the shorter woman whose face size is a little large in proportion to the rest of her body, contouring could be the perfect balancing solution. Constantine, the *visagiste* (skin and makeup expert) at the Elizabeth Arden Salon in New York City, suggests this method: LARGE FACE/ GENEROUS FEATURES

Using a contour powder that's one or two shades darker than your foundation (and after applying foundation) brush it . . .

1. Along the hairline on the forehead.
2. Underneath the cheekbone (especially if cheeks are pudgy or rounded) to create a hollow there.
3. On the tip of the chin.

Note: If you use contour powder in this way to "surround" the circumference of the face, it makes the face appear smaller.

To "shrink" a nose that is too large . . .
1. Brush some contour powder along the sides to narrow a wide nose.
2. To shorten a long nose, brush a little powder on the tip.

Hair

Ever have one of those days when you were tempted to skip work and call in sick simply because your hair looked funny? It's not an uncommon reaction because when your hair doesn't look right, nothing else seems to look right or feel right or go right. This gives you some idea of how important a flattering, manageable hairstyle can be to your self-image and to your self-confidence. But for the shorter

FOCUS ON: Pablo Manzoni

Among the beauty world's cognoscenti, Pablo has long been regarded as a daVinci of the makeup art. But, aside from his talents in that quarter, one soon discovers that this suave Italian gentleman is somewhat of a philosopher as well. Here, his delightful views on the many facets of beauty as they relate to the shorter woman . . .

"There is a fascinating charm about the smaller woman that is very special to me. In America, the attitude always seems to be 'bigger is better', but that's nonsense. European gentlemen are petrified of taller girls. There is an Italian proverb that goes, *'Piu piccolo l'amplèsso piu grande piacere'*: 'The smaller the grasp, the bigger the pleasure.' There is something so pleasurable about hugging and flirting with a smaller woman. Maybe it's because she seems so vulnerable. The reaction of the man is 'I am important to her because she needs me.' Now I know that American women might object to the term 'vulnerable,' but look—the most important people in the world are not afraid of showing emotion; it's really a test of greatness, the ability to admit being vulnerable. . . . I know that shorter women are always trying to make themselves look taller. By wearing very high heels, for instance. A girl friend of mine—very tiny, very pretty—used to wear those colossal wedgies. I would tell her jokingly that I expected one day to read in the paper: 'Tired of life, she jumped off her shoes and fell to her death.' Never mind the very high heels! There are other ways to look taller. There is a lovely little girl in the ballet who is the shortest one on the stage, but she keeps her chin up with such pride as if to say 'I am taller than you are.' It's very much a matter of attitude. I've noticed women coming into a beauty salon who look short because they feel unattractive. But when they walk out it's as if they swallowed a broomstick—they walk erect and they actually look taller because they feel better about themselves. . . . Then there are small women who try to look older by wearing a lot of makeup. It's very difficult to say how far you should go with makeup. It's in the face, the answer for each individual, personal need. You can't say 'so much of this, and so much of that'— you're not giving a recipe for a soufflé. All of this is empirical, I suppose, but in the way of a nitty-gritty how-to, I can tell you that too much makeup makes you look wrong, and too little amounts to a total waste of opportunity. Your makeup must be very polished and elegant. And for the office, at least, you should forget the ethnic look (like one of those dolls from an airport gift shop, you know). I feel, for example, that the use of artificial lashes is a mistake for the smaller woman because all of a sudden you have a proportion that comes horizontally out of someone who is not overly gifted vertically. . . . You should use lots of eye shadow in a pretty neutral shade like gray to give the eyes depth and mystery and appeal. You should use a lot of blusher because that is very attractive. Don't wear overpowering lipstick—gloss is much more appealing. And all your makeup should be discreet. . . . I think that fashion glasses are also marvelous on smaller women. They should be slightly over-sized and the lenses slightly darker on top than at the bottom (which, in a way, creates a vertical). There's immediate glamour in it. To me, a woman with glasses looks richer than a woman without. . . . When it comes to beauty, self-acceptance is so much more important than striking good looks. You can't use makeup to pretend you're something you are not. You must simply be yourself at your best. Again, so much of it has to do with attitude. When you are going out in the evening, for example, you should sit in front of the mirror, dim the lights, brush your hair back, spray perfume, and then say to yourself ten times: 'I am small, but I am exquisite. I am beautiful.' It's a healthy form of narcissism. If you are in love, so much the better. Because when you are loved and when you are convinced of your own self-worth, there is a sparkle to your eye which is very contagious and desirable. You even stand several inches taller because you're walking on air. . . . Usually, I prefer women who are not great beauties but who are intelligent and interest-ing. And if you are short and worry that people may regard you as a child, it's especially important to develop your intelligence. You must be very informed, very curious, very knowledgeable. When people recognize that in you, height doesn't matter. From my point of view, it's a pleasure to go out with a woman who is capable of ordering from a menu, who knows how to tip, who can get on a plane by herself. And what a sense of relief not to have to watch over somebody for fear she's going to get herself run over by a bus. . . . They say that small women have bigger brains and are more assertive. That's wonderful! Opinionated women will always be listened to more often because they have something to say, as opposed to the poor devil who never talks. Remember, it's through conversation that you reach someone else's heart. And it's through achievement that you get promoted. Inches mean nothing, except perhaps in the psychological sense: In America you have the wonderful expression that somebody 'grows on you.' And it's true. When a woman is self-confident, and happy, and interesting and intelligent, she'll grow taller in other people's eyes. And more beautiful."

woman especially, the right cut is not only beauty Essential No. 2, it could also be a means of creating the illusion of added height.

Cutting Remarks   The first thing to realize is that any haircut—short or long or in-between—shouldn't be based on your height alone, although height certainly does come into it. You and your stylist should also consider:

- *Your body type:* Your build and your weight have to be taken into account in order to keep your cut in proportion. As explained by Rafael of Le Salon in New York City, "The size of a woman's head has to be in proportion with the rest of her body. A thin, petite woman cannot walk around with a big head. If her hair has a lot of volume and is very thick, it can overpower her if it's worn too long. On the other hand, if a short woman is heavy and broad, she shouldn't look as if she had a 'pea head.' She needs enough volume and length in her hair so it looks right with her body."
- *Your head shape:* If it's large or small, long or wide, the cut or style you decide on should correct any "flaws" or enhance any assets.
- *Your face shape:* Hair can be a fabulous corrector, so by all means take advantage of it to widen a too-narrow face, narrow a round face, soften a square face, or reproportion a heart- or diamond-shaped face. The prettier a cut can make you look, the better.
- *Your features:* The right style can diminish a large nose or play up fabulous eyes—or do the opposite. "I did Liza Minnelli's hair," recalls Louis Alonzo of Pipino-Buccheri in New York City. "Ever since *Cabaret* she'd had a bulky cut that smothered her face and concentrated on her nose and overdramatized her eyes. It was just too severe. So I cut it, layered it, made it spikey and 'piecey.' It looked fabulous on her and much softer."
- *Your hair texture:* The trend these days (and three cheers, we say) is toward natural. Whether your hair is curly, straight, frizzy, wavy, thin and fine, or thick and heavy—the cut should go along with that. It shouldn't fight what you've got. If it does—if, say, you opt for a curly style when your hair has a tendency to be rail-straight—you could end up being a slave to it. Perms and straighteners come in handy, of course. But try not to resort to them unless you're really sure you want a change.

- *Your personality and life-style:* If you have the time and the inclination to fuss and experiment with your hair, trying different looks, different accessories, and so on, then let your stylist know that. On the other hand, if you're always on the go, or if you're "not good with hair," or if you're active in sports, you'll probably want to ask him for a wash-and-wear kind of cut that requires minimum attention from you.

There are short women who believe that long hair is always a no-no for them. Well, it can be—but only for *some* short women. As we said earlier, there are other things to take into consideration besides height. You also have to think about your body type, your hair type, and the style of the long hair itself.

THE LONG OF IT

A slim woman could look great in long hair if it isn't worn *too* long (way below shoulder length), if it doesn't have too much volume, or if the volume is controlled with a style that pulls the hair back off the face. "If a woman's hair is fine, thin, or wispy," says Rafael, "she can get away with a longer haircut. But shorter women should stay away from very long, draggy hair."

A heavier woman who's short may need more hair to balance her figure, but even in this case it shouldn't be worn very long and it should be kept off her neck. As Benjamin Moss (of the Benjamin Salon in New York City) sees it: "A lot of overweight women tend to grow their hair beyond their shoulders; they think they're giving the illusion of being taller because of this long line, but it's not true. If the hair is very long and tends to flatten down on her scalp, it just makes her seem shorter and wider than she is. Also, from the back view she loses the elongating line of the neck—she just looks all shoulders and head."

Time is another factor. A woman whose schedule (or patience) doesn't allow for long-hair upkeep might want to consider a shorter style or, at least, a long style that enhances her hair's natural bent. (If your long hair is straight, and you like to wear it curly, waved, or braided, that will take time.)

The versatility of long hair can't be denied, and shorter women who know how to make long hair work for their height are the first to praise its virtues. Such a one is Carlotta Karlson, the 5'2½" beauty editor of *Harper's Bazaar.* "I wear my hair long because I think that the look is me. There's one hundred percent more versatility to long hair—and that's really the prime reason I would never get mine cut. I can just let it go naturally free and curly. Or I can braid it, put it in a ponytail, or a French twist. Or I can pull it back with a ribbon or hair combs. There are probably about ten options of things I can do with it long. And that's one reason I think long hair is easier to take care of."

. . . AND THE
SHORT OF IT

Going from long- or medium-length hair to short can be a traumatic experience for some women. That's why you should think about the kind of short cut you want and need ahead of time, before the scissors go into action. When you do, the results can be fabulous. A few points to ponder . . .

If you are petite and have a small face, then short is probably the best length for you. But you may want to stay away from a cut that's cropped too close to the head lest it overemphasize the size of your head and make it seem much smaller in comparison with your body (what has been referred to as the pyramid effect).

If you're a bit on the heavy side or large-boned, short hair can look great on you, too—especially if it has some volume to it to balance your body type.

Active in sports or always on the go? Then short hair can be a godsend. Opt for a cut that's wash-and-wear and that doesn't fight your hair's natural tendency, and it will be even quicker and easier still.

Versatility used to be the chief bone of contention about short hair, but no more. Today's cuts and fashion trends offer so many options that short hair has become just as changeable as long. Says Louis Alonzo, "I put in a stabilized line when I cut. I do things like broken bangs, fringes on the sides, and so on, then I show the woman how to pull pieces back, wear it straight, wear it tousled. She can slick it back with setting lotion or wear side combs. Short hair can have tremendous versatility if you have the right cut." P.S. Short hair's also perfect for showing off jewelry, like earrings and chokers.

HOW LONG OR
SHORT CAN ADD UP
TO TALL

Here are some illusion-creating tips to keep in mind about hair and height:

- Hair that caps the head gives the illusion of making you seem shorter; such a style just "presses" you down into the ground.
- An asymmetrical style, on the other hand, brings the onlooker's eye upward at an angle. Hair that's pulled to one side, cut longer on one side, or pulled up with a hair comb on one side—all contribute to adding imaginary inches to your stature.
- Naturally curly hair worn in a short style will immediately

—and actually—give you a few inches more on top, especially if it's worn longer there.

- Or you can achieve the same effect as above if your short hair is cut narrower on the sides than on top.
- A hairstyle that shows the neck is also good because the neck then creates an elongating line. Showing the slight line of the ear has the same effect on a smaller scale.
- If long hair is worn up, it can have the same neck-lengthening effect as short hair. But do avoid upswept styles that are too intricate, or they could make you seem top-heavy.
- Keep knots and chignons high up in back of the head (or right on top if the style is soft and full and doesn't lend itself to schoolmarmishness). If either is worn low or centered in back of the head, it creates a horizontal when seen from the side.
- One method for adding volume to the top of the head: a soft perm near the roots of the hair to give the hair body and support.
- Very long, center-parted straight hair (from the sixties but still seen today) is not only shortening, it's also very high school and outdated.
- Coloring the hair can add a heightening effect, too. As Benjamin Moss explains, "If a woman has drab brown hair, for example, even if it's short, it can make her look shorter simply because it's dark around her face. The darkness pushes the body down. By slightly lightening the hair that frames the face, it gives the illusion of an extended line. Her whole body line extends upward into light."

Posture Points for Walking Tall

What we tend to forget is that good posture habits—when standing, sitting, and walking—also help the clothes you wear to look better and fall better on you, and they give people a more positive impression of you. (Next time you pass a shop window, catch a peek of yourself in the glass. Are you slouching or jutting forward like the prow of a ship? If you are, you can see for yourself what kind of impression you're giving the world at large.) . . . Yes, we all know the importance of good posture. As for the ways to *achieve* it, read on.

New York City Kinesio (Movement) Therapist Marianne Battistone believes that "the key to adding height is in knowing how to relax.

When muscles are relaxed, they are at their full length, and so by teaching muscles to know their resting state, it adds height to the body.

"*Shorter women often have a problem with self-image,* and so they wear very high heels to make themselves taller. That's why I see lots of foot problems with shorter women. They have toe joint problems, bunions, and arch aches. In addition, high heels cause tremendous postural problems—like lumbar spine tilt, which is when the tummy or backside stick out. That, in turn, causes low-back ache, which leads to neck tension. And finally, if women don't have correct posture, their abdominal muscles never obtain ultimate strength.

"*To make women aware of their bodies* (and teach them how to make themselves tall through their bodies), I show them a picture of the standing body in profile, and I point out the plumb line, which is the central mechanical axis of the body. Then I tell women to look at themselves in a mirror and compare their profiles—the sunken chest, the protruding tummy, the locked knees—with the correct way their shoulders, hips, knees, and ankles *should* fall. The best image is one of building blocks: When one block is centered upon the other, it takes very little for the blocks to remain upright. But as soon as one block is off-center, there's a lot of tension and gravity resistance, and the blocks become a precarious or tumbling pile. Similarly, when bones and joints are centered one on top of the other, movement is much more efficient.

"*The abdominal muscles,* a huge mass extending all around the ribcage, are antigravity muscles, which, when strengthened, keep proper posture alignment. To achieve the desired strength, there are three types of exercises that people must do during each exercise session: strengthening exercises, stretching exercises, and relaxation exercises. An ideal program would provide twenty to thirty minutes of posture exercise every morning or every night, in addition to any other exercise program you may be following."

Strengthening Exercises (Total time, about 5–10 minutes)

The Wall Push-Up:

1. Stand facing a wall, feet together and about 2½ feet from the wall, body straight (do not arch back), arms straight in front of you and palms against wall.
2. Following a moderate tempo, alternately bend and stretch the arms keeping legs and body straight and heels flat on floor

3. Do from 10–15 times
4. As you get more advanced, do the same procedure using a dresser and then a table as the surface you push against.

The lower the surface, the harder the exercise becomes and the more benefits you derive from it.

The Sit-Up:

1. Sit on floor, knees bent, legs slightly apart, back straight, arms straight out in front of you with hands clasped
2. Inhale. Then, on the exhale, pull stomach flat, round the back, and slowly roll backwards until you feel the abdominal muscles working . Hold that position for 6–8 seconds.
3. Return to original position; repeat 10 times.
4. As you get better at it, gradually achieve a lower back roll while increasing the holding time to 10 seconds.

Stretching Exercise (Total time, about 5 minutes)

Simple Stretch:

1. Sit upright on floor, legs and arms straight in front of you. Keep feet relaxed and together.
2. Relax shoulders, round back, drop head foreward and slowly reach toward toes as far as you can go comfortably.
3. Hold. Relax. Breathe until you feel muscles release.
4. Bend elbows, pulling body closer toward the legs. Hold. Relax. Breathe until you feel muscles release.
5. Return to original position.

Relaxation Exercise (Total time, 5–10 minutes)

The Sweigard Technique

This is a simple, guaranteed-painless method devised by Dr. Lulu Sweigard, PhD., who was known for her neuromuscular reeducation work with many actors and dancers at Juilliard. Says Ms. Battistone, *"Sweigard was actually able to measure height gain after people did her relaxation technique."* To do it yourself:

1. Sit on floor and hug knees to chest for about a minute, then . . .
2. Lie on the floor, arms folded gently across chest, knees bent and leaning on one another. Breathe normally.
3. Concentrate on each tension spot from head to toe. As you mentally focus on each area (eyes, facial muscles, shoulders, chest, and so on), allow the areas that feel tense to "let go." Then go back and . . .

    a. think of your skull "melting" into the floor
    b. think of your collarbone widening across the floor
    c. think of your spine lengthening from top to bottom
    d. think of your lower back widening across the floor
    e. think of your thigh bones dropping downward toward the pelvis
    f. think of your lower leg dropping downward toward your ankles
    g. think of your feet widening across the floor

4. **Do this** for about 5–10 minutes. As you do, every 2 minutes **or so,** inhale normally, then exhale in a slow hiss. Let the air **come out naturally** (as a balloon expells air; don't force it **out with your** stomach muscles).

20. Made to Measure: Alteration and Sewing Guidelines

"The money I've spent on alterations over the years would easily amount to the price of a whole new wardrobe (and I'd probably have to spend more money getting that altered, too!)."

—Maggie J., 5′1½″, 98 pounds

Shorter women are so used to their lot that they've taken the inconvenience of alterations for granted. Most are unfamiliar with the sensation of buying a dress in the afternoon and wearing it out the same night.

It's maddening, yes. And it's expensive, yes. But alterations are also necessary. A skirt that's too long—even by fractions of an inch—can throw the whole line of your look off-kilter. A blouse cuff that's too wide and hangs down below your wrist will be noticeable to others, even if you don't object to its trailing into your coffee.

The Whos, Ifs, and Whens of Altering

. . . Or when to take it in or up and when to give it up and take it in (to a tailor). If you are in the habit of buying the designer fashions at exorbitant prices, you can skip the rest of this chapter because, if and when they need altering, you probably take the extra process and price as a matter of course. And you do not need the following information if you yourself are a top-flight seamstress who designs or alters clothes with ease. *But* if you're moderately nimble with a thimble (that is, you know how to follow a pattern but aren't quite at the stage where you could design a garment without one), or if you don't even know the basics, read on.

Simple Alteration How-tos

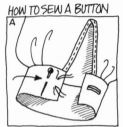

HOW TO SEW A BUTTON

PIN NEW BUTTON PLACEMENT

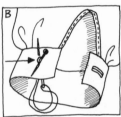

SEW A BASE FOR THE BUTTON

USE SLIGHTLY LOOSE STITCHES

WIND THE THREAD AROUND

This section is for the woman who doesn't own a sewing machine, who doesn't know how to sew, but who does want to learn some easy basics so she doesn't have to run off to the tailor for every little adjustment. Equipment for such alterations will include: a box of straight pins; a packet of different-sized sewing needles; thread in a variety of colors (your best bet for that is a small sewing kit, available at any variety store); sewing scissors; pinking shears; a seam ripper; and iron-on hem tape.

How to sew a button: Say you've just bought a long-sleeved blouse and the cuff buttons need to be moved an inch or so to make the cuff fit comfortably. (*Note:* When proper fit means moving the button so far over that it makes the sleeve itself overlap, you'll have to take the job to an expert to have the cuff reset or else bypass the blouse in the first place.) To do the minor move yourself:

1. *Use a seam ripper to remove the button,* leaving the broken threads on the cuff in place to act as a guideline.
2. *Slip wrist into cuff* and adjust to correct width (don't make it *too* snug) and pin in place with a straight pin.
3. *Slip a second straight pin* through the outer-corner of the buttonhole to mark where new button placement will be. Remove first pin, and make sure the second pin is exactly opposite the threads marking the old placement (see illustration A). Leave the second pin in place.
4. *Thread needle* with thread that matches the original as closely as possible. The length of thread to sew one button should be about 12 inches long. Knot cut ends together.
5. *Insert needle up through underside of cuff* (so the knot won't show), and sew two or three stitches on top of one another to form a base for the button (see B). Remove pin.
6. *As final base stitch comes up,* poke needle through button (make sure the right side of the button faces up), and push button down thread to base stitches.
7. *Using slightly loose stitches,* sew button to cuff (up through one hole, down through the other) in three or four complete rounds (C).
8. *On the last stitch* coming up from underneath, instead of

going up through the button again, pull needle and thread out between the button and the fabric and wind the thread two or three times around the stitches you've just sewn (D). This will make the button more secure and allow for the thickness of the top part of the cuff that will button onto it.

9. *To finish*, reinsert needle through cuff to underside of fabric and sew one loose stitch through fabric to form a small loop. Pull needle through this loop two or three times (to triple-knot it) before pulling thread (and the loop itself) taut. Cut off excess thread.

SEW A STITCH TO SECURE

Note: If the button itself has a shank—that little loop of metal or hole-in-a-stem underneath—you can skip step 8.

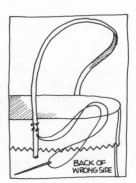

BACK OF WRONG SIDE

How to shorten spaghetti straps: You've got a skinny-strapped camisole or a sundress that would fit perfectly if your shoulders were just a few inches higher or if the straps were a few inches shorter. To make this last adjustment:

1. *Use a seam ripper* to remove original tacking stitches. (You may want to do this one strap at a time so you can use the original tacking method of one strap as a guideline for the other strap.)
2. *Try garment on backward* (yes, backward—the back is where you'll be resewing the straps), and use straight pins to secure straps at desired length.
3. *Try on garment again the right way* to see if strap length is correct. Readjust pins if necessary.
4. *When you're satisfied with the proper length*, cut off excess strap about an inch below the point at which it will be sewn.
5. *Double-thread needle* and knot as for button how-tos, step 4.
6. *Insert needle from inner side of strap*, and use four or five stitches to tack strap to inside of garment near top side (see A). Stitches should pick up threads from the inside of the garment only; they shouldn't be visible from the outside.
7. *To finish*, knot thread as described in button how-tos, step 9.

How to sew a simple hem: This info will come in handy for taking up hems on straight-leg pants, narrow skirts, and gathered skirts. Hem length for most garments should be no wider than 1¼ to 2 inches. On skirts, the more fabric in the skirt, the narrower the hem.

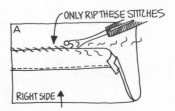

ONLY RIP THESE STITCHES

A

RIGHT SIDE

1. *First, use a seam ripper to remove the original hem* stitches (if the original hemline used machine-stitched hemming

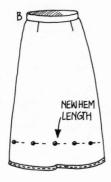

NEW HEM LENGTH

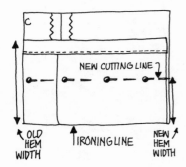

NEW CUTTING LINE

OLD HEM WIDTH   IRONING LINE   NEW HEM WIDTH

SLANT STITCH

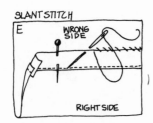

WRONG SIDE

RIGHT SIDE

CATCH STITCH HEM

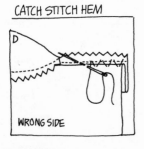

WRONG SIDE

tape, leave the tape intact where it attaches to the cut edge of the fabric and just remove the stitches that attach it to the wrong side of the garment (see illustration A).

2. *Try on garment* and use straight pins to mark desired hem length (B).

3. *Double-check evenness of hem* by measuring length from bottom of waistband to new hemline edge all around garment. (If you are hemming pants, you may want to make them slightly longer in back—say a quarter inch or so—so they don't droop over your shoes in front.) Adjust pins if necessary.

4. *Iron lightly along bottom of new hemline;* the ironing line will help serve as a guide when you get to the actual hemming.

5. *If new hemline allowance* is at or under the 2-inch allotment, you can restitch the hem as is (using one of the hemming stitches described below) and leave the original finished edge intact. However, if the hem allowance is much wider than 2 inches, it will have to be cut down and a new edge finish provided to keep fabric from unraveling.

6. *To cut off excess hem allotment evenly*, measure from ironing line to fabric edge and use straight pins to mark your new cutting line (C). But before cutting along this pin-line, be sure to note which hem-edge finish you'll be using:

   a. You can cut along pin-line with pinking shears (D), *or*

   b. If fabric is flat and lightweight, you can iron the edge under a quarter of an inch (if so, allow for the extra quarter inch when cutting), *or*

   c. You can cut edge with pinking shears, and instead of sewing hem, iron it in place with iron-on seam tape from the variety store (for lighter fabrics only).

7. *Hemming stitches:* Thread needle and knot *one* end of thread only. Then . . .

   a. *For sewing hems that are finished with stitched-on hemming tape or folded under,* you can use a simple slant stitch picking up just a few threads from the fabric of the garment as you sew each stitch (see illustration E).

   b. *For sewing hems that have been finished with a pinked edge,* you'd be better to use a catch stitch, again picking up just a few threads of the outer garment fabric as you sew each stitch (illustration F).

Note: Check the front of the garment occasionally as you sew to make sure stitches are as invisible as possible. If fabric has some stretch to it, keep stitches slack so that they won't break when the garment is stretched.

When dealing with anything more complicated than the three alterations just described (even if you want to hem a skirt that has a kick pleat, which can be tricky for the uninitiated), it's better to leave the job to a professional.

The Do-It-Yourselfer vs. the Pro

This section is for the fairly experienced sewer. You already know about moving buttons, taking up hems, taking in simple side seams on pants, blouses, and such. What you may need some help with is evaluating a garment you're about to buy for possible alteration problems and deciding when *not* to alter it yourself.

- *Lingerie:* Taking up simple hems on robes and nightgowns is easy, as you already know. But unless you're clever about hemming a slip (and willing to go through the trouble of doing it properly), best look around for a shorter slip, which fits when you buy.
- *Tops:* Taking in seams on blouses and side-seamed sweaters is easy. Narrowing an overly wide blouse shoulder, however, involves resetting the sleeves—not impossible surely but a bit of work, nonetheless. And if shoulder seams on a blouse are top-stitched, you have to be very careful to make the new seams look as neat as the original. As for narrowing the shoulder width of a sweater, you might want to try the solution in the box below.
- *Skirts:* If side seams have to be taken in, make sure the pockets won't get in the way of altering. And taking in a waistband needs time and care.
- *Pants:* If the crotch is too low, altering it is a real hassle; you'll practically have to remake the pants. Better leave this to a tailor or forget it altogether. Ditto if you need to narrow pants with top-stitched seams.
- *Jump suits:* Killers when they don't fit! If they're too long in the waist and/or the crotch and if they have a waistband, they can be shortened but with a lot of work. Again, leave this job to a pro. If the jump suit doesn't have a waistband and needs shortening, a pro could probably take care of that

too by either recutting and sewing to make a waistband (which would alter the style) or by ripping out and resewing the side seams and inner legs. Sometimes just belting the waist and blousing the top solves the problem. If that doesn't work, look for another jump suit, or be prepared to offer the tailor your first-born child in exchange for taking on the job.

- *Jackets:* Hemming an unlined jacket is easy, but by shortening it you may spoil the line of the jacket itself. Also, hemming or taking in side seams will affect the placement of pockets, which may have to be redone to compensate. As for narrowing a lined jacket at the shoulders, narrowing a lapel, or redefining the waist—these are all jobs for a very experienced and very patient sewer.
- *Dresses:* It depends on the intricacy of the design and the problem involved. A simple straight-lined dress is usually no problem if adjustments involve simple hemming, taking in side seams, or resetting a sleeve. If it has a waist that needs to be heightened or lowered, that too is possible, but it's involved: Call your tailor.
- *Coats:* When the necessary adjustments mean more than the slight moving of a button or two, always leave this one to a pro. A coat is one garment where any lack of expertise in alteration is especially evident.

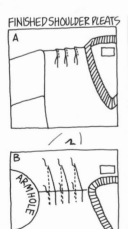

Give It the Bold Shoulder

A knitted sweater with a set-in sleeve presents a problem if the shoulders are too wide and fall below your own shoulder. You can't simply remove the sleeve and reset it as you would a blouse. But here's one solution you might try:

You can create a pretty pleated effect at the shoulder (and narrow the width of the shoulder in the process; see A) by sewing two or three darts along the shoulder line (B). In back, the darts are sewn all the way, just as you would sew regular darts. In front, they go down only a few stitches (use the backstitch on your machine to keep thread from loosening) so that darts form an open pleat; topstitch pleat. *Tip:* This method works best with thinner knits. And do pin in place before sewing to see if you like the effect.

You and Your Tailor

A reliable tailor is to the shorter, chic woman what a reliable butcher is to an expert chef: indispensable. Women who, because of their height or figure, have always had to rely on alterations to make their clothes fit properly, have usually gotten to know of some wonderful man (or woman) who does expert work at a reasonable price. (In some circles, the existence of such a tailor is a more closely guarded secret than Zsa Zsa Gabor's age, and if a woman friend thinks so highly of you that she recommends her tailor to you, it's considered bad form to bandy the information about lest the tailor's reputation grow so great that he raises his prices.) If you are one of the lucky ones, you know that such a tailor must be treated with loving care. What you might not have considered, however, is that the same tailor could be prevailed upon to copy some favorite pieces you already own. Say you have a pair of pants that fit you to a T. Often, a tailor can run up the same pants in different fabrics for you, even making minor style adjustments if desired.

On the other hand, if and while you're still searching for someone to do alterations, you might want to take advantage of the ones attached to the better department stores where you've bought a garment that needs to be fitted. In some cases (if the item is very expensive or if you need to raise the hem and the hem of the garment comes unfinished—as is often the case with men's pants), you may get free alterations or be charged a minimum fee. Also keep in mind: Pants cost less to hem than skirts, and unlined clothes less to alter than lined. And, of course, prices go up in direct proportion to the amount of work involved.

- *Special cases:* These could include very expensive clothes, very delicate fabrics, or fabrics that require knowledgeable handling (sequins, beads, and such), as well as clothes that are exceptionally well made and intricately constructed. All should be carefully ministered to by a good professional tailor.

Sewing

What we would like to do here is to employ a little gentle persuasion on the subject of sewing your own clothes from scratch. If you've already taken a few lessons—in a sewing class for adults or in your old home ec days in high school—and you are *firmly* and *irrevocably* convinced that you either can't or don't want to sew (or, as is often the case in these busy days, don't have a spare minute to)—fair enough. We don't want to nag.

But—if you don't sew simply because you never learned how and you think you might like to give it the old college try, we urge you to follow that thought as soon as possible. There are classes available all over the country at sewing centers, your local Y, or in schools that offer night courses for adults, to give a few suggestions. Why is sewing so great?

• *If you sew your own clothes, you'll be assured of having complete control of your fashion life.* Or as was stated by Judy G. (5′2½″, 100 pounds), a registered nurse from Illinois who answered our questionnaire:

"I enjoy sewing as a hobby, but I also enjoy being able to make just what I want in the exact material and color that I want. And I can make them with better quality and at a lower price."

This brings us to the next point:

• *Sewing saves you a bundle on clothes.* Even if you have to buy a machine, even when the material you buy is expensive (and we're all for quality material), you'll still end up spending at least half or less than half of what the same garment would cost ready-made.

• *As you get more proficient at it, you'll also be able to design your own clothes,* either by mixing several pieces from different patterns together or by winging it completely.

• *A really experienced sewer can even do knock-offs of designer originals* once she's examined how they're made close-up.

• *As for the time involved:* The better you get, the shorter it takes. (Even a moderately good sewer can usually run up a simple pair of unlined pants with zipper closing and side pockets in about two hours.) And as for shopping for material, the variety out there makes that chore a lot more pleasant than shopping for a piece of clothing that you both like and fit into. Fabric, after all, knows no height prejudice when you sew.

- *And, finally, one of the best reasons of all for learning how to sew—it's fun.* It's an art form, a very satisfying and practical way to express your creativity. And, for some women, that alone is reason enough. How about *you?*

PATTERN NEWS *From Mary Ann Feuss and Gail Dettlinger, fashion director and merchandise director, Vogue/Butterick Patterns:*

"We always get lots of consumer mail requesting smaller pattern sizes. And for a while we watched what was happening to ready-to-wear and saw the success of Petite manufacturers and designers and realized that the time had come to respond. Now the pattern market is reflecting the same boom in Petites as the retail market. . . . Until recently, we only started at size eight (our eight, by the way, is like a ready-to-wear size six) because of economic considerations. We are limited to the number of pieces in each pattern—the more pieces, the more expensive it is for the consumer. So if we made additional pieces (that is, cut them for an even smaller size than we had been doing), women of all sizes would have to absorb that additional expense. . . . The new pattern labels say 'Misses and Misses Petite.' In one package we give two sets of instructions (different cutting lines on one tissue)—one for Misses, one for Misses Petites. By making our patterns in dual sizes we also minimize the need for alterations. By fall '81 we expect to have forty styles available with dual sizing. . . . In deciding which styles to pattern for Petites, we have to use visual judgments. We want to do suits with short jackets and sleeve interest because they're softer-looking. With an A-line, tent shape, or float shape, a short woman just needs to change the hemline, but for more fitted dresses she needs a special pattern— and we'll be doing those for Petites, too."

Index